D1478632

The International Economic Order

By the same author

International Short-Term Capital Movements, 1937
The Dollar Shortage, 1950
International Economics, 1953, 1958, 1963, 1968, 1973, 1978, 1982
Terms of Trade, 1956
Economic Development, 1958, 1965, 1977, 1983
Foreign Trade and the National Economy, 1962, 1975
Economic Growth in France and Britain, 1964
Europe and the Dollar, 1966
Europe's Postwar Growth 1967
American Business Abroad, 1969
Power and Money, 1970
The World in Depression, 1929–1939, 1973, 1986
America in the World Economy, 1977
Economic Response, 1978
Manias, Panics and Crashes, 1978
International Money, 1981
A Financial History of Western Europe, 1984
Multinational Excursions, 1984
Keynesianism vs Monetarism, 1985
Marshall Plan Days, 1987
International Capital Movements, 1987
Economic Laws and Economic History, 1988

The International Economic Order

Essays on Financial Crisis and International Public Goods

Charles P. Kindleberger

Ford International Professor of Economics Emeritus
Massachusetts Institute of Technology

The MIT Press
Cambridge, Massachusetts

First MIT Press edition, 1988

© 1988 Charles P. Kindleberger

Printed and bound in Great Britain.

Library of Congress Cataloging-in-Publication Data

Kindleberger, Charles Poor, 1910–
    The international economic order : essays
on financial crisis and international
public goods / Charles P. Kindleberger.
      p.   cm.
  - Includes index.
    ISBN 0-262-11138-1
    1. International finance. 2. International economic relations.
  3. Business cycles. I. Title.
HG3881.K526 1988
337—dc19   88-22843
                       CIP

Contents

List of Tables

Introduction

This is the seventh volume of collected papers I have published since 1966, a number that may seem excessive to some people. When Peter Johns of Wheatsheaf Books flatteringly asked whether I would be interested in putting together a collection of recent papers, I first collected a hodge-podge and forwarded it to Ship Street in Brighton, England, an address that evokes echoes of *Treasure Island* and Long John Silver. Mr Johns was sensible enough to insist on an organizing principle or two. Each of the earlier volumes dealt more or less with a single given subject in international finance economics, economic history, or the multinational corporation. This collection is less of a unity, perhaps even a duality, as compared with the earlier volumes, but the separate sections on financial crises and international public goods are nonetheless somewhat related insofar as they deal with different aspects of the international economic order.

I got started in financial crisis and international public goods more or less by accident. Professor Wolfram Fischer, the Free University of Berlin economic historian, had planned a series of books on world economic history in the twentieth century, organized with a separate book to each decade, for a series of pocket books to be published by the *Deutsche Taschenbuch Verlag* of Munich. Visiting Harvard University, he offered a choice of decades to the eminent economic historian, Alexander Gerschenkron, who decided against participating and suggested that I, who was beginning to cultivate a taste for economic history, might be interested. Fischer took up the idea, and I chose the 1930s, a decade in which I first came into economics, along with many other young people (then) who were curious to learn how the world got into such an unholy mess. I finished the manuscript in the spring of 1971, although the Allen Lane version in English did not appear until 1973.

The point is that the troubles that surfaced in the international economic system beginning in the summer of 1971 and intensifying after the OPEC price hike in oil in November 1973, giving rise to the recession of 1974 and 1975, had nothing to do with my choice of subject. No prescience was involved. But by luck the book had relevance to the 1970s and 1980s, and it led me down two paths, one to financial crises more generally, the subject of the first part of this collection, the other to notions of international economic order under strong leadership—or disorder under weak or absent leadership—which are the meat of Part II.

The path from the depression started in 1929 to financial crisis over a longer time span is an obvious one. If 1929, what about 1920, and 1907, perhaps 1890, 1873, and so on? Financial crises are an agreeable subject in history because the troubles are those of others; one can indulge in *Schadenfreude* (joy over others' misfortunes) with a clear conscience because the others who had the trouble are dead. Those of us who fancy our prose styles have an opportunity to pour on the irony as we contemplate the follies of allegedly rational economic men. There is an abundant contemporary and historical literature on financial crises—a favourite recurring topic in the nineteenth century. I found myself inching back all the way to the South Sea and Mississippi bubbles, only to be told a couple of years later that I had missed out on some juicy ones from 1551 to 1653, associated with the Fuggers, Welsers, and Genoan bankers who were lending money on *asientos* to the Hapsburgs of Spain, and particularly to Philip II. I am trying now to repair that gap in my awareness. The result of pushing back from 1929 was two books, one entitled *Manias, Panics and Crashes* (New York, Basic Books, 1978), and a second, edited with Jean-Pierre Laffargue of the University of Paris I, based on a symposium held in Bad Homburg in the Federal Republic of Germany on *Financial Crises: Theory, History and Policy*, Cambridge, Cambridge University Press, and Paris, *Maison des Sciences de l'Homme*, 1982. I wanted to call *Manias . . .* Manias, Bubbles, Panics and Crashes but my editor thought that three substantives were all that a book title could carry. The two exercises missed out pretty largely on the Baring crisis of 1890, but I managed to work that into a paper for the *Festschrift* in honour of Wilfried Guth of the Deutsche Bank (Wolfram Engels, Armin Gutowski and Henry C. Wallich (eds), *International Capital Movements, Debt and Monetary System*, Mainz: v. Hase & Koehler, 1984), and included it in the collection *Keynesianism vs Monetarism and other Essays in Financial History* (London, Allen & Unwin, 1985). It must be told that I find rather more analogies between the present and the period 1888 to 1893 than between the present and 1929, but the latter is where I have done the most work and where the world's interest lies, as it is still fresh in memory.

The second train of thought on international public goods grew out of the last chapter of *The World in Depression, 1929–1939*. As I sought to pull the threads together, I found myself saying that the world of the 1930s was unstable because no country acted as a stabilizer. In words I am sick of writing: Britain could not so act, and the United States would not. In the 1973 version I developed three functions that a leader or stabilizer should discharge; in the 1986 edition, revised to take account of the growing literature on the 1930s and further reflection, I extended the list to five: provision of an open market for traded commodities in glut, and of a supply of those in acute shortage; a steady flow of capital so as not to cut off loans suddenly; coordination of monetary and fiscal policies among major nations; maintaining some coherent system of exchange rates; and serving in financial crisis as a lender of last resort, providing liquidity to halt liquidation, capital withdrawals and domino business and bank collapse. These were international public goods that did not emerge spontaneously from a market system, and had to be provided. In the absence of world government they had to be provided by some leading country.

These ideas seem to have appealed to the growing group of political scientists who worry about economic questions. They modified the vocabulary: what I called leadership, they called hegemony. But they more or less accepted the idea that world economic stability is a public good that has to be provided, if at all, by some country that takes charge, accepts responsibility, acts as a leader. Leaders need followers, to be sure. Political scientists are exploring whether when one leader abdicates, the habits of cooperation built up in its hey-day can become institutionalized into what they call regimes.

The notion of international public goods, the reader of Part II will gather, is at variance with the neo-classical version of economics, that all is well if only markets are left alone to do their thing. In my view it is useful to make a distinction between trend and crisis. On trend, markets are needed to allocate scarce resources among limitless wants, and on the whole function adequately without intervention. But markets occasionally get out of whack and into crisis; on such occasions they need direction. The question of when to stand aside and when to intervene would seem to be a question for art and intuition, not for science. The chapters in Part II argue with neo-liberal economists whether private maximizers, joined in markets, can alone and as a rule, produce a good society, or whether some attention to the public good, economic responsibility perhaps, and assistance to the market to fix on standards, may not be required.

I should perhaps explain that my interest in the political dimensions of international economics did not begin with *The World in Depression*, although this has attracted the most attention. On my return from the war and government service to academic life, my first book, *The Dollar Shortage* (New York, Wiley and The Technology Press, 1950), contained an appendix entitled 'The Distribution of Income, Political Equilibrium, and Equilibrium in the Balance of Payments.' This was a draft paper that had been rejected by some economic journal I have forgotten, and was added to the book in conformity with the New England slogan 'use up, wear out, make do'. It develops in rudimentary form some of the ideas on inflation and trade deficits worked out contemporaneously by Henri Aujac, the French economist, in 'Inflation as a Monetary Consequence of the Behaviour of Social Groups', *International Economic Papers*, No. 4, original in *Economie Appliquée*, vol. 7, no. 2, April–June, 1950, (pp. 19–38), that later blossomed into the notion of structural (as opposed to monetary) inflation and in books edited by Fred Hirsch and John Goldthorpe, *The Political Economy of Inflation* (Cambridge, Mass. Harvard University Press, 1978) and written by Mancur Olson, *The Rise and Decline of Nations: Economic Growth, Stagflation and Social Rigidities* (New Haven, Yale University Press, 1982). In 1951 I published an article 'Group Behaviour and International Trade', connecting political clout to economic action (reprinted in *Economic Response: Comparative Studies in Trade, Finance and Growth* (Cambridge, Mass., Harvard University Press, 1978), and in 1970 a book entitled *Power and Money*, with a subtitle that tickled at least one of my friends, *The Politics of International Economics and the Economics of International Politics* (New York, Basic Books). The book was not a commercial success, failing of adoption for use in classes, as it fell between the carefully-separated stools of economics and political-science courses.

Many of the chapters started as lectures on some special occasion or in response to a particular invitation. It happened that I was lecturing to the Economics Club of Basle, Switzerland, on October 19, 1987 when the New York Stock Exchange collapsed with the largest (508-point) drop in the Dow Jones industrial stock index in its history. That paper, suitably brought up to the minute, would have made a dramatic entry in this collection, but was accepted by an international economic journal located in Basle, KYKLOS, which had a prior claim. As it happened, however, I had an engagement of long standing to lecture on an appropriate topic, and use this as the opening gun of Part I.

There is no need to discuss the provenance of each of the essays, lectures or talks since this is indicated at the start of each. Chapter 7,

'A View from Experience', is perhaps worth a word. Senator Bill Bradley of New Jersey and Congressman Jack Kemp of Buffalo, New York, the one a Democrat, the other a Republican, both formerly professional athletes, held a so-called 'Congressional Summit' on exchange rates in Washington in 1985. It was organized with split-second timing, and along with others, I was allotted five minutes on a panel scheduled from 2:35 to 3:15 PM on November 12. It has not hitherto been published but may be worth inclusion as a model of compression. 'Distress in International Financial Markets', Chapter 8, is also unpublished. Given as a talk to the Economics Club of Stockholm in December 1982, shortly before I returned to the United States from four months in Sweden, it was accepted by a Scandinavian economics journal subject—to convert it from a talk to a scholarly paper—to substantial revisions that I never got around to making.

Chapters 6, 15 and 16 were name lectures—the Jones lecture at the State College of New York at Geneseo, the Fred Hirsch memorial lecture at Warwick University in England, and the Frank D. Graham Memorial lecture at Princeton, respectively. Chapter 9 was a presidential address to the American Economic Association. And all chapters, as indicated, were commissioned for one or another purpose except for Chapter 13, on 'Standards', which was produced on my own initiative for a seminar at the Institute of International Economic Studies, Stockholm, and submitted for publication to a refereed journal.

The international flavour of the papers is unlikely to escape notice: two were written in Sweden, one in Finland, one to honour a Japanese economist, another a British, and various of them appeared in England, Switzerland, Italy and Hungary. Globalization has overtaken the intellectual markets of the world as well as those for goods, money and other assets. But globalization has some distance to go, as Parts I and II each complain, in the integration of economic policies to produce the international public goods that private markets do not provide, perhaps on trend, but thus far certainly not in crisis.

I am acutely conscious of the repetition of ideas that runs through the chapters. This is a collection, not a monograph and it is too much to ask an academic economist to discard each of his ideas after merely one use. I apologize to the reviewers who are more or less obliged by their calling to read the essays through at one time. To have deleted repeated notions, however, would have subtracted from the unity of the parts for the sake of the whole, when the work is likely to be consumed by the average reader in bite-size portions.

Charles P. Kindleberger

Lincoln Cent, Massachusetts
January 1988

Part I
Financial Crises

1 Is There Going to Be a Depression?[1]*

The title of this chapter seemed slightly alarming when Father Devereux assigned it tó me last summer. After October 19, 1987, now known as Black Monday or the day of the Dow-Jones Industrial Index meltdown, it seems as if Father Devereux was prescient, that in raising the question, he knew something that not all of us knew. I wonder whether he went strenuously short of stocks in the market or whether his vow of poverty enjoins him against taking advantage of superior wisdom.

Most of you know the epigram of Paul Samuelson that the stock market has forecast nine of the last five recessions. The question now is whether Black Monday belongs in the same folder as Black Thursday and Black Tuesday 1929, 24 and 29 October to be precise, although the press continuously tries to slip in 28 October. Was the stock-market crash last October a symptom of a deeper malaise in the world economy as thirty-three economists from thirteen countries assembled last December by the Institute of International Economics in Washington maintain, linking it with a sharp drop in the bond market of the early months of the year (IIE, 1987)? Or was it something transitory and ephemeral like a summer storm that clears the air? In contrast with the gloomy forecast of the thirty-three economists, which, to be sure, could be saved by governments taking their advice to avoid the difficulties they see ahead, thirty business forecasters predicted at the end of last year that 1988 won't be so bad: real GNP up 2 percent—not as good as the 3.7 rate of growth for the first three quarters of 1987, but positively positive, with unemployment just a little over 6 per cent, as contrasted with 5.9 per cent at the end of last year (*New York Times*, 1987).

There are two contrasting views of what the stock market means for the real economy, and a consequent pair of contrasting opinions what

---

* A lecture given in the Alex. G. McKenna Economic Education Series at St Vincent's College, Latrobe, Pennsylvania, 21 January 1988.

3

any particular movement of share prices may mean. On the one hand, 'rational expectations' is a theory that markets are rational and that asset prices are set by markets at levels that reflect real values, taking into account all available information. On this showing a collapse of the stock market reflects some unexpected news that portends real changes. Jude Wanniski looked to find such news to explain the 1929 crash, and discovered it in the action of a subcommittee in one of the houses of Congress, which resisted an attempt to hold down a tariff on a minor item, i.e. a carbide compound. This indicated, he asserted, that the Hawley/Smoot tariff, then progressing through the houses of Congress, would pass, be signed into law by President Hoover (nine months in the future) and evoke worldwide retaliation and a vast shrinkage of foreign trade (Wanniski, 1977, p. 130). This seems too small an event to have produced so large an effect.

In October 1987 there was equally no outstanding event that would explain the largest absolute (and among the largest percentage) decline in the Dow-Jones Industrials Index—508 points in one day. There was poor news—it would be excessive to say it was bad—that the United States deficit was up instead of down, despite two and a half years of depreciation of the dollar; and Secretary of the Treasury James Baker had some undiplomatic words to say about the lack of cooperation he thought he was getting from the West German monetary and fiscal authorities. Again the effect seems oversized in relation to the 'cause'.

The second view is that the stock market, and many other markets—for commodities, foreign exchange, real estate, and even reputations—take on from time to time an independent path, governed by fads or largely psychological factors. Rational expectations ascribe market prices to 'fundamentals'—demand, supply, structural changes, changes in policy and the like. The psychological view emphasizes that price changes can start off in this way but get caught up in movements of their own. Market 'feel' is needed to know when to get in and when out. 'People who bet on fundamentals,' said that foreign-exchange trader for the Federal Reserve Bank of New York a few years ago, 'lose their shirts' (Coombs, 1976, pp. 116, 235), and his judgment was vindicated in 1983 and 1984 when a number of economists specialized in international finance could not believe the dollar could go up all the way from February 1982 to February 1985 in the face of a large deficit in the balance of payments, and sold the dollar short.

The view to which I subscribe combines rational expectations and the psychological model. A change in fundamentals alters profit opportunities. Investment patterns change, and sometimes,—I emphasize that there is nothing inevitable about the path—there is a follow-the-leader pattern that leads to 'over-shooting', called by Adam Smith,

John Stuart Mill and other classical writers 'overtrading'. Monetarists assert that this cannot occur if the money supply is held steady or grows at some foreordained rate consonant with the rate of growth of the whole economy. It is true enough that if the monetary authorities follow the real-bills doctrine, which thinks it is sufficiently stable to expand bank credit with increases in output, monetary expansion parallel to the expansion in real output may make the economy unstable—again I emphasize the 'may'. But even when 'money', somehow defined, is growing in the economy at some regular pace, euphoria can lead to overtrading.

Innovations in credit instruments may produce a change in how money should be defined, and if definitions don't change, velocity calculated on the basis of the old definitions rises. The euphoria may become so widespread and intense as to amount to a mania or bubble. Peter Garber is not sure bubbles exist—a bubble being defined as a movement of prices well beyond what would be called for by the fundamentals (1977). The measurement problems, and for historic bubbles, the data problems, become complex. For simple-minded economic historians, it may be enough to say that if the contemporary world thought that the tulip bubble, the South Sea bubble, the Mississippi bubble, the canal mania, the railway mania, the 1919–20, 1928–9, and the last months of the five-year 1982–7 stock market booms were bubbles, manias, 'new eras' and the like, they were.

Postulate a bubble, mania, short-sharp boom. When the bubble is pricked, or cold water or the cold light of rationality cools down the mania or boom, then the price for the asset that has gone through the roof comes down again. Does this mean there will be a recession or depression? In their classic study of money in the United States, Friedman and Schwartz insist that the stock-market bust of October 1929 was basically unrelated to the depression that followed down to 1933 (1963, Chapter 7). The fault, they claim, lay in mistakes in monetary policy, and in particular, in allowing the money stock to shrink. Presumably they now feel that provided the money stock holds steady in the next years, there will be no recession or depression following Black Monday. I disagree about 1929, but am uncertain about 1988.

In 1929, the collapse of stock prices spread to commodities because banks were so tied up in trying to unscramble brokers' loans that they were unable to make their usual advances to commodity brokers. These last were thus unable to buy their usual amounts of standardized commodities shipped to New York on consignment, and commodity prices plunged. In the spring of 1930 there was a flight to quality in foreign bonds: first-class issues held up in price, third-grades declined.

The same phenomenon was observed in domestic bonds in September of that year. Between, there was probably a shift to quality in municipal bonds and mortgages, with investors trying to get out of the riskier issues. The decline in stock prices, commodity prices, low-grade bonds and mortgages put pressure on the banks. Farm banks had been failing since 1925 as agricultural prices drifted down to the third quarter of 1929 before dropping faster. Bank failures spread to the Southeast, to South-central Tennessee and Arkansas, to New York City where the Bank of the United States failed,—or in some views, was allowed to fail—in December 1930.

The liquidity pressures spread abroad, and beginning in May 1931, the tenpins started to topple. There were panics in foreign exchange withdrawals, bank failures, business bankruptcies. In earlier writing I have claimed that if there had been a lender of last resort internationally, the deflation could have been halted short of the depths of 1932 and 1933 (Kindleberger, 1986, Chapter 14). This view is contested by an astute observer of financial history, D.E. Moggridge, who believes that more extensive real therapy was needed, something on the order of the Marshall Plan after World War II, to correct the severe imbalances in the real and financial economies—real imbalances resulting from the recovery of European production in many lines without a corresponding shrinkage in extra-European output that had grown to replace wartime losses in Europe;—financial ones associated with war debts, reparations, overvaluations of the pound, undervaluation of the French franc, and a host of other distortions (1982).

Perhaps I put too much stress on the role of the lenders of last resort. The basis for attaching importance to it is that the market, like children, can stand a heap of ruin, and that if spreading collapse from the implosion of bubbles can be prevented, the normal recuperative powers of markets can bring things around. As I view the economic history of the last century or so, I have the feeling that the panics of 1847, 1857, 1866, 1907, and 1921 in Britain proved transitory and without deep-seated consequences, because there was a lender of last resort, while the panics of 1873 in central Europe and the United States, and of 1890 and 1929 were so wide, so deep and so prolonged because of its absence. Financial panics are often compared with meteorological phenomena, and probably should not be separated into mere financial panics and those that lead to prolonged and serious depression. There should perhaps be a Beaufort scale for measuring storms, or a Richter scale for earthquakes, rather than a binary division, summer thunderstorms vs hurricane or typhoon.

Let me come up to date and discuss whether Black Monday of October 1987 means depression, or merely a blip that knocks a point and a fraction off the rate of growth. Our thirty-three economists from thirteen countries are worried about the world financial economy and its imbalance as reflected in the large US deficits in the national budget and the balance of payments, substantial surpluses in Japan, Germany, Taiwan, the possibility that foreigners will stop buying US securities and plants in support of the dollar, and initiate a 'free fall', which would be inflationary. There is also understandable concern for Third World debt and its impact on economic growth both in the developing countries themselves and in the developed countries which have been lending and selling to them (Bryant and Portes, 1987). The business forecasters, on the other hand, are concerned specifically with the outcome in the United States—more or less as a closed economy—and worry whether business investment, household spending for consumption, and housing will hold up. One macro-econometrician ascribed the 1930s depression to the stock market via a wealth effect, people whose stocks have fallen severely in price feeling poorer and spending less (Mishkin, 1978). There does not seem to have been a similar effect when the 1919–20 boom in commodities and stocks collapsed in 1921. The difference—to use some *ad hoc* reasoning, that my old teacher Wesley C. Mitchell dismissed as implicit theorizing—may have been due to the length and steepness of the rise. In 1929, security prices had been rising for a long time, if spectacularly from March 1928 to September 1929, giving time for people to regard their gains as real wealth rather than merely paper profits likely to melt away. The stock market had risen consistently from 1982 to 1987, to be sure, but a great deal of the rise had been concentrated into a few months from June to August of the latter year. Whether investor psychology regards the October collapse as a loss of wealth, or merely the disappearance of paper profits may well affect spending this year and in the years to come.

In all this, my concern, derived from a study of financial history, focuses on the financial system, and whether the sharp deflation in stock markets spreads to other markets for assets and goods. First, however, let me make a point about world financial markets.

It is a cliché that world financial markets have been integrated or globalized. It was also a common belief before 19 October 1987 that astute investors could diversify their holdings by keeping assets in a number of countries. Such a tactic has proven to be of little value because most share markets in the major countries of the world fell together (*New York Times*, 1988). The Tokyo market, as it happened, fell less than New York—some thought in advance that because price/earnings ratios were three times as high as those in the United States when push came to shove it would fall earlier and further. In the event, Japanese financial authorities set limits on daily price changes (as is done in United States commodity markets), and sometimes instructed investors when and what to buy. But it is seldom recognized that the same worldwide phenomenon occurred in 1929: all stock markets fell together, although the degree of world financial integration is now thought to have been much less. What this suggests is that there are psychological connections between asset markets in different countries, as well as connections through money movements, arbitrage (for identical securities and commodities), and income changes spilling over into trade—psychological connections that move faster than changes in money supplies produced by the balance of payments, or changes in spending through the foreign-trade multiplier. Investment diversification may be more readily effected through the shares of multinational corporations than through buying the shares of domestic corporations in a number of countries. This is a question worth deeper research. The findings may require revisions in the textbooks on international economics.

But let me get back to the current outlook. Economic historians among whom I count myself a late recruit, are better at describing the past than foretelling the future. While the more it changes, the more it is the same thing, it is also true that generals often fight the last war, and economists the last depression, with less than complete success. Like the rest of the world, including people who have not written books on the 1929 depression, I analogize from that episode, or perhaps I should say experience. Where I look for insight is into what may happen to commodities, to international indebtedness, to foreign-exchange markets, and to domestic assets of varying degrees of quality. Let me address them one at a time.

I judge that commodities pose less of a threat today than the one they carried out in 1929 and 1930. In the first place, the financing is different. In 1929, many international commodities were sold on consignment, and required financing that was not forthcoming. Today they are bought and financed in the export market. Credit troubles in importing markets pose little threat.

Moreover the background conditions of today differ from those of the 1920s. Then there were serious surpluses in basic commodities and prices had been sagging since 1925. In the 1970s, the world was dominated by sellers' markets, not buyers'. It is true that the steps taken to halt inflation in 1979 and 1981 had produced a decline in a number of raw-material and foodstuff prices, notably grains, coffee, cotton, tin and copper, but this movement seemed to run its course in the spring of 1987 when prices turned up again. The stock-market crash of October was not paralleled by a commodity-price plunge. The danger rather lies in inflation.

Few economists or economic historians attach the significance I do to the relationship between commodity prices and exchange rates. When an exchange rate changes, it must alter the relative prices of competitively-traded commodities in two countries with a changed exchange rate. I contend that in a buyers' market, the prices of internationally-traded commodities will stay the same in the depreciating country and decline in the appreciating. This is what intensified the depression in the United States and the gold bloc in 1931 when sterling went off gold (and the dollar and gold currencies appreciated). In a sellers' market, on the contrary, appreciation leaves traded-goods prices unchanged, while depreciation raises them. This is what happened in the 1970s. If an exchange rate moves in a sine wave, first down and then up, traded-goods prices in a buyers' market will continuously decline—first remain unchanged, then decline, then remain unchanged, then decline—in a ratchet. In a sellers' market, on the other hand, the sine-wave path of a currency makes the ratchet work to raise prices. When markets are more or less balanced between buyers' and sellers' condition, it is likely that prices will move partway up in the depreciating currency, partway down in the appreciating, with no ratchet taking over. This appears to be the fortunate position of the world in 1987 and 1988.

There is one commodity in a special position—oil, wracked by the success of OPEC in 1973 and 1979, but getting the price so high that more oil was discovered and produced than could be sold at the peak price, then falling on evil days in the Iran–Iraq war that led to inability within OPEC to agree on sustainable output quotas. Such non-OPEC members as Mexico, Canada and the United States over-invested because of the intermediate OPEC success. A number of companies are threatened with trouble of one kind or another, and previously ebullient areas like the Southwest United States and Alberta in Canada face a long dreary road to work their way back to health.

The exchange market poses a different problem in commodities like automobiles and electronics that are traded in oligopolistic markets. The deficit in the current account of the United States that rose sharply with the appreciation of the dollar did not decline symmetrically with depreciation, as a number of companies—especially Japanese—lowered their local-currency prices rather than raise dollar prices, in an effort to hold market share. Profits were cut, and on this account the tactic is presumably not supportable in the long run. It has sometimes been regarded as dumping, giving rise to calls for countervailing duties. But it explains—along with the J-curve that depreciation makes the balance of payments in local currency worse before it makes it better as volumes adjust more slowly than prices of competitive commodities—why the deficit in the US balance of payments has been so long sustained following depreciation of about 30 per cent from the dollar's February 1985 high.

Is a foreign-exchange crisis likely? Debate turns on whether a so-called 'free-fall' of the dollar, (should it occur) would be harmful to the US economy or not. So long as the G-7 central banks are committed to something like the Plaza agreement or the Louvre agreement, however modified, the dollar will be supported by public authorities if private investors should experience revulsion from it. This is the lender-of-last-resort function at the international level. But like any lender-of-last-resort exercise, it requires political acceptance. If the financial authorities of, say, Japan and Germany become locked in disagreement with those of the United States over where the responsibility for stabilizing exchange markets lie, the markets might fall freely between two or more stools.

At a conference on the dollar in December 1987, Professor James Tobin of Yale University held that fear of a free fall of the dollar was unwarranted. With flexible exchange rates, the currency can fall to a point where the volume of sales is matched by the volume of purchases. I am unpersuaded. A precipitous fall in the dollar could raise the prices of internationally-traded goods to such an extent that various distributional coalitions, as Mancur Olson calls them, dig in to raise prices, wages, interest rates, whatever their source of interest is (1982). Government interest rates, of course, will rise automatically when the Japanese banks and insurance companies stop buying them, or worse, start to sell them as may have happened briefly in the spring of 1987. Social Security and government pensions are protected by cost-of-living allowances. Only private pension and long-term contractual arrangements would bear the brunt of the gap to be closed. In Paul Erdman's imaginative novel, *The Crash of 1979*, the dollar went into a free fall when the Arab oil-producing countries dumped their holdings on the market, and there was no support. This led to American households rushing down to the supermarket to stock up on goods, and a huge, irreversible rise in goods prices. The Erdman novel is of course fiction, but a similar real movement occurred in Mexico in mid-December 1987. There are those who think the United States is getting more and more like Latin America, with electricity brown-outs, student protests and rampant inflation. To be sure, inflation would answer the question posed in the title of this lecture. It is not depression, but another if different pathological economic condition.

Probably few people reading this watch enough late movies to have seen one with Myrna Loy and William Powell, in which Powell, the politician, announced that he was against inflation and against deflation, but for flation. (I am ashamed to say I have forgotten the title and am not clear how I would look it up.) But while a foreign-exchange crisis holds out the possibility of inflation—an undervalued exchange rate had a great deal to do with the German hyperinflation of 1921–3—the major danger posed by the Black Monday crash is of deflation. I hope I may be said to have disposed of the possibility of danger from the side of commodity prices, such as was so deadly in 1929–30. There remain, as I have said, various markets for debt that are under threat. The possibility of trouble lies in debt defaults of such a magnitude that they pose serious dangers to the banks, dangers of a size and extent such that the safety-net machinery in place is overwhelmed and its repair, extension or replacement encounters political obstacles. I can suggest what I have in mind in relation to June 1931. The Hoover moratorium on war debts and reparations announced on June 19 was to be followed by a lender-of-last-resort loan from the United States and France to support the Reichsmark. France wanted to discuss the moratorium; the Young plan established two classes of reparations payments, the conditional and unconditional. Did it apply to both or only to the conditional? And if France was going to help Germany with a loan, would the latter give up its proposed customs union with Austria and cancel the pocket battleship it was building? While these issues were being negotiated over three weeks, withdrawals and capital flight from Germany proceeded at an accelerating rate so that it became necessary to suspend convertibility of the Reichsmark.

On the international front today, there is of course 'Third World debt', the monies borrowed by many less developed countries from banks in the United States and Europe. Last May Citicorp led a parade of banks setting up reserves against losses from this source, and last month the Bank of Boston actually wrote off some of these loans. Earlier this month the Morgan Guaranty bank produced a complex scheme for new borrowing against the collateral of 20-year US Treasury zero-coupon bonds which provided the ultimate principal repayment, although Mexico of course faces the necessity to pay interest regularly. With these new bonds of guaranteed principal, the Mexican government will buy a much larger amount of old debt (at a discount). The proposal is imaginative, although not without problems. The fact that the banks had gone overboard in lending to these countries was evident to many as early as 1977; the banking world in the United States seems to have taken notice of the fact only in August 1982 when Mexican debt had to be rescheduled for the first time. The International Monetary Fund played a role in this and in other private debt rescheduling. It lays down conditions which the debtor countries regard as offensive, but which the Fund and the banks involved feel are required to render payment of debt service practical.

All sorts of questions are involved from the monetary and fiscal policies of the debtor, to interest rate caps, forgiveness, periods of grace and so on. The issues are highly political. Thus far the world of debtors and creditors has muddled through from country to country and crisis to crisis. There have been numerous suggestions that the matter should be addressed in a world economic conference. In my opinion that would be harmful. There is insufficient agreement in advance to be relatively certain of a positive conclusion. A stalemated conference would exacerbate the problem. Muddling through in Darwinian fashion is my preferred solution. Admittedly the result of getting through cannot be guaranteed. The positions of the different debtors—oil producers, oil consumers, countries that invested the money, and countries that have spent it on imports and military adventure—all differ. So do those of the banks: some regional banks believed themselves dragged along into Third World lending by euphoria and want to get out and stay out. Money-center banks include those which invested cautiously, and others that did not. An overall solution that will fit all countries and all banks in the creditor countries is utopian.

As I write before the end of the year the investment houses in Wall Street are sounding gloomy. Prospects for year-end bonuses have been dashed by heavy fourth-quarter losses, some by specialists on their inventories, some by underwriters of such issues as the privatization of British Petroleum where the issuing houses made commitments before 19 October. A number of mergers were called for to stave off bankruptcies. Even strong houses cut back on expansion plans of the last couple of years, gave up whole departments, reduced the numbers of employees. But this looks more like recession than depression.

A greater sense of unease, if not disease, emerges from the field of corporate debt issued in recent years both to finance takeovers of one company by another, some friendly, some hostile, or by companies preparing themselves to stave off hostile takeovers by bidding up the price of their stock and adding debt. Part of the rise of the stock market in New York from 1982 to 1985 came from the substitution of debt for equity. Debt service will be a heavy burden on a number of corporations in the years ahead if inflation is staved off but interest rates remain fairly high. Some corporations may fail. There is something of a debate in financial circles whether the high rates on so-called junk bonds—those below investment grade—are high enough to cover the risk of default. I do not know enough to have an opinion. But the market bears watching.

Next mortgages: thrift institutions in the Southwest and in California are suffering from construction and mortgage loans on overbuilt office buildings and luxury apartments. Speculative builders of very expensive housing elsewhere in the country may experience difficulty in selling their buildings, and so may the banks that have lent to them. The thrift institutions that had acquired large portfolios of loans before the 1970s rise in interest rates, especially suffer from disintermediation, as depositors take their savings out of low-interest deposits to invest them in money funds, certificates of deposit, and to some extent, moved by euphoria, in the stock market. The Federal Savings and Loan Insurance Corporation has had to be expanded by Congressional appropriation to take care of the remaining deposits of the distressed thrift institutions. The Farm Loan Bank Agency equally called for a capital increase. Luckily there was no prolonged political hassle over these rescue steps, as there might have been if the troubles had occurred in the Northeast, rather than the Southwest and West, and the Populist tradition of President Johnson, Wright Patman, and if you like William Jennings Bryan had resisted saving Wall Street.

Some observers expect trouble from consumers' loans. Consumer debt has risen continuously in recent years to all-time highs, and consumer bankruptcies from inability to meet debt service are inching up. The Tax Act of 1986 puts limits on the deductibility of interest on consumers' loans from income subject to taxation, but not that on mortgages; some consumers are borrowing against the increased equity in their inflation-price-increased housing—what used to be called second mortgages—for consumption rather than for investment purposes. The continuous decline in the savings ratios of households—in the face of the supply-side theory that reduced taxes in the 1981 act would raise savings and investment to speed up growth—does not augur well for household health. But if savings were to rise too rapidly, as is unlikely, it would be harmful to national income which relies importantly on autonomous consumption, perhaps more in the modified Keynesian world of today than on investment.

The stock-market crash by itself is thus not enough to bring on a serious depression; spread of disintermediation to simply one of the many fields of debt would not be fateful and could be contained. Prospects for the future depend rather on two possibilities: one that foreigners stop buying and actually sell their dollars and dollar-denominated assets to such an extent that the monetary authorities feel it necessary to raise interest rates sharply to attract and hold foreign investors, with serious repercussions on the bond and mortgage markets, and secondly, that perhaps one, or more probably two of the segmented credit markets runs into serious trouble leading to rescue operations by the monetary and fiscal authorities which are themselves hobbled by lack of leadership in devising the appropriate measures, or by political divisions that render the authorities catatonic and incapable of effective action. The thirty-three economists from thirteen countries are concerned about the first of these scenarios for disaster, although James Tobin exhibits abundant sang-froid. As I recall the spread of liquidity crises from one market to another in past troubles—not always the same markets to be sure, and not always closely related—I am alive to that source of trouble.

An interesting question is whether commodity, equity, junk-bond, foreign-exchange mortgage, and consumer-credit markets should be regarded as isolated and separate, or as linked. If the chance of trouble in any one market that could not be promptly and effectively halted by lender-of-last-resort action were 1 in 10, and real trouble would come if two markets were battered with disintermediation and liquidation, should the chances be multiplied, or added? If multiplied, the risk of real trouble is 1 in 100; if added, it is one in five. My reading of history suggests that asset and credit markets are intimately connected, and that real trouble that is not promptly handled would be likely to spread, and possibly overwhelm the safety net of deposit insurance and lender-of-last-resort action. But I take great comfort in the responsiveness of the authorities, both Democratic and Republican, to the crises in Chrysler, New York City, Lockheed, First Continental, the Hunt silver collapse, etc. etc. The world has learned, or relearned, a lot since 1929–32. The problem comes down to the will and force to apply the lessons of that period.

I have many times suggested that the problem is far easier at the national than at the international level. Nations have governments that are assigned responsibilities. Some may dither, and some may be incapable of action because of political gridlock. The presidential campaign in the United States this year is widely marked by candidates' assertions that they can produce the necessary leadership in government. Not all such assertions are credible.

In the international field there is no government, and at best weak institutions such as the United Nations, the Organization for Economic Cooperation and Development, World Bank and International Monetary Fund, the G-5, G-7, G-24, G-30, the Group of 77 which actually consists of more than 130 countries, and so one. Responsibility is not firmly lodged. Countries and country-leaders will have to rise to the occasion as it presents itself. I see no way to predict whether financial crises will be met with effective action so that summer storms will quickly give way to plain sailing. Sometimes they do, sometimes they don't. If one believes in free will, rather than dialectical materialism and inexorable social forces, one is likely to be more cheerful. True believers with a strong prior that markets never make mistakes are unhappy as they contemplate the power of government to mess it up and leave the economy in a muddle. As a student of history with a congenital optimistic streak, I choose to make no firm predictions. We shall see what we shall see.

REFERENCES

Bryant, Ralph C. and Portes, Richard (eds) (1987), *Global Macroeconomics: Policy Conflict and Cooperation*, London: Macmillan in association with the International Economic Association and the Centre for Economic Policy Research.

Coombs, Charles A. (1976), *The Arena of International Finance*, New York: Wiley.

Erdman, Paul (1976), *The Crash of '79*, New York: Simon and Schuster.

Friedman, Milton and Schwartz, Anna J. (1963), *A Monetary History of the United States 1867–1960*, Princeton, NJ: Princeton University Press.

Garber, Peter M. (1987), 'The Dollar as a Bubble', paper presented to the Brandeis University Symposium, The Economics of the Dollar Cycle, December 4, unpublished.

Institute for International Economics (1987), *Resolving the Global Economic Crisis After Wall Street*, Special Report 6, A Statement by Thirty-three Economists from Thirteen Countries, Washington, DC: Institute for International Economics.

Kindleberger, Charles P. (1986), *The World in Depression, 1929–1939*, revised ed., Berkeley: University of California Press.

Mishkin, Frederic S. (1978), 'The Household Balance Sheet and the Great Depression', *Journal of Economic History*, vol. 38, no. 4 (December), pp. 918–37.

Moggridge, D.E. (1982), 'Policy in the Crises of 1920 and 1929', in C.P. Kindleberger and J.-P. Laffargue, eds, *Financial Crises: Theory History and Policy*, Cambridge: Cambridge University Press, pp. 171–87.

New York Times (1987), 'What Lies Ahead: 40 Views', December 20, p. F.4.

—— (1988), 'How Markets Fared Around the World in 1987', January 4, p. D.3.

Olson, Mancur (1982), *The Rise and Decline of Nations: Economic Growth, Stagflation and Social Rigidities*, New Haven, CT: Yale University Press.

Tobin, James (1987), 'Eight Myths about the Dollar', paper presented to the Brandeis University Symposium, The Economics of the Dollar Cycle, December 4, unpublished.

2 Overtrading, Sometimes Followed by Revulsion and Discredit*

The title of this chapter is the same, in translation from classical economist English, as that of my *Manias, Panics and Crashes*, adopted because I like the mouth-filling rhetoric of Adam Smith and John Stuart Mill. I propose to summarize that book concisely, and to show how the model in it (which originated by Hyman Minsky) applies to 1929 and today.

The model starts with what Minsky calls a 'displacement', that is, an autonomous shock, financial or real, which closes down old and opens up new opportunities for investment. Financial displacements include an unexpected success in security flotation that encourages more; debt refunding that lowers interest rates and sends rentiers on to riskier investments to maintain their incomes; mistakes in recoinages or monetary policy, most notably in recent times attempting to lower interest rates in the United States in 1970 and 1971 in an effort to help re-elect President Nixon when the Germans were trying to raise them, the joint pressures flooding the Euro-currency market with dollars and kicking off the bank lending to Third World countries well before the need for recycling the OPEC gains of 1973. Real displacements are the start of wars, the end of wars, good harvests, bad harvests, mineral discoveries, opening up of new lands in the United States in the 1830s and 1840s, in Argentina in the 1880s, sharp price increases as in the OPEC 1973 and 1979 price hikes, innovations, canals in the 1790s, railroads in the 1840s in Britain, computers in the 1980s. Overtrading and revulsion are frequent in foreign exchange as the recent history of the yen and the dollar demonstrates. One could go on to mention investment fads—shopping centers, real estate

* A lecture before the Bank Credit Analyst's symposium in New York City, 22 September 1986 and published in The Bank Credit Analyst Special Monograph on 'The Escalation in Debt and Disinflation: Prelude to Financial Mania and Crash?', Montreal, Canada: BCA Publications, 1987, pp. 50–62.

investment trusts (REITs), office buildings, condominia in Southern California . . . But enough.

The displacement leads to new investment which may (or may not) grow in cumulative fashion. Under rational expectations—a theory of monetary economists holding that markets digest all the available information according to some reasonable economic model and grind out an appropriate set of prices and the right amount of investment—an excessive response is impossible, or at least unlikely. But rational expectations as a hypothesis rests on the presumption that the market has one mind, one level of intelligence, one set of information, one objective function or goal, when in fact there are many different groups involved with heterogeneous capacity for responding to a given impulse. Some invest early for synergy with other projects; some for income; some to make short-run capital gains; some late after the market has been rising for an extended period and they belatedly catch on. As some make capital gains, others become infected with what may politely be called an appetite for income and wealth, but more bluntly are avarice and greed. The asset or assets in question rise in price. Euphoria sets in and a boom. The boom in one asset may spread—from one or more objects of investment to others, from one or more countries to others. Possible trouble arrives if prices in two or more markets climb to unsustainable heights.

A number of monetary economists think that overtrading is readily forestalled by a monetary policy that ensures that the quantity of money grows at some steady appropriate rate. This surely is the correct policy on trend. But if the excitement is sufficiently high, it is unlikely to be contained in this fashion. Markets and bankers are innovative, and in new circumstances can monetize credit in new ways. When money consisted almost entirely of specie, it was extended by the development of bills of exchange, including chains of such bills as one man drew upon another, and the second back on the first, by the addition of bank notes, and then bank deposits and in more recent times CD's, credit cards, money funds, NOW accounts, super-NOW accounts, etc., etc. The most imaginative and most terrifying innovation in recent history has been the use for speculative investment in Kuwait in 1982 of post-dated cheques, instant money of appalling quality that at least had the advantage of making US nineteenth-century experience with wildcat banking look tame.

If overtrading or overshooting based on expectations of continued price rises continues apace, it is likely to be followed by a period of 'distress'. Distress occurs when the expectation of continued price increase begins to erode and the possibility of a price decline comes to be considered. There is great uncertainty. The period of distress may be extended or brief. Not enough is known about how markets form expectations to be able to say a great deal on the subject. Economists are for the most part interested in 'fundamentals', variables such as national income, the balance of payments, investment, savings, government spending and the like; markets are often guided by psychology which may converge to or differ from the fundamentals. Distress is a term borrowed from corporation finance, and means in that connection that the officers of a corporation can reasonably contemplate the possibility—but only the possibility—that the company can go bankrupt. In a broad financial market distress is the realization on the part of a significant portion of the market that prices are too high and will have to be adjusted downward.

The downward adjustment may be gradual and orderly or it may be a precipitate revulsion, a crash of prices and even a panic of market participants. The gradual movement or rush out of liquid assets into real or long-term financial assets rising in price in the period of euphoria may be followed by orderly liquidation or by a rush of illiquid into liquid assets. The way to halt a panic, should it occur, is well known. There should be a lender of last resort, who quiets the excited rush into money by assuring the market that money will be available. The lender of last resort must be identifiable and accept the responsibility for quietening things down. In periods of national revulsion it is usually the central bank, sometimes the Treasury, sometimes even money-centre banks. In international crises, the problem is more difficult: international institutions may not have the resources or move fast enough, and a national lender or national lenders pose questions of choice of country or countries and of institutions within them. In addition, the function poses problems of moral hazard, as in insurance. If investors or countries know they are going to be rescued, the resolve to act prudently declines.

This then is the model: displacement, followed by euphoria (overtrading) and possibly distress, possibly further revulsion (a crash and/or panic) leading again possibly, unless alleviated by a lender of last resort, to deep discredit, serious trouble for the banking system and economic depression. How does this model apply to 1929, and what is its relevance today?

It is to my mind shocking that economists and economic historians do not agree today, fifty years after the event, on what brought on the stock-market crash of 1929 and the depression of the 1930s. There is disagreement first between the monetarists and the Keynesians. Monetarists think that 1929 somehow produced a stock-market crash and a mild recession which was magnified into a major depression by mistakes of monetary policy. On occasion they go so far as to ascribe the recession to the fact that the money stock was not growing in 1929, even though it did not decline. They reject a role for price changes, on the grounds that for every loser by prices declines, a seller, there was a gainer, a buyer, and to think otherwise is to be guilty of 'money illusion'. The crash and depression were of American origin, a phenomenon that spilled over to Europe and the rest of the world. Bank collapse had nothing to do with the stock market. They find no role for exchange rates.

The Keynesian reply to the monetarists is that the trouble started in spending and spread thence to money. The foremost defender of this position is Peter Temin, who, however, does not attempt to identify the cause of the decline in spending. This has been done by W.W. Rostow, who thinks it lay in the exhaustion of the wave of investment in automobiles, gasoline and suburbs after World War I, and differently by Clarence Barber who ascribes it to the end of the housing boom after the population spurt following the war. For Temin the proof that spending declined first and not the money supply lies in analysis of movement of the interest rate along the lines of the Hansen–Hicks IS-LM model. With the interest rate on the vertical axis and national income on the horizontal, the test of whether it was the IS (investment/savings) curve that moved or the LM (liquidity/money) curve turns on what happened to interest rates. If the interest rate went down, it was spending that shifted, with a shift *along* the LM curve; if the interest rate went up, the autonomous shift occurred in money. Since the interest rate fell after January 1930, Temin believes in the Keynesian, not the monetarist, explanation.

The analysis on both sides seems to me too simple by half. It leaves out:

1. The halt in foreign lending in the middle of 1928 when the New York stock market started moving up, cutting investment in Germany, Argentina, Australia, etc., leading to depression in Germany, early depreciations of the Argentine peso and the Australian pound, and putting pressure on world prices of wheat, meat, wool, etc.;
2. The increase in interest rates in 1928 and 1929 as the call-money market was turned to in order to finance the mania in stocks. This hurt automobile and housing purchases, and started US national income down from the June 1929 peak;
3. The steady rate of bank failure in the farm country as farm prices fell from 1925 and were unable to support the weight of farm mortgage debt contracted during World War I and the run-up of farm prices in 1919–20;
4. The January 1929 failures of the *Bodenkreditanstalt* of Austria and

the Williams Deacon Bank in Manchester, England, the former rescued in a merger with the *Kreditanstalt*, itself to fail in May 1931; the latter in a secret lender-of-last-resort operation by the Bank of England;

5. The need to rescue the two major Italian banks in the spring of 1930, both done secretly by the Bank of Italy, the banks having been weakened by large holdings of industrial shares that declined first in 1923, again in 1926 when the lira was revalued upward, and finally in the 1929 collapse in securities that spread around the world from Wall Street after Black Thursday and Tuesday, 24 October and 29 October.

6. The spread of liquidation and price declines from the stock market in October 1929 to commodities, especially those imported that were then conventionally shipped to New York on consignment and sold to brokers on arrival. Absorbed in trying to liquidate brokers' loans in the call-money market after out-of-town banks and 'all other' lenders withdrew, New York banks cut off lending to other borrowers. Without credit, commodity brokers could not bid for materials dumped on the mercantile exchanges. Import commodities—especially cocoa, coffee, hides, rubber, silk, tin, and zinc—fell 10 per cent to 25 per cent in price in three months, a movement that defies a Keynesian or a monetarist explanation. Export commodities and sugar, imported but owned by US companies, both financed in the interior, fell in price much less;

7. The spread of security liquidation from stocks on the New York exchange to second-grade securities, including municipal bonds and mortgages that later brought about the collapse of Caldwell and Co. in November 1930 and the Bank of the United States in December, after months of fighting off bankruptcy in a struggle for cash;

8. A persuasive demonstration of changing economic expectations as early as March 1930 after interest rates had fallen well below 1928 levels, when second-grade foreign bonds declined in price as high-grades held up, with the same phenomenon repeated in the US domestic issues in September 1930. The earlier wedge between sound and unsound issues in foreign bonds makes it difficult to believe that the depression started in the United States and spread abroad;

9. Deflationary pressure after September 1931 when the pound left gold and depreciated drastically. Keynesian and monetarist analyses ignore the exchange rate. In a world of inflation, however, depreciation raises the prices of exports and imports, while appreciation leaves them unchanged; when the world is on the verge or has started down the road of deflation, on the other hand, depreciation leaves prices unchanged and appreciation such as occurred to the dollar and the gold bloc lowers them. There was an additional monetary effect on the United States after the decline of sterling from the conversion into

gold in New York of $750 million in dollar deposits owned by the gold bloc—France, Belgium, the Netherlands and Switzerland—that induced the Federal Reserve inadvisedly to raise its discount rate, a solid point for the monetarists. But Keynesians and monetarists both ignore the impact of appreciation on prices, convinced as they are of the non-existence of money illusion. The dynamics are against them. Producers facing falling prices know immediately that they have lost, and so do their banks when they fail to service loans. The banks may fail, and many did in 1930 and 1931. Consumers, however, are slow to realize that they have gained and to increase their spending. Few of them start new banks.

In the last years, the monetarists have admitted one international element into their analysis, the Hawley–Smoot tariff of June 1930. In one extreme version, relying on rational expectations, Jude Wanniski blames the crash of the stock market on it, even though the act was not passed and signed until nine months later. Rational expectations require some outside unexpected event to change prices to the extent that the market fell on Black Thursday and Black Tuesday, being unwilling to accept the conventional explanation that the Hatry crisis in London tightened interest rates there, which drew British funds out of brokers' loans in New York which started to unravel the credit support for the stock market. In searching the press, Wanniski found that a subcommittee had voted against a motion to lower the tariff on some carbide product. In his interpretation this was a signal to the stock market that the Hawley–Smoot bill would be enacted and signed and met with widespread retaliation. Most monetary economists merely observe that the tariff was deflationary, although in the usual macroeconomic analysis, tariffs expand domestic spending and are stimulating unless they meet with retaliation that overwhelms the effect.

In my judgment the depression of the 1930s was so wide, so deep, and so long because there was no lender of last resort. Local lenders of last resort had propped up the British Williams Deacon bank in 1929, and the Italian banks in 1930. The Federal Reserve system was not especially interested in saving the distressed farm banks because it thought there were too many weak ones. Caldwell and Co. and the Bank of the United States, neither a very salubrious firm, were also allowed to fail. The real weakness, however, was the absence of an international lender of last resort. The British could not come alone to the rescue of the Austrian banks, as the detailed history of the *Kreditanstalt* shows, and when the collapse spread to Germany in June 1931, the United States and the French would not. The French wanted to impose political conditions on Austria, and to debate for three weeks the exact conditions to be applied in the German case, during which time the German banks and foreign exchange position went under. The essence of last-resort is that it be done rapidly, without conditions, and with details to be worked out later.

In due course, from 1934 when the Reciprocal Trade Agreements Act was passed, or from the 1936 Tripartite Monetary Agreement that provided cover for a devaluation of the French franc, or possibly only from the Atlantic Charter of June 1941, the United States moved to take up the world responsibilities that Britain had relinquished. Earlier, it failed to see the need, both when the crash and depression began and a decade before that. Then, it refused to take any leadership in resolving the financial imbroglio of war debts, reparations and commercial debts on the one hand, and the overvaluation of sterling, undervaluation of the French franc, making for a piling up of French claims on London, on the other.

THE 1960s AND 1970s

The world economy has survived well on the whole—in many cases brilliantly—for four decades after World War II, compared to its collapse in depression little more than a decade after World War I. In part this was because the United States took the lead in steering clear of many of the mistakes of the 1920s and 1930s, escaping the tangle of war debts and reparations with Lend–Lease and UNRRA, not to mention the British loan and the Marshall Plan. Bretton Woods provided for stability of exchange rates until 1973 and loans for economic development. The position was sustained particularly well until the Vietnam War in the second half of the 1960s, when bit by bit new problems arose. The international lender of last resort function had been worked out in March 1961 with the so-called Basle Agreement that provided for swaps among the central banks of the leading financial countries. Then came a series of shocks—the flooding the the Euro-currency market with dollars in 1970 and 1971 as already mentioned, the Nixon–Connally shock of August 1971 when the United States slammed down the gold window after breaking up the London gold pool in 1968, the move to flexible exchange rates in the spring of 1973, the Nixon embargo on soybean exports to Japan that depended on them in the summer of 1973, the oil shock of November 1973, and inflation. As the dollar moved down and up again in a world of sellers' markets and inflation, the ratchet which had lowered world prices in the deflationary 1930s this time raised them. World oil prices fixed in dollars, for example, were raised each time the dollar depreciated, but not lowered when it appreciated. Each full cycle of the exchange-rate sine wave thus pushed prices higher.

Euphoria in financial markets was happily rather scattered, so that excesses could be contained in local settings and financial crises did not propagate widely. With the adoption of floating there were spurts of speculation in foreign exchange by the Herstatt Company of Cologne and the Franklin National Bank of New York, resulting in 1974 failures that might have ricocheted through the financial world had it not been for agreement among the central banks that each would be responsible for the obligations of its nations' banks anywhere in the world—the so-called Basle protocol of 1975. The Hamilton Security Bank of Chattanooga got caught up in lending on mortgages in Atlanta, and the United States National Bank of San Diego provided the first billion-dollar bank failure in November 1973. These setbacks were the result of a recession in 1974–5 but were kept from spreading by the federal deposit insurance put into effect in 1934.

At the end of the 1970s came another OPEC oil shock and a run on the dollar which was fended off after some years of benign neglect by intervention in the foreign exchange market and a squeeze at the end of October 1979. A new recession combined with a programme of tight money by the Federal Reserve System produced another wave of difficulties, especially after oil prices started declining in 1982.

THE 1980s

Outside the financial area, there were near bankruptcies, saved by government intervention, of New York City, of Lockheed and the Chrysler Corporation. Nearer the financial arena was Bunker Hunt's attempt to corner the silver market, that required the Federal Reserve to prop up Bache and Co. that had advanced funds to Hunt that he could not immediately repay. Hunt lost $1 billion in this failed effort, defeated by expanded new production, the melting down of silverware at high prices, and reclaim—an episode that recalls the equally disastrous attempt of one Denfert-Rocherau in 1888 to corner the world copper market, defeated by similar forces. Luckily the Hunts had three billion dollars of wealth so that after Bache had been assisted the loss could be absorbed and did not spread. There were further bankruptcies of firms dealing in government securities via the 'repo' market that got leveraged too far and bet the wrong way—Drysdale Securities and Lombard–Wall, not to mention E.S.M. Securities of Fort Lauderdale, Florida. But the major problem occurred in four batches: disintermediation, as it affected the thrifts; loans of farm banks concluded at the peak of inflation of farm prices in the 1970s and badly hurt by the decline in grain and meat prices; banks that had loaned heavily on oil; and Third World syndicated bank loans.

The thrifts have now been through the worst, it would appear, with interest rates falling substantially in 1986. A problem remains in that the FSLIC (Federal Savings and Loan Insurance Corporation) has run out of money, and a number of banks, savings and loan associations and state systems remain in trouble. Acute spots are found in Maryland, Ohio, which got caught up in the E.S.M. failure in Florida, and in California where, in addition to thrifts stuck with old mortgages at low interest rates and the necessity to borrow on CD's at much higher interest, there are some banks like Crocker National of San Francisco that got caught in the boom in million-dollar condominia in Southern California that have fallen sharply in price and are worth less than the mortgages. The government is trying to help on an *ad hoc* basis, by shifting rescue funds from the Federal Home Loan Banks to the FSLIC, and to ease restrictions against interstate takeover of failing banks so as to lighten the burden of making good their deposits. It is important not to have to ask for special legislation to raise new funds at a time when the federal budget is widely unbalanced and Gramm–Rudman–Hollings legislation calls for a relentless march to balance. Extended debate over who is to blame for what would upset financial markets and possibly incite attempts at further liquidation of assets that are sound in the long run.

Farm banks remain a serious problem, and the danger extends, of course, to such providers of farm supplies as machinery and fertilizer, although these have been working on their troubles for some years. Farm banks are in difficulty, as are the farmers themselves, not to mention the government agencies designed to prop up farm banks. There was a brief prospect of increased export sales because of the Chernobyl disaster, but it did not last, and a likelihood of further losses on sales to Spain and Portugal which are joining the European Common Market—an issue still under negotiation. But the potential for claims on government support remains.

The fall in the price of oil has already brought down Penn Square in Oklahoma and contributed to the reorganization of the Continental Illinois Bank in Chicago which bought $1 billion in oil loans from Penn Square. But troubles remain in Texas, Oklahoma and Alaska in the United States, not to mention Canada and other oil producers in various parts of the world such as Mexico, Venezuela, Indonesia, Peru, etc. In part, the problem of oil merges into that of loans to Third World countries, but some countries such as Brazil and Argentina benefit from the decline in oil prices, while others suffer on both oil and non-oil account.

The crisis in Third World debt is sometimes said to have surfaced in 1982 with the Mexican oil crisis of that year, but it was widely recognized to exist as early as 1977, even though some bankers such as Walter Wriston of Citicorp refused to acknowledge it. The world as a whole had the reality borne in with the Mexican crisis of August 1982, followed by the necessity to negotiate new arrangements in the debts of Argentina, Brazil and a series of lesser situations. A number of voices have been raised calling for a world economic conference to renegotiate the debts of Third World countries. Most observers, however, favour a case-by-case approach, sometimes called 'muddling through'.

Third World debt, as it happens, is not the only substantial pile of debt representing overtrading. A run-up in stock prices has been financed by low-grade bonds—called 'junk bonds'—issued to finance or resist corporate takovers. Consumer debt on instalment purchases and credit cards is at an all-time high, as is mortgage financing. Banks encourage homeowners to borrow against the equity in their houses with second mortgages. Felix Rohatyn has said that the world has become a junk-bond casino.

There is a temptation to compare the 1980s with 1929 and 1930, equating the Third World debt to the tangle of reparations, war debts and commercial bank lending to such countries as Germany; the 1929 stock market to the 1986 bond market (the 1986 stock market not being high by comparison with 1929 after adjustment for the rise in prices); the decline in commodity prices, especially oil, to the shakeout in commodities that accompanied the stock market crash of 1929; and of course farm prices with farm prices, against the background of excessive borrowing against the value of farms, 1920 as against 1982. One could go on and compare the failure of the Franklin National Bank to that of the Bank of the United States, both suburban banks that belatedly went into New York City and catered to risky loans in an effort to make their way; the Butcher banks in Tennessee and Kentucky of 1982 to Caldwell and Company in Nashville in 1930 that brought down a chain of banks in Tennessee, Kentucky and Arkansas.

The differences, however, are significant. In the first place, instead of the fluctuating exchange rates of the 1930s that were deflationary in a deflationary world, and those of the 1970s, inflationary in an inflationary world, we have, first, an attempt since September 1985 to bring about more exchange-rate stability, and second, a world poised between inflation and deflation. These have meant that the rise of the dollar to a height in February 1985 and its subsequent 40 per cent decline as I write produced no ratchet either in an inflationary or a deflationary direction.

Secondly, initiatives have begun to coordinate macroeconomic policy in a way that was barely thought of in the 1930s with its belief at the time that the gold standard would produce coordination automatically. It is true that in July 1927 a meeting at the Long Island home of Ogden Mills, US Secretary of the Treasury, gathered the representatives of the principal central banks—Benjamin Strong of the Federal Reserve Bank of New York, Montagu Norman of the Bank of England, Hjalmar Schacht of the Reichsbank, and Charles Rist of the Bank of France—to concerted action to ease the pressure against Britain. This was an isolated incident, along with the appeal forty years later of Secretary of the Treasury, H.H. Fowler, at Chequers in England, in 1968, to adjust monetary policy in aid of the United States balance of payments. The world now realizes that more is needed, although negotiating difficulties as to which country moves first inhibit action. Recognition of the need, however, is a giant forward step.

Thirdly, and most important, the world understands the need for an international lender, lenders of last resort. This awareness was absent in 1930–2, when instead of helping, countries tended to look after their own short-run interests, often at long-run cost. The lessons articulated by Henry Thornton in 1802 and Walter Bagehot in 1873 were forgotten. Today they have been fully relearned. Last resort lending takes place among the financially-developed countries through the swap network that produces instant credits for central banks in periods of crisis. These swaps are not extended by developed to developing countries because of a lack of trust that the position would be reversed at the end of six months, whether by an undoing of the crisis and a return of capital flight home, or by funding the outstanding balance through the International Monetary Fund or otherwise.

The arrangements for last-resort lending to Third World countries in crisis have an *ad hoc* quality that is hard on the nerves: reliance mainly on the International Monetary Fund which tries to drive the money-centre banks to carry old loans forward and make new loans, while the money-centre banks do the same to the regional banks that would dearly love to get paid off and bow out. The IMF has two disabilities as lender of last resort: it takes time to make decisions, whereas sometimes a crisis billows up so fast that time is not available; secondly it feels that need to lay down conditions as to macroeconomic behaviour of those whom it rescues, when those conditions inevitably have political dimensions that on occasion lead to breakdown. That the problem is not a new one is underlined by the fact that those imposed by American and French bankers in August 1931—following, to be sure, the recommendations of the British May Committee about cutting down the dole to balance the budget—brought about the collapse of the Labour government and led Britain to abandon the gold standard.

The slowness of the IMF to make decisions about rescue loans has been remedied after a fashion by bridging loans and such expedients as the United States buying a billion dollars worth of oil from Mexico for the stockpile. If many more devices of this sort are required at a time when the United States budget is unbalanced and the Congress is committed to its reduction, lender of last resort action may give rise to political problems among the rescuers as well as among the rescued.

Conditionality imposed by lenders, even international lenders like the IMF and the World Bank that are struggling to get new resources to operate on a larger scale and to develop new techniques, is inevitably resented. Thus far with few exceptions, Third World countries have avoided the defaults that plagued the 1930s, since they are highly conscious of their need for capital to achieve high rates of growth and aware that past default has led to exclusion from international borrowing for a generation. There is, nonetheless, some limit beyond which they are unwilling to be pushed in the direction of austerity which is hard to sustain politically.

There is, however, a number of possible bases for disquiet on which reasonable economists may differ:

In the first place, there is a weakening of the United States' appetite for and capacity to fill the role of stabilizer of the world economy, including that of lender of last resort. The US share of world income has fallen since World War II from something like 40 per cent to 16 per cent. Germany and Japan have risen in economic strength, continue to support the system without challenging it, but exhibit no inclination to take over the stabilizing role. A number of suggestions have been made for a duumvirate—Japan and the United States—or a troika—Japan, Germany and the United States—that together take over the function. There are strong theoretical reasons, however, to think that shared responsibility approximates no responsibility. The change of the United States from a creditor to a debtor nation—while it cannot be pinned down in time precisely because of difficulty of measurement—weakens the capacity of this country to assist others in trouble. Less debilitating perhaps than the accumulated deficits in the government budget and the US balance of payments is the persistent deterioration both in the rate of personal savings and in productivity increases, suggesting that the country is aging and following Britain into economic senility a century later.

Secondly, the prospect of shocks to the world economy has in no way dimmed. The energy picture is still uncertain, given the political difficulties and the possibilities of war in the Middle East and in North Africa. Political upheavals in Central America and South Africa cannot be excluded. Alexandre Lamfalussy of the Bank for International Settlements notes that the financial systems of the main Western industrial countries are going through not one, but in some cases as many as four, interconnected revolutionary processes: disinflation, internationalization, innovation in financial instruments, and deregulation, in each of which, he claims, economic theory can do little to guide the world. Displacements or autonomous shocks to the system are inevitable, and are likely to lead to destabilizing feedbacks. Finally, there are possible shocks from terrorism and nuclear disaster, on which I hestitate to comment.

Thirdly, there are indications of rising national preoccupation at the expense of international concerns—protectionism in trade and declining foreign aid while domestic spending is skimped because of budget constraints. The present Republican Administration is strongly opposed to protectionism, but is pushed in that direction by parochial interests.

Where the balance of the three positive and three negative prospects comes out, it is difficult and probably impossible to judge. To forecast confidently on the basis of some econometric model calls for more faith that I am able to muster. On balance, I suspect that the good side—lack of pressure from a foreign-exchange ratchet, initiatives in coordinating macroeconomic policy and stabilizing exchange rates, plus awareness of the need for crisis management—outweighs the negatives of a weakening United States economy, the prospect of continued shocks, and increasing preoccupation with local and national interest at the expense of the international interest. That highly tentative conclusion, however, may merely reflect an inherently optimistic temperament that comes from a eupeptic digestive system inherited from my forebears.

NOTE

1. This is not a scholarly article, and those who want support for its didactic statements, or further detail, are invited to see the revised (1986) edition of my 1973 book, *The World in Depression, 1929–39*, along with the 1978, *Manias, Panics and Crashes*.

3 Reflections on Current Changes in National and International Capital Markets*

The invitation to present views to the House of Commons Treasury and Civil Service Committee on changes under way in international credit and capital markets, with emphasis on Third World debt, 'securitization', and energy and agricultural loans, especially outside the United States, emphasizes that one may proceed as one sees fit. It is hard to find much new to say about Third World debt, but I offer some reflections late in the chapter on muddling through from crisis to crisis, plus useful limited initiatives of the Baker variety, as against what the BIS 1986 Annual Report calls 'grand solutions' (p. 5). On securitization, I can offer no information and few views beyond those contained in the BIS Study Group (Cross) Report (1986), the new Kaufman book (1986), and the daily press. I should like, however, to link the discussion to some continuing themes of financial analysis, relating especially to intermediation and disintermediation, direct dealing versus dealing through entrepot centres, and the occasionally disequilibrating effects of innovations in finance, or autonomous shocks of various kinds, but especially financial ones. Finally on energy and agricultural loans especially outside the United States, my knowledge is again limited, but I should like to make a few remarks about debt in general and its potential for financial crisis, for debt deflation leading to depression, the lender of last resort function and its dilemmas, together with the choice in the case of financial distress or crisis, between grand solutions and muddling through.

* This chapter was written in the summer of 1986 in Helsinki when I was James S. McDonnell Distinguished Scholar at the World Institute of Development Economics Research of the United Nations University. I am grateful for WIDER's support. It was published as Appendix I to the Minutes of Evidence of the Fifth Report from the Treasury and Civil Service Committee, House of Commons, Session 1986–7 on *International Credit and Capital Markets* Volume II, London: HMSO, ordered to be printed 16 March 1987, pp. 111–19.

INTERMEDIATION AND DISINTERMEDIATION

The insertion of an intermediary between lender and borrower performs one or more of several functions: intermediating by size: borrowing small amounts and lending large; by liquidity or term: borrowing short and lending long; by credit risk: borrowing from risk-averse lenders and lending on operations with greater risk; and in the early days of banking, by social standing: borrowing from commoners and lending to the nobility or the sovereign. The risk of lending to the sovereign who was above the law meant that the king could borrow only through an intermediary, such as his intimates whom he was likely to repay—Sir Stephen Fox in the reign of Charles II (Clay, 1978), on collateral such as the royal jewels, or by getting a group of merchants to guarantee the loan, the City of London in England, or the Hotel de Ville in early modern France. The comparable demand for intermediation of credit risk today is furnished by the OPEC countries' refusal to lend directly to Third World borrowers after the price rises of 1973 and 1979, or to sell oil to less-developed countries on credit, as was frequently suggested, but their insistence on depositing the monies from oil sales in Euro-market banks and letting them do the lending. A current suggestion that abundant Japanese savings be invested directly in Third World countries (WIDER Study Group, 1986) may well run into the same reluctance to proceed without mediation.

Economic growth requires more and more effective financial machinery and more and more effective intermediation. Raymond W. Goldsmith asserts that the ratio of financial assets to gross national product, called by him: the financial intermediation ratio (FIR) starts at about .25 in less developed countries and builds with growth to about 1.75 when it tends to level off (1969). This finding is out of date; the ratio of only non-financial debt to GNP in the United States has risen from 1.4 to 1.60 (Cross Report, p. 215).

Disintermediation is of various kinds. It can hit a given set of financial institutions, as when savers draw money from thrift institutions to invest in higher paying money-market funds, or on a national scale in financial crisis when holders of illiquid financial assets seek to convert them into cash or short-term government securities. Cash and central-bank notes backed by short-term governments are sometimes regarded as 'outside money' which cannot be reduced by disintermediation, whereas inside money—bank deposits of various kinds—may rise through intermediation or fall through disintermediation, and typically does so in the course of a business cycle. Moreover an acute bout of disintermediation represents a financial crisis.

ENTREPOTS VS DIRECT TRADING

Up to the middle of the nineteenth century, the history of foreign trade was dominated by the development of successive entrepot centres to which merchants with goods went to sell and merchants seeking goods went to buy. Venice, Bruges, Antwerp, Amsterdam and London successively served in this capacity, possessing quasi-monopolies in their time of the knowledge of what goods were available where and what were wanted where. As this information became widely disseminated, however, it was found that the transport costs of bringing goods to the centre and then shipping them away again could be economised by direct dealing between producing and consuming localities. Entrepot centres gave way to direct trading, and Sweden, for example, bought its wool in Australia, rather than going to London for it. Re-exports died away.

Centralised trading lasted much longer in money than in merchandise because the cost of moving money was small relative to its value. Financial centres formed within nations and on a world-wide basis as areas with excess funds went to a central place to invest it, while localities needing capital went there to borrow. Small centres and local banks persisted because of the difficulty of concentrating credit knowledge about millions of households and hundreds of thousands of firms in a single place, but economies of scale in central dealing continued long after they had been lost in merchandise trade. All this seems now to be in process of change. New issue markets in bonds were perhaps the first to spread around the world. Secondary markets hung on, as the cost of buying or selling a small number of bonds would not cover the costs of searching local markets for the best price (Kindleberger, 1974 (1978)). Satellite communication and computers are now making it possible to search worldwide relatively cheaply and on that account reducing the need for a central place for bond or share trading.

For bank loans, moreover, the advantages of the large commercial bank as an intermediary between savers such as insurance companies, pension funds and well-to-do individuals on the one hand, and large corporations on the other are also being eroded by the technological advantages of linked computers in transmitting and storing information. Direct trading is taking place at the top of the market as prime borrowers deal direct with institutional lenders. The Cross report puts it that the large international banks have lost their comparative advantage to international securities as a channel for credit interme- diation for high-grade borrowers (1986, p. 2). This is not only because credit information is no longer monopolized, but also because of market concern that the credit standing of major non-financial corporations has risen (*ibid.*, p. 15) while that of banks has fallen because of disinflation and the decline in prices of many of their assets (*ibid.*, p. 129). To disinflation, I would add 'overtrading'.

INNOVATIONS

The Euro-currency market that developed in the 1960s and '70s increased the volume of financial intermediation. Banks dealt to a considerable extent with non-banking depositors and borrowers, but on an enormous scale with one another in order to achieve a desired balance of their books in terms of liquidity, currency, interest-rate and credit risks. Corporations frequently borrowed long in the Euro-market and redeposited the funds short, happy to pay the spread so as to be sure of having funds available when they were required. This churning contributed to the expansion of bank balance sheets that led monetary authorities to be concerned for bank capitalization and to lay down requirements of higher capital/asset ratios. Since bank earnings had been squeezed by intense competition in the Euro-currency and national markets, many banks foresaw difficulty in raising equity capital. One move was to steer away from the market for bank shares, and to raise money that counted toward improvement of the capital/asset ratio in the form of subordinate debt. Another was to shift from loans to various innovative devices to serve their customers without adding to the balance sheet. Note-issuing facilities (NIFs)—underwriting a line of credit on the issuance of Euro-notes that would be taken up as a rule by others—some small banks but largely non-banks—involved disintermediation for the major banks. The underwriting banks earned fees instead of interest income. A variety of currency and interest-rate swaps provided the means of accommodating banks and non-banks alike to comfortable positions with respect to currency, term, and interest-rate risk. In addition, securitization, i.e. the bundling of similar loans into a package that could be sold in equal fractions to the market, took assets off the books and earned another fee. The interest-rate risk of a term loan was avoided by this securitization: as a rule a residual default risk remained, because the initiating bank usually bore some responsibility in the case of significant borrower failure.

If prime customers moved to security markets, moreover, the banks could do so too. The Glass-Steagall bill in the United States still prohibits certain types of security trading, but there are ways around the restriction in municipal bonds in the United States, and in dealing in Euro-bonds through foreign branches. Fees, commissions, trading and other non-interest income which had been 24.9 per cent for the six largest New York banks rose to 31.3 per cent in 1985 (*New York Times* (hereafter *NYT*) 16 April 1986). For an aggressive bank like Citicorp, non-interest income in 1984 was 60 per cent of the total (*NYT*, 9 July 1985) while the Bankers Trust Company which was one of the first banks to declare itself interested in merchant banking rather than ordinary commercial and personal business, 1985 non-interest income amounted to 43 per cent (*Financial Times* (hereafter *FT*) 17 July 1986). Innovation typically starts among US banks which have the widest and deepest financial markets and spreads to Europe and Asia. German, French and Dutch banks lag in the process, it would appear from limited information. The gross commission income on security trading of the Dresdner Bank in 1985 amounted to 32 per cent of the sum of that and gross interest income (*FT*, 25 July 1986); and interest income constituted 68 to 70 per cent of the income of the Amro bank in Amsterdam (*FT*, 16 July 1986) and 80 to 90 per cent of the income of French banks (*FT*, 22 July 1986).

Securitization started in the United States as a means of improving the market for residential mortgages. Mortgages were sold by banks and insurance companies to two governmental agencies, the Federal National Mortgage Association (Fannie Mae) and the Government National Mortgage Association (Ginnie Mae), that bought mortgages and issued their own securities against them. The evolution of the mortgage market in the United States provides an illustration of the gradual move from local to regional to national to international credit markets. Originally, and to a considerable extent still, mortgage loans were available only locally, largely from thrift institutions such as savings banks and savings and loan associations. As building proceeded faster on the west coast then in the east of the United States, savings banks in California advertised for deposits in the *New York Times*. Insurance companies collected funds nationally and invested them where the demand was greatest. After World War II, special mortgage credit insurance available to veterans helped build a national market. Then came packaging, first by government agencies and then by banks and insurance companies, equalizing mortgate rates nationally. The last step, in 1986, was the sale of some packaged mortgage loans in European markets.

The success in packaging mortgage loans has led to parallel efforts by banks to take other loans off their books against securities sold to the public—instalment loans, automobile paper, and in the United Kingdom, bundles of officially-guaranteed export credits. Where there is no government guarantee, the risk of default as a rule rests with the issuing bank, though some bundles are sold without recourse. The bank earns an issuing fee, may earn a fee for collecting and distributing the interest income, and where it holds a residual risk, earns a fee on that account. The risk, of course, is an off-balance sheet item that has to be evaluated.

The suggestion has been made by a number of economists, mainly monetarists who believe in perfect markets such as Allan Meltzer and Milton Friedman, that commercial banks burdened with Third World debt sell that off. One or two prices have been quoted as high as 80 per cent of nominal value, but this is always with recourse, as I understand it, and the residual liability in this category is substantial. A *New York Times* account of 9 June 1986 notes that some US banks have sold Mexican debt without recourse at 55 that has been resold at 60 to an American manufacturing firm that takes it to Mexico to exchange against pesos with a nominal dollar value of 90. The firm in this case agreed to maintain its investment in pesos for at least thirteen years, i.e. to 1999. It is not likely that a large amount of Third World debt can be worked off in this fashion. The Cross report emphasizes that US and European banks are reluctant to take the losses involved in selling these loans at deep discounts, and that most business in these loans consists of swapping to improve portfolios. Apart from swaps, outright sales amount to approximately $1 billion a year, a figure that compares with a cumulative total to the end of 1985 of loans sold by US banks, apart from packaging of $45 billion (1986, pp. 136–7).

PARTIAL VS GENERAL EQUILIBRIUM

The crucial question with respect to innovations is whether they correct a position that was in need of adjustment, and stop there, or whether there is a tendency in a highly-competitive financial climate for them to be pushed too far. The Minsky-Kindleberger model used in my *Manias, Panics and Crashes: A History of Financial Crises* (1978) assumes a 'displacement'—an autonomous change in the system, or shock—that leads to a new set of investment opportunities that may go too far, producing what Adam Smith, John Stuart Mill and other classical economists called 'overtrading', that sometimes leads to 'revulsion' and 'discredit'. The displacements are sometimes real—the outbreak of war, the end of a war, a good harvest, a bad harvest, discoveries, inventions, such a shock as the oil price hike by OPEC in 1973 or 1979. They are sometimes financial. Among financial displacements are gold discoveries, debt conversions that lower interest rates sharply and induce those with prospectively lower incomes to take greater risks in an effort to maintain them. An important contributor to overtrading in Third World debt was the mistake of the Federal Reserve System in 1970–71 in trying to lower interest rates to stimulate economic activity in the United States before the 1972 presidential election at a time when the Bundesbank was running a tight-money policy to restrain inflation. Dollars poured out of the US into the Euro-currency market, to Germany where the Bundesbank redeposited them in the Euro-market. The Euro-currency banks, awash with liquidity, started lending to Third World debtors in 1971 and 1972 before the OPEC shock.

Similar financial displacements may arise from financial innovation. The BIS (Cross) report puts it in terms of the new products being under-priced so that market demand takes them beyond prudential risk limits (1986, p. 201). Where the spread of innovations is drawn out, the last to adopt the new techniques are under temptation to carry them too far in an effort to displace the first who have established positions with the best customers. In the case of Third World syndicated bank loans, the regional banks that were drawn in at the end may not have the stamina to stay the course when it becomes clear that the approved therapy is to hang on, shovelling good money after bad, and lend more. If only a few of the regionals pull out, their participations can be absorbed by the large creditors. It happens, however, in such an international crisis as 1931—and in the breakdown of cartels—that the unravelling starts at the fringes.

As a further example of a displacement leading to overtrading in the financial area, there is McKinnon's criticism of 'repression' in financial markets in less developed countries (1973). Repression in this context means favouring certain segments of the capital market—government, foreign trade, multinational corporations and large companies—and discriminating against or repressing others. A number of countries in Latin America were impressed by the argument, deregulated the financial system. In each case, bank lending was carried to excess and ended in crash (Diaz Alejandro, 1985).

In partial equilibrium an innovation may correct a maladjustment or exploit an opportunity for greater efficiency and all other things remain unchanged, or *ceteris paribus*. In general equilibrium change may lead to further feedbacks and loops of the sort suggested. The Cross report expresses it in a series of questions: Do innovations produce enough profit to cover potential losses? (p. 199); does diversification reduce risk or induce money-managers to take greater risks because the portfolio is balanced? (pp. 207, 214); does financial innovation substitute for or add to existing instruments (p. 216). The

Report concludes in assuming on balance that with innovation the banks have taken on more risks (p. 232).

In all this the Miller-Modigliani theorem is relevant as a first approximation. Risks are not reduced by such innovations as limited liability as much as shifted (1958). Floating rate notes (FRNs) reduced the interest-rate risk of the lender, but increased that of the borrower. The same is true of swaps, both currency and interest rate, except in cases where the swapping parties have exactly opposite exposures. And a market participant that reduces one risk may be moved thereby to take on more, thus possibly increasing the risk for the system as a whole.

ENERGY, AGRICULTURAL AND OTHER DEBT

The opinion of the secretary of the Commons Committee, expressed in his letter to me, that the crisis of Third World debt is over is one that I am not sure I share. I come to that topic later. I want first, however, to broaden the discussion from energy and agricultural debt outside the United States to debt more generally, and I am afraid, because of ignorance, mostly that in the United States. Energy and agricultural debt present peculiarly acute problems at the moment in view of the struggles of banks in Oklahoma, Louisiana and Texas to keep afloat, not to mention the problems of Canadian banks enmeshed in the troubles of Dome Petroleum, and the difficulties of Pertamina in Indonesia, national oil companies in Bolivia, Egypt and Venezuela and Pemex in Mexico. A rise in agricultural and farm prices in 1979 led to excessive borrowing not only in the United States but in Canada, Australia and New Zealand. The *International Herald Tribune* (hereafter *IHT*) reported on 19–20 July, 1986 that four more farm-belt banks had failed. The Farm Bank Loan Board that takes over farm debt is virtually out of funds and will be supplied from other governmental bodies rather than run the gauntlet of an appeal to the Congress at a time when budget balance is an acutely sensitive question.

But there are other difficulties. Those of the Bank of America which wrote off $640 millions in the second quarter of 1986 were blamed on losses in oil and real estate; the two are of course connected as the hardest hit commercial realty market seems to be in Houston, Texas, the capital of oil country. The failure of the large conglomerate in steel, LTV, was because of its assumption of very large debts. Such as observer as Henry Kaufman writes about the mountain of debt in the United States, with record levels reached in those of government, given the federal budget deficits since 1981; on mortgages, both residential and commercial, with overbuilding especially in office space and hotels; of consumers, both installment payments and automobile financing; or corporate debt, that in considerable part arises from a wave of corporate takeovers that have been leveraged with so-called 'junk bonds', debt rated below BAA by Moody's. Real estate investment trusts (REITS) in which banks packaged real-estate equity were an innovation of the 1970s that collapsed, but are said to be making a comeback. Another form of finance is the commercial sale and leaseback of real property, especially undertaken by a number of banks to improve liquidity. The present discounted value of the long-term lease is broadly equal to the amount received from the sale of the building, on which perhaps capital gains must be paid if they are not sheltered by operating losses, but the balance sheet is improved by the addition of cash while the lease goes off balance sheet. The buyer of the building is typically leveraged with more debt.

The Cassandras find this disturbing. Felix Rohatyn of Lazard Freres, New York, asserts that the world has become one junk-bond casino (1985). The takeover movement directly and indirectly reduced the volume of equity shares outstanding as it increased the amount of debt, which accounts for some considerable part of the rise in the New York stock market between August 1982 and June 1986. Debt is growing 'much faster' than GNP, the ratio rising from 1.6 to 1 in 1964, to 1.7 to 1 in 1974 and reaching almost 2.1 to 1 in 1984 (Kaufman, 1986, p. 36; see also chart, p. 120).

This burst of borrowing got its impetus largely from the inflation of the 1970s that made it easy to shrug off debt and discouraged saving except through institutionalized means such as pensions and insurance contracts. My MIT colleague Franco Modigliani won the Nobel award in 1985 for his work on the life-cycle hypothesis in consumption. This asserts that households save through the early years and dissave in the later. This is surely the case of savings through pensions and insurance, and considerable dissaving takes place when pensions are drawn on and assets may have to be liquidated to pay for recreational travel and medical expense in old age. In consumer credit and mortgages, however, the opposite is the case: large dissaving occurs in the early years of household formation and saving takes place later in the life cycle to pay down mortgages and pay off instalment loans. Recently in the United States an innovation that especially encourages dissaving is the refinancing of old mortgages to take account of the rise in real estate values and the amounts contractually paid off—a movement that has burgeoned with the decline of interest rates since 1982. Some dissaving out of pension funds has also occurred as funds have been reorganised to take advantage of excess monies beyond contractual liabilities from turnover of workforce whose pensions were not vested. Kaufman's extrapolations to 1999 do not seem to me to be more than shrewd guesses, but he sees US credit markets rising to $16 trillion at the end of the century, as compared with $8 trillion at the end of 1985, with an increasing share that has already risen from 85 to 94 per cent intermediated by institutions, including pension and insurance reserves, money market and other mutual funds, and deposits in commercial banks and thrift institutions (*ibid.*, pp. 194,199).

In Kaufman's opinion the peak of intensity of financial innovation has not yet been reached. The Cross report observes that the successes of innovations in recent years have encouraged banks and non-bank financial institutions to establish groups to search out new ways to make profits or to sustain them in a competitive world setting. It predicts that many banks will be unable to retain corporate business, that size will be needed to take large positions quickly in response to customer needs, and that a smaller number of institutions is likely to emerge with a presence in the market (1986, p. 237). After noting the existence of 'hari-kiri bonds', priced at a loss by Japanese banks in an effort to break into the Euro-market, an American newspaper story asserts that a shakeout is looming in the industry. A New York observer is quoted as saying 'It's going to be war', and another: 'The best are going to survive but in the long run there may not be room for a second tier. You'll have two or three major Japanese firms, two or three European firms, and perhaps seven or eight American firms at the top. Getting to that level, though, is where you'll see the real scrambling' (*NYT*, 1 April, 1986, p. D1).

THE LENDER OF LAST RESORT

As I write, the failure of the First National Bank of Oklahoma, absorbed into the First Interstate Bank of California, and the second quarter 1986 giant loss of the Bank of America have the world waiting for the other shoe to drop, whether in Texas or the farm belt. Third World debt is also tense, with negotiations under way with Mexico, Venezuela and Argentina, a quasi-default in Peru, and potential problem situations throughout the Third World. Even in such a developed country as Australia a mini-crisis broke out at the end of July 1986, involving foreign debts of A$80 billion. I come presently to the question whether these problems are best tackled one at a time as they reach the critical stage, or whether a more schematic and organized approach to the totality is called for. First, however, I want to say something about the role of the lender of last resort.

Fears of another 1929 or 1931 are not warranted, in my judgment, because responsible authorities throughout the world understand the necessity for a lender of last resort. The therapy is not without its own problems or side-effects. Moral hazard is serious; if the major banks know that they are going to be rescued no matter what happens, they are less inclined to act with all due diligence. This seems to me to have been especially the case in the virtually manic spate of Third World lending in the decade from 1971. Again, there are insider-outsider problems: members of the Establishment who are about to fail may be rescued, while pushy outsiders are allowed to go to the wall. Where there are special instrumentalities for farm, real estate or bank salvage (as the Italians call it), old legislative limits may be reached while the problems are still cresting, calling for new legislation that raises political issues not always easy of resolution.

In addition, it is not always clear who the lender of last resort should be: within countries it is usually evident: the central bank for commercial banks, the treasury or parastatal agencies for other seriously-threatening cases. In international crises there is usually a choice which may on occasion by paralysing: the swap system of the Group of Ten, the International Monetary Fund, and where bilateral ties are strong, a foreign national treasury. In the case of the IMF, morever, decision-making among the many parties involved in instructing the directors is slow, whereas crises may have to be resolved in hours, or at most days. Bridging loans may be hurriedly put together, but where amounts are large and cooperation of many parties is required, there may be difficulty in assigning responsibilities.

The Cross report makes a point that the decline of the banking system because of the growing strength of large non-bank financial institutions weakens the system as a whole by depriving it of, or at least weakening the capacity of the large banks to play the role of lender of next-to-last resort (1986, p. 238). The point is well taken. In the United States in the nineteenth century, when there was no central bank and the treasury acted in that capacity fitfully, the money-centre banks leaned against the wind in moderating financial stringency caused by the country banks, now overlending, now dumping loans for cash (Sprague, 1910). Again in the summer of 1929, anticipating the hasty withdrawal by out-of-town banks of call loans to New York stock-exchange houses, New York banks cut back on their own loans to get ready to cushion the impact of withdrawal by others (Kindleberger, 1973, rev. 1986, chap. 4).

Because of moral hazard there should be some ambiguity about whether there will or will not be a lender of last resort, and occasionally a significant firm or bank in very bad shape should be allowed to fail 'to encourage the others'. There may be merit in forbidding inept executives that allowed their institutions to fail to receive a golden handshake on dismissal, the terms of any original contract provision for such having been negated by misfeasance or malfeasance. The acid test is not the standing of the individual firm or bank in the community but whether its failure would generate significant external diseconomies in promoting a rush for liquidity and spreading disintermediation. This refers to bank runs within countries and to a free fall of an exchange rate. On this score it is sad but true that weeding out a number of small firms or banks in the competitive battles ahead will not undermine the safety of the system and can be tolerated so long as the larger ones hold firm.

The crucial point is the credibility of the system in the eyes of the market. This applies especially to Third World debt where it seems a lot to ask the industrial countries to furnish support in one or more of a number of ways—taking over the LDC loans of the banks and writing them down, subsidizing interest payments, providing new direct loans to LDC governments from DC governments, granting new infusions of credit to the IMF and the World Bank, etc. etc. . . . So long as private capital in these countries continued to flee abroad for safety. I cannot judge the validity of the Morgan Guaranty Trust Company's estimates of Latin American capital flight—$100 billions in mid-1986, with Mexico responsible for $50 billions (*NYT*, June 8, 1986, p. C1), or $50 billion between 1983 and 1985 of which Mexico $17 billion, Brazil $7 billion, and Venezuela $6 billion (*NYT*, May 27, 1986, p. D1). The estimates are rough and debatable. I do have a view, however, about the prospect for reversing the present haemorrhage. A report, *Rebuilding Cooperation in the Americas* by the Inter-American Dialogue, calls for a massive flow of resources to Latin America: $12 billion per year from commercial banks, $1 to $1.5 billion each from bilateral lending and in foreign direct investment, $4 billion from multilateral agencies, and $1 to $2 billion in recaptured flight capital (1986, p. 12). The amount mentioned for the commercial banks seems high, given the resistance. Direct investment poses an interesting change of view: during the inflationary late 1960s and 1970s, Latin American countries wanted debt that could be worked off by world inflation rather than direct investment that would share in inflationary profits. Now that inflation has come to an end they reject debt and seek equity investments.

The estimate of the return flow of capital seems especially dubious. If confidence in the exchange rate and in macroeconomic stability can be established, the estimate is far too low. If confidence is not re-established, it is too high as the direction of capital is likely to continue to be outward. Some part of the uncertain estimate of capital flight represents illegal profits of the drug traffic which will stay hidden from Latin American authorities under any circumstances.

The worst-case scenario is the possibility that Latin American firms and households retain their dollars and use them in domestic transactions because of distrust of local means of payment. Such currency substitution, as it is called, has occurred in other pathological monetary conditions—Germany in 1921–23, for example, or Israel until recently. This complicates money management in both countries, not least by making it difficult to understand what is happening.

The essential question is whether the difficulties posed for international credit conditions and capital markets by the debts of the Third World and those in energy, agriculture, real estate, and corporations that are in distress will be settled piecemeal over time by an evolving process—call it muddling through—or whether it requires more thoroughgoing planned and organized treatment—a second Bretton Woods or Marshall plan—what the BIS 1986 report calls somewhat pejoratively a 'grand solution'.

MUDDLING THROUGH VS THE GRAND SOLUTION

Whether one is prone to solve these questions by frontal attack and some once-and-for-all agreement supported by legislation in a number of countries, or prefers to proceed as the way lies open, responding to successive problems and crises as they arise, is to a large extent a matter of temperament. Americans typically seek written constitutions to tidy it all up, whereas the British character is more apt to take the hurdles one at a time. There is something to be said on each side. A shrewd political scientist, Harold Stein, once told me that President Roosevelt was right in 1941 to announce a programme of 50,000 airplanes a year, a staggering number at the time, to galvanize the country into action, whereas President Truman and the Department of State and Interior were right in 1946 to conceal their goal of exporting 40 million tons of coal annually from the United States to Europe and the rest of the world because the industry would have been overwhelmed by such an ambitious goal and might well have given up. In the event the goal was achieved piece-meal.

A further contrast is illuminating. During the war, American and British forces each permitted what was called euphemistically an excess of foreign currency in their troop pay accounts, as they redeemed enemy and occupation currency in dollars and sterling, either through lack of financial astuteness—more bluntly stupidity—as some thought, or deliberately to promote troop morale. The sums were substantial. In Britain, as I understand it, the matter was put to Parliament which voted an appropriation to make good the sterling deficit. In contrary fashion, in the US the army slowly scraped dollars out of other accounts, for example, requiring occupation officials and forces to pay dollars for quarters rental, while they paid German landlords in marks, and paying marks for cameras to be sold for dollars in the post exchanges. After four or five years, the deficit in dollars and excess of occupation currency was closed out, though at some cost, I happen to think, in financial integrity.

Which road to take is rarely an ethical question, but usually one of art as well as temperament. It is posed by the economic recoveries after World Wars I and II. I happen to believe that recovery could have been achieved by the market after mid-1931 if there has been a satisfactory lender of last resort for the Credit Anstalt in May, but that the Marshall plan was necessary in 1947. D.E. Moggridge disagrees on the first score and holds that more thoroughgoing action, resembling the Marshall plan was required in the 1920s (1982).

The record of Bretton Woods is on the side of the grand solutions, along with the Marshall plan, though it must be acknowledged that the agreement was imposed on the conference by the United States rather than freely negotiated (Van Dormel, 1978). Against these successes are two historical episodes of the interwar periods, the World Economic Conference of 1927 under the auspices of the League of Nations that reached a number of tariff agreements on which no action was taken anywhere, and the World Economic Conference of 1933, broken up by an erratic demarche of President Roosevelt, that reached no agreement apart from a derisory one in silver. I side with the evolutionary rather than the constitutional approach. A mild aphorism that I produced at the Kemp-Bradley summit on exchange rates in Washington, DC on 12 and 13 November, 1985 was picked up by some of the press: 'I doubt it is useful to have a meeting of bodies before there is a meeting of minds'.

There is no dearth of proposals for global solutions: from Peter Kenen and Felix Rohatyn for writing down LDC debt by the developed countries, by Jagdish Bhagwati for a debtors' cartel, from Allan Meltzer, Milton Friedman and Mike Faber, the last of the Institute of Development Studies, Sussex, for selling or even auctioning off the debt among the creditor countries (*IHT*, 21 July, 1986). None seems to have much likelihood of agreement within the debtor or the creditor groups, given their different exposures, much less between the two. Even if one side could formulate a coherent solution, an attempt to impose it on the other side runs grave risk of rejection, and breakdown, with deleterious consequences for world stability through effects on banks in the developed world and on Third World access to credit and continued growth.

Nor is there lack of suggestions for drastic steps in domestic banking. Flannery and Guttentag propose that banks should be required by examiners to mark their assets to market, rather than value them at cost, a step that would force many to close their doors (1980). Ian Giddy recommends that off-balance sheet contingent liabilities be valued as a 'put option' according to one of the several formulae available, and counted with balance-sheet liabilities for setting reserve requirements (1985). Henry Kaufman calls for a degree of reregulation. There is doubt that any of these steps is practical: the difficulties of marking to market were referred to above and in case of Third World loans the market is thin or non-existent. Treating off-balance sheet items as put options is too complex to be understood widely outside academic finance and more sophisticated banking circles. Reregulation poses awkward problems because deregulation has gone so far with official tolerance if not blessing that it would probably be necessary to exempt much of what has happened under grandfather clauses.

Muddling through in Third World debt has two aspects: one, the Baker initiative to keep the pressure on the commercial banks, and through them on the regional banks, to roll over maturing debt and advance new, and two, the propagation of concessions won by given debtors in negotiation with their creditors to other debtor countries as their negotiations come up, under implicit most-favoured-nation treatment. Further in the international field it takes the form of such steps as the Basle 1975 protocol following the failures of the Herstatt and Franklin National Bank, making clear that each central bank accepted responsibility for backstopping the banks of its own nationals wherever located. This agreement, to be sure, became somewhat ambiguous when the Bank of Italy refused to make good the liabilities of the Banco Ambrosiano unit in Luxembourg on the ground that it was not a branch but an independent entity. Far-reaching initiative was taken, again by the US Secretary of the Treasury, James Baker, at the Plaza Hotel on 22 September, 1985 to move in evolutionary fashion toward greater exchange-rate stability. One-step-at-a-time technique is clearly called for when central banks and academic experts lack agreement on the design of an ultimately satisfactory system, but can agree that flexible exchange rates have been too volatile. Acceptance of the goal of greater stability by the five paves the way for further practical steps such as may emerge from the report on the international monetary system to be produced by the US Treasury for President Reagan on the future of the international monetary system.

In domestic banking systems, pressure continues to be applied to increase capital ratios, write off bad loans, devise prudential steps to deal with particular off-balance sheet liabilities, and to reorganize troubled banks by having them taken over, changing their executive leadership, and in the worst cases, liquidating them. Takeovers of insolvent banks in the United States have been helped by further deregulation, permitting out-of-state banks, in certain circumstances, and with certain exceptions, to take over banks in other states.

Further scheduled deregulation, such as those of 1 October 1986 and 1 January 1987 in Britain have given rise to considerable uncertainty and an attitude on the part of authorities that resembles watchful waiting.

WHEN AND HOW WILL IT END: WITH A BANG OR A WHIMPER?

The present position is sometimes compared with 1929, with the implication that the world is poised on the verge of a serious debt deflation. I believe that the outcome is excluded by the fact that the lender of last resort function is now so well understood in international terms. In 1929 the doctrine as developed from Henry Thornton (1802) and Walter Bagehot (1873) was thought of exclusively in national terms. There may be slip-ups in future, institutional or political, but the appropriate economic response to debt deflation spreading internationally is generally agreed.

Suppose, however, that lender of last resort therapy is called for on a massive scale, and a large injection of money into the system occurs as a central bank takes on a large volume of assets, domestic or foreign, depending upon whether the financial crisis is domestic or foreign. How does one get the genie back into the bottle, so to speak, or clean up after the big monetary spillage? It is useful to deal with ideal types, first of a domestic, and then of an international rescue or salvage operation.

The polar means of clearing up after a financial crisis in which say the central is a lender of last resort are one to work the collection of bad assets off slowly, and two to inflate. Working them off slowly is the technique used by the Bank of England in the nineteenth century. Whereas the Bank had a rule that it would discount only London paper with two good names, in crisis it frequently violated this as Clapham has described in detail. In the course of various rescue operations the Bank acquired a copper works, iron foundry, coal mines, a plantation in the Caribbean, and of course all manner of failed banks which it liquidated and sold off gradually to recover its money and shrink the money supply. In the case of the three American 'W' banks that were first rescued in 1836 and then allowed to fail in 1839, the Bank of England took fourteen years to get them off the books (Clapham, 1945, II, p. 157). The modern equivalent is the US Reconstruction Finance Corporation established by President Hoover in December 1931. This made rescue loans on various sorts of collateral, and gradually got paid off during the later 1930s, only to be metamorphosed into the Defense Plant Corporation at the outbreak of war, to lend government funds to build and equip new factories, or extensions of old, to produce war materials and inputs. After the war these were sold into private ownership and the corporation liquidated.

In contrast stands the Istituto per la Riconstruzione Industriale (IRI) which was formed in Italy in January 1933 to hold a series of frozen assets that the Bank of Italy had acquired over the years—at the outbreak of World War I, in the recession of 1922, in the recession caused by the 1926 'quota novanta' that raised the Italian lira from 150 to the pound to 90 (and badly battered the prices of stocks owned by the banks), and again with the further collapse of the stock market in 1930–32 (Toniolo, 1980). The original intention had been for IRI to sell off these assets as markets picked up, but recovery was slow, and in March 1934, the Istituto was authorized to organize its holdings, regrouping them by industry, and furnishing them with direction and control. In 1936 when the Italian banks were forbidden to own equity shares in producing corporations, the hope of selling off IRI's portfolio to a perennially weak capital market was abandoned. Much of these bad assets was thus monetized, leading to long-run inflation. The choices then for cleaning up after a domestic lender of last resort operation are by a piecemeal process of liquidation as the opportunity presents, somewhat like the present process of privatization of nationalized industries in a number of countries, or inflation.

In the international sphere, I have already expressed a preference for working off the Third World debt problem slowly, case by case, albeit recognizing the importance of the developed countries maintaining income high, interest rates low, and protection down, and of the LDCs on their part, working toward the restoration of national confidence in the stability of prices and exchange rates. If the developed countries are forced to take over some part of the syndicated loans from the banks, I would urge against an attempt to close the books by exchanging them for Latin American real assets, such as mines, wells or plant transferred to foreign ownership.

A word is perhaps useful on possible exchange crises among developed countries, with special reference to the dollar where the mountain of debt and the distress of the banking system are most evident. Assume that the United States is seen not to be getting its debt position under control and that European and Japanese private interests lose their appetites for dollar assets. If a massive capital outflow from the US should get under way, would European and Japanese central banks operate the swap network to hold the dollar steady, or would it go into a free fall, leading to inflation? The decline of the dollar from March 1985 to the present has not raised US prices significantly, to be sure, but that is because world commodity prices especially in foodstuffs and raw materials are falling in recession.

In such a financial crunch, in my judgment, the swap network should be invoked, although the amounts involved are likely to be so large as to overwhelm it to a degree. Other steps might be called for: recourse to the IMF as the others of the Group of 10 forced on the UK in 1979 or the sale of a substantial amount of US gold if other central banks were willing to accept it. If the swap network were invoked, and the position had not reversed itself in six months, the foreign official claims on the United States might have to be funded into something on the order of 'Roosa bonds', i.e. long-term government bonds with exchange guarantees and provision for resale when the original holder ran into financial trouble.

The swap arrangement should be relatively free of risk of disturbing markets if private European and Japanese investors sold their US assets and bought equivalent long-term assets at home, while European and Japanese authorities bought the US assets sold by their private nationals, and sold long-term assets out of their portfolios to the market at home. If long-term assets of the central banks were insufficient to sterilize the acquisition of US claims in this fashion, they could be created. Something like the British Exchange Equalisation Account might have to be established, though with the ability to create medium- and long- rather than short-term maturities, to prevent the swaps from unduly enlarging the money supplies in the countries acquiring dollars. The operation would be tense, but it is institutionally possible to work out a solution both stable and internationally equitable.

CONCLUSION

Let me summarize in a series of concise statements:

1. While a new wave of financial intermediation is under way with such devices as leveraged buyouts, some disintermediation is in progress as banks get assets off their balance sheets.

2. Investing by institutions that accumulate savings in the securities

of prime corporate borrowers, bypassing the banks, is a form of direct trading that inevitably follows a system of centralized intermediation as communication and information storage and retrieval become technologically easier and cheap.

3. Financial innovation takes place in waves. It runs the risk of over-trading, that may be followed by financial crisis.

4. Overtrading or euphoric and in some cases manic investment in response to perceived opportunities for profit in Third World debt, energy, farm, real estate, both commercial and residental and corporate takeovers has gone to excess in the 1970s and the early 1980s.

5. Such overtrading is unlikely to lead to revulsion and discredit because the role of the lender of last resort in financial crisis is well understood.

6. It is desirable not to seek far-reaching solutions to the problems caused by overtrading, but to proceed on a case-by-case basis.

7. If lender of last resort action on a large scale is called for, it too should be tidied up after the resolution of the financial crisis on an *ad hoc* basis.

REFERENCES

Bagehot, Walter (1873), *Lombard Street: A Description of the Money Market*, London: John Murray.
Bank for International Settlements (1986), *Recent Innovations in International Banking* (the Cross Report) Prepared by a Study group established by the Central Banks of the Group of Ten Countries, Basle: BIS (April).
——— (1986), *Fifty-Sixth Annual Report*, Basle (June 9th).
Clapham, Sir John (1945), *The Bank of England: A History*, 2 vols, Cambridge: Cambridge University Press.
Clay, Christopher (1978), *Public Finance and Private Wealth: The Career of Sir Stephen Fox, 1627–1716*, Oxford: Clarendon Press.
Diaz Alejandro, Carlos F. (1985), 'Goodbye Financial Repression, Hello Financial Crash', *Journal of Development Studies*, December.
Financial Times (1986), various issues.
Giddy, Ian (1985), 'Regulation of Off-Balance Sheet Banking', in Federal Reserve Bank of San Francisco, *The Search for Financial Stability: The Past Fifty Years*, San Francisco: Federal Reserve Bank of San Francisco, pp. 165–77.
Flannery, Mark J. and Guttentag, Jack M. (1980), 'Problem banks: Examination, Identification, Supervision', in Leonard Lapidus and others, *State and Federal Regulation of Commercial Banks*, Washington, DC: Federal Deposit Insurance Corporation, vol. II, pp. 171–226.
Goldsmith, Raymond W. (1969), *Financial Structure and Development*, New Haven, Connecticut: Yale University Press.

Inter-American Dialogue (1986), *Rebuilding Cooperation in the Americas*, Washington, DC: Aspen Institute of Humanistic Studies.
International Herald Tribune (1986) various issues.
Kaufman, Henry (1986), *Interest Rates, the Markets and the New Financial World*, New York: Times Books.
Kindleberger, C.P. (1973, rev. 1986), *The World in Depression, 1929–1939*, Berkeley, California: University of California Press.
——— (1974 (1978)), *The Formation of Financial Centers: A Study in Comparative Economic History*, Princeton Studies in International Finance, no. 3, reprinted in *idem. Economic Response*, Cambridge Mass.: Harvard University Press, pp. 66–134.
——— (1978), *Manias, Panics and Crashes: A History of Financial Crises*, New York: Basic Books.
McKinnon, Ronald I. (1973), *Money and Capital in Economic Development*, Washington, DC: The Brookings Institution.
Modigliani, F. and Miller, M.H. (1958), 'The Cost of Capital, Corporation Finance, and the Theory of Investment', *American Economic Review*, vol. 48, pp. 162–97.
Moggridge, D.E. (1982), 'Policy in the Crises of 1920 and 1929', in C.P. Kindleberger and Jean-Pierre Laffargue (eds), *Financial Crises: Theory, History, and Policy*, Cambridge: Cambridge University Press, pp. 171–87.
New York Times (1985, 1986) various issues.
Rohatyn, Felix (1985), presentation to the Kemp-Bradley summit on exchange rates, Washington, DC, 12 November, 1985.
Sprague, O.M.W. (1910), *History of Crises under the National Banking System*, Washington, DC: US Government Printing Office, for the National Monetary (Aldrich) Commission.
Thornton, Henry (1802), *An Enquiry into the Nature and Effect of the Paper Credit of Great Britain together with the Evidence*, reprinted London: Frank Cass, 1962.
Toniolo, Gianni (1980), *L'economia dell'Italia fascista*, Rome: Laterza.
Van Dormel, Armand (1978), *Bretton Woods, Birth of a Monetary System*, New York: Holmes and Maier.
WIDER Study Group (1986), 'The Potential of the Japanese Surplus for World Economic Development', Tokyo: mimeographed.

4 International Capital Movements and Foreign Exchange Markets in Crisis: the 1930s and the 1980s*

THE MODEL

I propose to discuss the crises of the 1930s and the 1980s in their international financial aspects in terms of a model that starts with an autonomous shock or 'displacement' that reorders profit opportunities, followed by euphoria and excessive investment, leading to what may be called 'distress' as expectations of continued price rises and profits from investment peter out. This may lead to crash, when expectations are fully reversed, unless this can be contained by a lender of last resort. This is the model discussed in my *Manias, Panics and Crashes* (1978), though the treatment of 1929 to 1933 was minimal in that book compared to my *The World in Depression, 1929–1939* which did not use the model.

I put great emphasis on the international aspects of both crises. In this I am not widely followed by most American writers on the 1930s who regard it primarily as an American depression which spilled abroad. In my view, on the contrary, intense international interaction across boundaries produced both the boom and the collapse. The mechanism was only partly and belatedly the foreign-trade multiplier. Much more significant was the transmission of price changes in commodities and financial assets, partly by arbitrage, partly by two markets, side by side, revaluing identical goods or securities by similar amounts without actual sales between them, some purely psychological contagion both of euphoria and of pessimism, and some communication of monetary ease and stringency by capital flows and movements of gold and foreign-exchange reserves.

* A paper prepared for section 5A for the Ninth International Economic History Congress, held in Bern, August 1986, and published in Ivan T. Berend and Knut Borchardt (eds), *The Impact of the Depression of the 1930s and Its Relevance for the Contemporary World*, Budapest: Academy Research Center of East-Central Europe, Karl Marx University, 1986, pp.437–55.

The Displacement of the 1920s

The end of the European war in 1918 produced a change in world demand and supply conditions. With Germany out of action for a time, British investors saw a set of golden opportunities in steel, coal, ships, textiles. Prices of commodities and securities were bid up in 1919–20, and collapsed in 1920–1 to form a classic bubble and bust.

Over the longer term, profound changes had taken place. The world outside Europe had expanded production of primary products during the war—notably sugar and wheat. Rapid technological change in the United States stretching back of the war to the Ford assembly line, led to a boom in automobiles and the associated industries of tyres, rubber, gasoline, not to mention such durable consumer goods as radios and refrigerators. Increased ease of transport required road construction and led to a redistribution of housing. A demographic burst after the war, and northward migration from the south during it, stimulated housing construction.

In finance, a special fillip to foreign lending was given in 1924 by the success of the Dawes loan in the United States, a loan undertaken to prime the pump of German reparations. The loan was oversubscribed eleven times in New York and widened the horizons of American investors who, previously for the most part, had not considered foreign portfolio investments apart from Canada.

The Boom

European recovery from the war had been achieved by about 1925. Britain was still depressed because of the overvaluation of the pound, restored to par in that year, and because of the burden of debt still carried by many business concerns since the 1919–20 bubble. Attempts to lower prices and wages led to strikes. In France, financial tumult lasted until July 1926 when Poincaré stabilized the franc at an undervalued rate, inducing a return flow of capital to France that piled up as Bank of France claims on London and New York. World commodity prices reached a peak in 1925 before easing gradually. In some commodities such as sugar and coffee, affected by long lags of production behind price stimuli, heavy stocks began to accumulate over the market from the middle 1920s, as production belatedly responded to the 1919–20 price peak. Germany undertook a burst of borrowing by states and municipalities—over protests by President Hjalmar Schacht of the Reichsbank. The periphery—Australia, Argentina, Brazil, Chile and others—continued a boom of import substitution and direct investment begun during the war, financed in great measure by US foreign lending.

The last stage of the boom was in stock-market prices, especially in

New York's Wall Street. Prices started to advance in the spring of 1928, and new records were set in the volume of trading which went beyond four million shares a day. Stock purchases were leveraged by one-day brokers' loans. Interest rates tightened in the second half of 1928 and throughout 1929, leading individuals and even business firms to invest in brokers' loans when they were not themselves directly investing in stocks such as General Motors, General Electric, Radio Corporation of America, the Insull public utilities, on margin. The rise of interest rates cut off lending on foreign bonds, and attracted short-term funds from abroad, producing a sharp reversal in the flow of capital from the United States.

DISTRESS

Between the boom when expectations are euphoric, and the crash when they have turned in the opposite direction is an intermediate stage when expectations hesitate and begin to change. It may be protracted or brief. Crisis may be precipitated by some event such as a suicide, defalcation, collapse of a bank, or the distress may continue for an extended period with the financial and business world waiting with bated breath for a turn for the better or worse.

World commodity prices had begun to slip from 1925. The financial position gradually worsened as the undervalued franc piled up claims on the overvalued pound. Germany paid reparations for a time with governmental budget surpluses, offset by state and municipal deficits (James, 1985), and with foreign exchange made available by the state, municipal, and industrial foreign borrowing. When that halted in the second quarter of 1928, the position perceptibly worsened as borrowing was shifted overwhelmingly to a short-term basis. Countries unable to obtain increased short-term credits such as Australia and Argentina ran down their foreign-exchange reserves to cover current-account deficits and waited. The inability of the great powers to settle the tangle of reparations, war debts and commercial debts, in each of which one or another power had conflicting interests, meant that this uneasy situation was temporized.

Particular trouble spots developed in Italy where the overvaluation of the lira in 1926 drove down the stock market and weakened the large 'mixed' banks that invested in industrial equities and debt; and in Austria, deprived of her economic hinterland by the treaty of Trianon and suffering from exchange losses and frozen bank loans in the failure of the speculation against the French franc in 1924. The Bodenkreditanstalt would have failed in January 1929 had it not been taken over by the Österreichische Creditanstalt, which paid, as it later proved, too much for its bad assets. In the same month the William Deacons Bank in Manchester, England, with frozen cotton-textile loans, was rescued by the Bank of England, but quietly so as not to give rise to alarm.

In July 1927, central bankers of the United States, France, England and Germany met on Long Island to see whether a way could be worked out to help Britain as it lost gold to France. The solution was to lower interest rates in New York, and to have the French take gold there rather than in London. The decline in interest rates is sometimes blamed for having given a fillip to the New York stock market the following spring. It was not a dilemma situation, however, as was to be the case two years later in 1929 when the stock market was booming but business was declining, and the Fed raised interest rates. In 1927 there was a slight recession in the United States, largely the result of the Ford Motor Company changing from the Model T to the Model A; lower interest rates were thought desirable both for American business and to ease the British position.

The peak of business in the United States was reached in June 1929, and income and output started to slide gently downward thereafter, largely, it may be judged, because of tightening interest rates as funds were drawn into the brokers' loan market. Money was attracted into this market from abroad which spread the tightness to European markets. Paul Warburg of the Federal Reserve Board warned that the stock market was too high. Investors paid him no heed. The German depression proceeded apace and the Frankfurt Insurance Company collapsed in August 1929. A rumour holds that France started to draw its balance out of London in gold in the same month after her Foreign Minister, Cheron, thought himself insulted at The Hague by the British Foreign Secretary, Snowden, but the evidence is doubtful. In any event, a highly speculative London firm owned by one Clarence Hatry, who used fraudulent collateral to bolster his borrowing capacity, failed in September 1929, tightening London interest rates. British money was brought back to London from New York, increasing the stringency in the brokers' loan market there. The New York stock market collapsed on 24 October, Black Thursday. New York bankers tried to rally the market by moving on to the floor of the Stock Exchange conspicuously placing orders to buy shares. The effort failed, as the device had done on previous occasions in other security markets. Governor George Harrison of the New York Fed, exceeding his instructions from Washington, bought $160 millions of government securities in the week ended October 30, to add to bank reserves and relieve the stringency, and another $210 million in November. The effects were not immediately noticeable in arresting the decline of stock prices.

The stock-market crash is often dismissed as irrelevant to the subsequent deep depression but it was significant in two respects. It spread price declines to security markets in other countries, through arbitrage and through bear-market psychology, and it drove down prices in commodity markets. The latter mechanism operated through tightening bank lending. New York banks had been preparing for months for the withdrawal of loans by other participants in the call-loan market by cutting down their own advances. When they were obliged to fill in to take the place of withdrawals to the extent possible, they rationed loans to other borrowers. Since most commodities imported into New York were shipped on consignment and bought by merchants with the help of bank loans, a cutback in lending to commodity brokers produced a downward shift in the demand for commodities and a sharp decline in commodity prices. Those commodities financed within the United States—exports, or such an import as sugar produced abroad on plantations owned in the United States—fell less than rubber, silk, cocoa, coffee, hides, etc. Moreover, prices fell not just in the United States but worldwide, through markdowns taken from New York prices and perhaps through arbitrage. The speed with which the price deflation spread from securities to commodities, worldwide, makes any mechanism relying on the quantity theory of money in the United States out of the question as an explanation of events.

The New York money market had recovered by January 1930, with interest rates lower than they had been in two years, but with commodity prices, US imports and hence world exports, sharply off. A number of countries, notably Argentina and Australia, running out of reserves and unable to borrow abroad, saw their exports decline. They had little choice but to depreciate their exchange rates. In a world of heavy stocks and widespread deflation, depreciation does not raise prices, but appreciation lowers them—the contrary of a position of world inflation and moderate stocks in which depreciation raises domestic prices and leaves world prices unchanged. The depreciation of the Argentine peso and the Australian pound began in December 1929. Uruguay and New Zealand followed suit in early 1930. These depreciations put further pressure on world prices, especially of wheat and wool.

Keynesians pay little attention to price levels, despite the fact that Keynes himself in 1931 was concerned about price declines and debt deflation. Monetarists hold that since losses from price changes are matched by gains of others, to concern oneself with prices is to be guilty of the error of money illusion. Such a view is mistaken, however, because of the dynamics of the case. With sharp price declines, commodity producers are made immediately aware of their losses, while consumers are slow to become conscious of their gains. Moreover, banks of producers may see their loans become frozen, whereas the consumers who gain in the long run do not start new banks. Some Keynesian analysis includes a wealth effect in a consumption function and explain the depression in part by the mark-down of stock-market values as it reduced consumer wealth and hence consumer spending (Mishkin, 1978). A more direct effect, however, goes back to Irving Fisher's debt deflation. When prices fall sharply and stay down, both producers who have contracted at higher levels of prices, and their banks, are threatened with bankruptcy.

Interest rates fell in January 1930 as credit markets eased up, and the New York bond market recovered to float the largest volume of foreign bonds in the second quarter of any quarter of the decade. From a strictly financial and monetary point of view—for real money, i.e., nominal money deflated by prices, had risen—it appeared that the difficulties were over and the stage set for recovery. The persistent low level of commodity prices in relation to outstanding debt, however, gradually turned expectations pessimistic. The evidence is furnished by the wedges that developed between high-grade bonds and those of low quality.

In the foreign field Aaa and Aa bonds held up through 1929 and gained in price during the first nine months of 1930, whereas Baa bonds, the poorest quality, fell through 1929 to a low at the end of the year, recovered for the first three months of 1930, thereafter falling moderately to June before dropping further to September and then collapsing. Yields went from 8 per cent in June 1930 to $8\frac{1}{2}$ per cent in August and 10 per cent in September (Sachs, 1982, p. 227). The explanation for the last plunge is probably the victory of the Nazi party in the German elections of September 1930. The profile of bond prices (inverted yield curve) prior to September, however, clearly shows the loss of confidence in the international position after March 1930. A similar picture for domestic bonds in the United States shows the wedge between government bonds and corporate Baas developing later, in August 1930 (Friedman and Schwartz, 1963, p. 304). As Temin points out (1976, pp. 103–8), these comparisons by grades understate the differences in bond categories, because those bonds that deteriorated most were regraded downward, removed from the existing category, and thus raised the average price of the category from which they were excluded. Schumpeter expressed what was happening in highly qualitative terms: 'People felt the ground give way beneath their feet' (1939, p. 911). Distress turned into acute pessimism.

The Crisis
Banking difficulties began in the depression—after the Bodenkreditanstalt and William Deacons difficulties of January 1929—in Italy in the spring of 1930. Weakened by the 1921–3 bubble and its bursting, and by the *quota novanta* of 1926, the Italian mixed banks were hard hit by the further fall of security prices after October 1929. By March 1930 they were deeply concerned, as expressed in reports at their annual meetings. Steps were taken secretly to bolster them by selling off assets to the Banca d'Italia at book-value prices. Some failing provincial banks were 'salvaged' as the Italian expression has it, in the summer of 1930. By the end of the year, and again in early 1931 before the failure of the Austrian Creditanstalt, the Banca d'Italia had undertaken massive infusions of credit into the Credito Italiano and the Banca Commerciale Italiana.

The first banking difficulties in the United States were not those of the Bank of the United States, allowed to fail in December 1930, but come from the bankruptcy of the Caldwell chain, centred in Tennessee but stretching into Kentucky, North Carolina and Arkansas, a month earlier (Wicker, 1980).

The collapse of banking in Europe in 1931, starting with the Creditanstalt in May and spreading to Germany in July, Britain in September and reaching Japan in December, is too familiar to merit recital. I would make an important neglected point, however, that the depreciation of sterling by 30 per cent from September 21 to early December 1931, representing a 40 per cent appreciation of the Reichsmark, the US dollar and the currencies of the gold bloc, was highly deflationary for the world for reasons indicated earlier: in a world of deflation, depreciation fails to raise domestic prices, but appreciation lowers them. In addition, the gold bloc responded to its losses in sterling by a run on the dollar, converting $750 millions into gold in the days and weeks after September 23, 1931, and forcing, or leading, the Federal Reserve System into the error of raising its discount rate in depression to correct its balance of payments.

No Lender of Last Resort
The spread of bankruptcies from May 1931 to the ultimate devaluation of the dollar in March and April 1933 could have been averted, in my judgment, if there had been an international lender of last resort, ready and willing to bolster the Austrian schilling, and if necessary,

the German Reichsmark and the pound sterling. Some international help was given these currencies but it failed to measure up to Walter Bagehot's prescription of 'lending freely, if at a penalty rate'. It was, in fact, too little and too late, not to mention highly controversial, including, as far as France was concerned, political conditions. Franco-American lending to Britain in August contained conditions interpreted by the lenders, and British monetary authorities, as economic—requiring the British government to balance its budget, including an allocation for debt reduction by cutting the dole—but which was viewed by a wing of the British Labour Party as ideological and political interference—'a bankers' ramp'. The failure of international last-resort lending in the 1931 crisis was stated in *The World in Depression* to have been due to the on-going shift in world economic leadership from Britain to the United States, the former too weak to rescue Austria and Germany, the latter not yet conscious of the need, the opportunity or the benefit to itself. The apposite British statement was that His Majesty's Government had loaned to Central Europe as much as it conveniently could—a confession of incapacity. On the American side, the rationale was 'No throwing of good money after bad', whereas the essence of last-resort lending is that the only means of recovering bad money is to send good after it.

This view of the 1929 depression is not accepted by D.E. Moggridge, who takes rather the position that in the circumstances of 1931 a lender of last resort would not have helped. He is not a deflationist who wants purification by liquidation, but holds the belief that the difficulties were so deep-seated, of a structural character, that they required a more far-reaching therapy, on the order, say, of the Marshall Plan after World War II (Moggridge, 1982). There is force to this position. Overproduction of primary products, the disequilibrated structure of exchange rates, and the knotted tangle of reparations, war debts and commercial debts would remain after debt deflation had been arrested. By May 1931, moreover the depression was well advanced. Prices had fallen some 20 per cent in the United States, and only a few unconventional economists with no great followings were ready to recommend attempts to raise prices by such means as revaluing gold (but not changing exchange rates) or by means of a programme of public works adopted internationally.

The system still retained recuperative powers, however, and if the deflationary pressure had been halted fairly early in the spring of 1931, it is possible that the depression could have been limited to roughly one half of its ultimate devastating extent. Against this view are the weak recovery to 1937, largely investment in inventories, which collapsed in September of that year when expectations of further price increases were reversed, and the fact that real recovery waited on expenditure for rearmament and war. So much is admitted. There is no way to settle the issue. Nonetheless my instinct tells me that the appropriate therapy for a continuing debt deflation is to halt it by national and international last-resort lending. The current experience of the 1980s may throw some light on the subject.

PARALLELS TODAY

Displacement
The trigger of the international crisis of the 1970s and 1980s is generally regarded as the sharp increase in oil prices following the Yom Kippur War between Israel and Egypt. In my opinion, this neglects a significant antecedent cause, the attempt by President Nixon in the United States to help insure his re-election by promoting economic expansion, through, among other means, cheap money. In 1971, under the chairmanship of Arthur F. Burns, the Federal Reserve System embarked on a policy of lowering interest rates. Given the fact that the Deutsches Bundesbank was engaged in trying to contain inflation by tight money, and that the two markets were closely joined by the Euro-currency market, this was a serious mistake. By means of what is now called 'currency substitution', money created in the United States lowered interest rates in New York. Funds flowed to the Euro-currency market in, say, London, reducing interest rates there, leading companies in the Federal Republic to refinance their outstanding debt. Borrowing Euro-dollars and paying off Deutschmark debt, they sold the dollars to the Bundesbank which redeposited them in the Euro-dollar market or New York. This liquidity deficit in the US balance of payments rose from a level averaging $4 billion a year to $20 billion in 1971 and $30 billion in 1972. Money creation was pushed much further in the United States than would have occurred if the US and West German markets had not been joined. The Euro-currency market became flooded, and Euro-bankers searched for loan outlets. Their attention fastened on Third World countries engaged in programmes of economic development, this in 1972 and 1973, well before the OPEC price rise in oil and the necessity for recycling oil revenue.

This sort of sudden extension of investors' horizons is not new in economic and financial history. The unexpected success of the Dawes loan in 1924 attracted US attention to foreign bonds, as already related, and echoed the effects of the Baring loan in 1817 that excited British foreign lending, the Thiers *rentes* of 1871 and 1872 that led French banks to speculate in bonds. Sudden reductions in interest rates from successful conversions of government debt have had a similar impact, resulting from a sort of backward-bending supply curve on the part of investors who found their income reduced and were tempted to try to maintain it by more risky, higher yield investments. This occurred in 1822 in Britain, and contributed along with the Latin American revolts from Spanish domination to a frenzy of lending to newly-independent governments and investing in Latin American mines. The Goschen conversion of British debt from 3 per cent to $2\frac{3}{4}$ and $1\frac{1}{2}$ in 1887, foreshadowed as early as 1884, contributed to the investment boom starting in 1885 that collapsed with the Baring crisis in 1890. More contemporaneously, I believe that the Rome Treaty in 1957 excited foreign direct investment by American corporations less by changing the profitability of potential investments than by calling attention to profitable opportunities already in existence that had gone unnoticed. Investors maximize within limited horizons, and an unexpected event such as the success of a security issue or a sudden decline in interest rates, may widen or shift a given horizon.

Recycling
The sharp rise in the price of oil from $3 to $12 a barrel in November 1973 created a large balance-of-payments surpluses on current account for the so-called 'low absorbers' among oil producers, notably Saudi Arabia, Kuwait and Abu Dhabi, and large deficits for many countries of the world, including both developed countries such as the United States and countries of the Third World that produced no oil. OPEC countries deposited their profits in the Euro-currency market; Third World oil importers borrowed them. The Euro-currency market in effect recycled the monies from the oil producers to the oil consumers. One oil expert suggested that it would be helpful for financial stability if the producers sold oil partly for cash and partly for credit (Levy, 1982, p. 260). The proposal lacked attraction for the producers, who preferred claims on international banks to those on developing countries. It evoked memory of the French proposal of the 1920s that Germany borrow in New York to pay reparations to France, an idea that appealed neither to American investors nor to Germany as a debtor. Some recycling was undertaken in any event, to the detriment of world financial stability, in the Dawes loan and the American investments in German state and municipal bonds, plus bank deposits, already discussed, that furnished the foreign exchange with which Germany paid reparations until mid-1928. Recycling in the 1920s through bonds differs, to be sure, from that of the 1970s through banks, in that default on debt to individual bond holders, despite its effect in reducing wealth and spending, has much more circumscribed

macroeconomic effects than default to banks on a scale that endangers their safety.

Boom

The 1960s and '70s witnessed a series of independent booms in the United States, affecting at one time or another transport aircraft, supertankers and ore carriers, California real estate, Real Estate Investment Trusts (REITs) and after 1973, oil. A boom and collapse in a single commodity or asset is not likely to have serious macroeconomic consequences. The booms that led to distress and panic in the nineteenth century usually involved two or more objects of speculation: cotton and public land in the 1830s, wheat and railways in 1847, cotton and shipping in 1866, real estate and railroads in 1873, Argentine, Australian and United States real estate, plus Chilean nitrates, and breweries in 1888–1889. In the 1960s and '70s, the manic desire to get rich quick was more or less safely contained in one area at a time until the boom in oil coincided with the wave of syndicated bank lending on sovereign risk to Third World countries.

Oil enjoyed a double peak, the first in 1973 as noted, and a second in 1979 when war broke out between Iran and Iraq, taking both for a time out of the world market as suppliers. The first price increase stimulated recovery from existing fields, exploration, and development of discovered fields everywhere, but notably in the North Sea and the North Slope in Alaska. Companies such as Dome Petroleum in Canada expanded enormously on the basis of bank loans. Such a bank as Penn Square in Oklahoma City financed a series of wildcat explorers, and marketed the loans to metropolitan banks such as the Continental in Chicago. American and European banks loaned widely for a time to Africa, and then to Latin America and Eastern Europe. Bank leaders such as Walter Wriston, Alfred Costanzo and Irving Friedman of The Citibank in New York insisted that there was little or no risk that the loans would not be fully serviced.

It is important not to convey the impression that there were no problems outside oil and the Third World. As farm prices fell, farmers found difficulty in paying mortgage interest on land bought at high prices and the farm machinery industry, including notably International Harvester and Massey-Ferguson suffered heavy losses covered by bank loans. In Germany the Dresdener Bank was hurt by the troubles of the closely-associated Allgemeine Elektrizitat Gesselschaft to which it had advanced large sums. The UK Midland Bank bought Crocker National Bank of San Francisco which loaned heavily for luxury condominia in Southern California, costing $1 million or more each, and selling badly.

Foreign Exchange Rates
The breakdown of the Bretton Woods system would lead us too far
afield, but a contributor to the financial turbulence of 1980s has been
the system of flexible exchange rates, adopted in 1973 (prior to the
OPEC price hike), when it proved to be impossible to restore stability
to foreign-exchange markets with a 10 per cent devaluation of the
dollar, worked out with great difficulty in 1971. A good many
economists had believed that flexible exchange rates made adjustment
automatic, gave monetary authorities independence to adopt any policy
they chose, and made equilibrium in international finance foreordained.
They believed that floating would dry up international capital flows
except of the stabilizing speculative variety, as ordinary investors stayed
away from foreign lending and borrowing because of exchange risk.

This analysis proved overly sanguine. Capital continued to move
between countries as many investors considered interest return and
safety dominant over exchange risk. Current accounts adjusted slowly
since prices moved faster than quantities; trade followed what was
called a J-curve with the first impact of depreciation a decline in export
values and an increase in the value of imports. This led to still further
depreciation, in the absence of official intervention, and an overshooting
of equilibrium levels. First depreciation went too far, and then
appreciation went too far. The result was structural inflation in an
inflationary world; depreciation raised domestic prices and appreciation
did not reduce them. The ratchet was the opposite of that in the
deflation of the 1930s. It worked especially in oil, priced in dollars.
When the dollar depreciated, the oil price was raised; when it
appreciated, the dollar price of oil was not reduced but prices in
depreciating currencies rose. This meant that with every cycle of the
dollar exchange rate which returned to the same position, oil prices
and indeed the prices of internationally-traded goods in general rose.
When the supply caught up in about 1980, however, the ratchet that
had operated from 1973 to that time subsided.

Early in the experience with fluctuating exchange rates moving in
wide swings, a number of banks came to believe that they could earn
substantial profits from foreign-exchange trading in which they took
open positions. The failure of the Franklin National and the Herstatt
banks, one American with an Italian ownership interest, the other in
Cologne in the Federal Republic of Germany, led to the tempering of
this belief.

The 1980 election in the United States brought to power a government
committed to 'supply-side economics' and produced a new displacement
in the world structure of exchange rates. The theory held that a
reduction in tax rates would quickly produce a stimulus to work,

investment and output that would restore budgetary equilibrium at lower tax rates because of higher yields from increased national income. Like the view that flexible exchange rates converged to equilibrium positions, this belief proved illusory. The tax cuts, together with increases in military spending, produced substantial deficits in the US budget. To head off a possible renewal of inflation, the Federal Reserve in 1982 applied the money brake. Inflation kept subsiding but high real interest rates cut spending in housing and through instalment purchases. They also attracted capital from abroad to the United States which bid up the dollar. Appreciation of the dollar further assisted in reducing the rate of inflation, but had the unwanted result of producing record deficits in the balance of payments of the United States, stimulating imports and crowding out exports. Tight money further increased the difficulties of the Third World countries in raising the interest rates they were required to pay on their adjustable-interest-rate loans.

In combination with another quasi-ideological view that banks along with other industries should be deregulated, high interest rates also led to trouble among US thrift institutions. Unregulated money-market funds paying market interest attracted savings out of savings banks and savings and loan associations, which continued to be limited in their ability to pay more than $5\frac{1}{4}$ per cent on deposits. This required the thrifts to buy funds on the open market. With returns from their portfolios of mortgages on the whole fixed, though high at the margin and in increasing numbers of cases at adjustable rates, extensive disintermediation took place everywhere, except among the relatively ignorant depositors in blue-collar neighbourhoods. A substantial number of savings banks and savings and loan associations failed and had to be merged or taken over by governmental institutions. As this is written, the largest S & L in the United States, the American Savings and Loan Association of California, managed by the Financial Corporation of America, is experiencing a run on its deposits.

Distress
Shortly after the second oil shock in 1979 it became clear that markets were far from equilibrium in many areas, and that the world financial system was in distress. That recognition differed in time from place to place, sector to sector, individual to individual, and some institutions, like the Citibank in New York, resolutely refused to recognize that lending to Third World countries had been excessive until in August 1982 Mexico faced difficulty in meeting its debt service. Mexico had expanded oil production at a rapid rate since 1973 largely on borrowed money, and as oil exports levelled off, continued to borrow money to

maintain service on its outstanding debt. Banks were becoming increasingly reluctant to lend more, or to renew old loans. In the overt crisis, an emergency arrangement was worked out with leading banks, under the leadership of the International Monetary Fund, calling for continued bank lending and a programme of rigorous macroeconomic austerity in Mexico. Since such negotiations are time-consuming, and the expiration of loan contracts produced a short-term crisis, the US government advanced $1 billion against future deliveries of oil and the Federal Reserve made a large bridging loan. The IMF faces several weaknesses as a lender of last resort: it takes time to reach decisions, and it cannot create money, but rather only advances monies made available to it by the member countries. Moreover, the amounts so made available are fixed at any one time, and can be raised only slowly by a series of legislative acts in the member countries, with the total time taken governed by the slowest to approve. For a Hungarian emergency loan, also in the summer of 1982, the B.I.S. advanced a bridging loan until the creditors could be assembled and work out a reorganization of the debt. But this was a small amount—$100 million—and for sums in the billions, bridging loans are available only from the major central banks with money-creating powers.

The Mexican crisis was followed by further troubles in Latin America—in Brazil in the fall of 1983, and in Argentina in the spring of 1984. Both countries were oil importers, with debts piled up to international banks during the years from 1971. Some relief came from the easing of oil prices after 1981, but Brazil had been financing a major expansion programme, and Argentina had run large budget and balance-of-payments deficits in its unsuccessful Falklands war. In addition to the cumulative troubles of oil importers, the high absorbers among the oil-exporting countries found themselves in difficulty when oil production was cut back to slow the decline in price.

In 1983 and 1984 distress in international financial markets came from the accumulation of Third World debt amounting to more than $700 billion, from high interest rates, a high dollar in foreign-exchange markets (most debts had been contracted in dollars). Some alleviation occurred through economic expansion in the United States. Other negative elements were falling raw-material prices in general, and the threat that markets in developed countries would be cut off by protection. The high dollar exchange rate, making for heavy US imports and a large current-account deficit, hurt especially import-competing industries in the United States such as textiles, clothing, steel, copper, automobiles, and gave rise to pressures for tariffs and quotas. The free-market ideology of the Republican administration furnished some defence against this pressure, but was slowly crumbling.

The beliefs or ideology of the Republican administration favoured not only tax reduction and deregulation in financial markets, but, as already indicated, non-intervention in foreign exchange. The previous administration had had a similar if less marked belief in benign neglect of the fate of the dollar, but on October 31, 1979, this was quickly abandoned when the dollar came under bear attack and started to sink rapidly. There is a question whether the present Administration would follow this precedent in similar circumstances. Many competent observers expect the massive cumulating deficits in the US current account, which would ordinarily make for depreciation, at some point to overcome high interest rates currently holding the dollar up. When a reversal of the market's expectation will occur, if at all, cannot be predicted. Acute uncertainty in this area is characteristic of what is meant by distress.

The Lender of Last Resort

In the 1930s, the *domestic* lender of last resort function was understood fairly well—witness the rescues of the William Deacons banks and the Bodenkreditanstalt in January 1929, the US open-market operations in October and November 1929, and the Italian salvage operations of 1930 and early 1931. There were lapses; the Caldwell banking chain fell without rescue in November 1930, the Bank of the United States in December 1930, and the Danat bank in July 1931. The Bank of United States failure took place after extended discussion at the time of what action to take, and was later sharply criticized (Friedman and Schwartz, 1963, pp. 299–300). The inaction of the German authorities in the case of the Danat bank is characterized as 'unthinkable' today (Irmler, 1978, p. 287). It may have been tolerated in the 1930s because of Chancellor Brüning's conviction that the only way to rid Germany of the burden of reparations was to precipitate economic collapse—a heroic and costly therapy.

At an international level, however, in the 1930s, attempts at last-resort lending were made for Austria, Germany and Britain only hesitatingly and on an inadequate scale, as set out above, in grievous contravention of the Bagehot prescription of lending freely (if at a penalty rate). The Bank of England with a century and a half of experience in the matter understood the necessity but lacked the resources. The United States and France perceived the need only dimly, responded to a degree, but in the final analysis stood aside.

After World War II, last-resort lending was initially international, not domestic, and took the form of the swap network, developed at the B.I.S. during the British foreign-exchange crisis of March 1961. This statement perhaps fails to give adequate recognition to the Group

of Ten agreement of 1960 that provided ancillary lending facilities to
the IMF for coping with foreign-exchange crises among the financially-
developed countries—a change required by the fact that the original
IMF design provided facilities for current-account deficits only in the
mistaken belief that capital movements could be contained by foreign-
exchange controls. From 1961 the swap network was extended by
countries, increased in amounts and used to meet foreign exchange
crises in Britain, Italy, Canada and ultimately the United States. In
the 1967 crisis, however, the IMF intervened early instead of the
swap device, and laid down conditions for the conduct of British
macroeconomic policy. Until that time, financially developed countries
had trusted each other completely so that last-resort lending among
them had been immediate, unconditional, and by reason of the rapid
increase in amounts made available, adequate in amounts (Coombs,
1976).

National last-resort lending, apart from the normal run of failures
of small banks, came into prominence in 1974 with the threatened
bankruptcies of the Franklin National and the Herstatt Banks. The
Federal Reserve System swung in behind the Federal Deposit Insurance
Corporation in the United States and made good the liabilities of the
Franklin National at home and abroad. This obliterated the distinction
between domestic and international last-resort tasks, as increasingly
required by the internationalization of financial markets. The Bundesbank hesitated in the Herstatt affair, first agreeing to guarantee the
bank's liabilities to domestic creditors, and only later, after a disturbing
delay, extending that guarantee to foreigners. Discussion of the
implications of failure to protect foreign creditors took place in March
1975 at the B.I.S. and produced the so-called Basle Concordat. The
leading central banks undertook in future bank failures to take care
to foreign, as well as domestic creditors so as to forestall the spread
of bank runs from one country to others. The agreement was subject
to strain later, however, when the Vatican-owned Banco Ambrosiano
failed, and the Banca d'Italia refused to make good the losses of its
Luxemburg subsidiary on the ground that it was a separately owned
Luxemburg entity and not a branch of the Roman bank. Some residual
ambiguity perhaps remains also in the case of consortium banks owned
by several banks of different nationalities.

The lender of last resort function developed fairly rapidly in the
United States. From its inception in 1933, the FDIC started to insure
the deposits of failed banks only for small depositors, the initial limit
having been set of $10,000. The rationale, of course, was that larger
depositors were well informed and able to protect their funds
themselves, without government help, judging the strength of banks

and keeping their funds only in strong banks. With growth, inflation, and increased appreciation of the dangers of runs on banks, this amount was raised postwar to $40,000 and then to $100,000. In addition, protection was extended from deposits to certificates of deposit (CDs), which were marketable debt instruments. The near collapse of the Continental Bank in Chicago in 1984 led the authorities to extend their guarantee, by one agency or another, to all creditors, wherever located, and of any amount. The implications of this position—whether to extend it to small banks with no likely repercussions, what it means for 'moral hazard' or the possibility that the insured bankers will take undue risks in loan-making, and how, after a near failure in which the authorities are required to create large amounts of liquidity to make good bad assets, the quantity of money in circulation is sunk again—have not been explored to any great extent analytically, and remain to be worked out in practice.

Pervasive change and possible danger are being encountered in a related area because of adjustable-rate loans, including mortgages. These began as an innovation in the Euro-currency market, with interest on loans adjusted every six months to some negotiated premium over the London Interbank Borrowing Rate (LIBOR), and spread to the United States. Adjustable rates relieve banks of the risk of a sharp increase in interest rates (and borrowers of the risk of loss from a sharp decrease) and leave banks only with the risk of creditor default. The interest-rate risk does not disappear, of course, but is taken on, on the up side, by the borrower. This explains the difficulties of Third World debtors in an environment of rising interest brought on by US tight monetary policy, introduced to combat inflation when fiscal policy was lax. Commercial banks nonetheless faced interest-rate risk indirectly to the extent that higher interest rates made the residual risk of default greater.

Conditionality
In the 1930s commercial banks sometimes imposed conditions on their foreign lending, as in the case of the Morgan loan of 1924 to France to provide funds to combat speculation against the franc; conditions were sometimes imposed officially as illustrated by the Franco-American requirement in August 1931 that the British government balance its budget by cutting the dole. This last condition brought down the Labour Government. In earlier weeks pressure to pursue 'sound policies' had been exerted on Germany, both in the loan negotiations of June 1931 and in the Standstill Agreement of the end of July. In the 1980s conditions are usually laid down by the IMF and are sometimes imposed on debtors and creditors alike. Those on the

debtors are the subject of considerable controversy, with the IMF insisting that the conditions serve only the purpose of insuring adjustment, recovery and ability to continue debt service, while opponents charge that they are ideological in character, insufficiently sensitive to the political pressures faced within the borrowing country, and based on a narrow monetarist as opposed to a structural view of the cause of difficulty (Williamson, 1983).

The creditors, on the other hand, are required by the IMF to keep renewing their loans and in some instances to lend more. This has created a major strain between the major international banks, which have been the leaders in banking syndicates lending to Third World debtors, and the smaller regional banks which feel uneasy, want to be repaid and get out of a line of business which they little understand. It is relevant to observe that Britain was pushed off the gold standard in 1931, and the United States in 1971, not by the large creditors demanding to be repaid in gold, but by the smaller countries that felt no responsibility for the system as a whole.

Refunding
Early in the postwar period, as one or another country got into trouble by overborrowing and became unable to repay the World Bank or foreign governments for development loans, there developed the 'Paris Club' of government officials and representatives of international financial institutions that arranged for refinancing, stretching out the terms of loans providing periods of grace when debt service was suspended, and frequently lowering the interest. Default in form was strictly avoided, although from an economic viewpoint much of the borrowed money has been wasted by, say, Nkrumah in Ghana or Sukarno in Indonesia. The discounted value of the contract after Paris Club adjustment was markedly reduced even though the nominal amounts involved were generally unchanged.

In the initial attempts to settle the Mexican, Brazilian and Argentine commercial bank debts, new loans were forthcoming from the IMF and usually at IMF insistence from the banks, old loans were renewed but at market rates of interest, generally with a higher mark-up over LIBOR. The loans were seldom stretched in time, nor were the borrowers granted a period of grace. After the Mexican settlement of 1982, however, and especially after the Brazilian agreement of the fall of 1983, debtor countries began demanding concessional terms. No debtor cartel was organized; each country negotiated by itself, and most governments, if not parties in opposition, stayed clear of threatening default, with the severe consequence that implied for access to world capital markets. In the century and a half before 1970, each default was followed by a period of a generation in which the defaulter was denied access to loans. Nonetheless, commercial banks as well as government and international financial institutions seemed readier to grant extended terms, periods of grace, and initially at least modest concessions on interest rates, such as a shift in the Mexican agreement of September 1984 from the New York prime rate as a base for adjustable interest to the slightly lower LIBOR rate, and cancellation of the renewal premium.

The lender of last resort function is thus undergoing metamorphosis. For the most part debtor countries remain anxious to avoid default, but markets now strive to find new ways to share the losses between borrowers and lenders, both government and commercial. Despite criticism of 'muddling through', economic authorities steer clear of the dangers of a grandiose attempt at an overall settlement among leading creditors and debtors, as recommended by many, among them Felix Rohatyn, Peter Kenen and Jagdish Bhagwati. Where there is no meeting of minds, and no strong leadership, extended debate over world debt and financial stability threatens a repetition of the World Economic Conference of 1933 debacle, rather than the semi-durable success of the Bretton Woods Conference of 1944. In these circumstances, distress persists.

REFERENCES

Coombs, Charles A. (1976), *The Arena of International Finance* (New York: Wiley-Interscience).
Friedman, Milton and Schwartz, Anna Jacobson (1963), *A Monetary History of the United States, 1867–1960* (Princeton, NJ: Princeton University Press).
Irmler, Heinrich (1976), 'Bankenkrise und Vollbeschaftigungspolitik (1931–1936)', in Deutsche Bundesbank (ed.), *Wahrung und Wirtschaft in Deutschland*, (Frankfurt: Knapp).
James, Harold (1985), *The Reichsbank and Public Finance in Germany, 1924–33: A Study of the Politics of Economics during the Great Depression* (Schriftenreihe des Instituts für Bankhistorische Forschung e.V., Band 5), (Frankfurt: Fritz Knapp).
Kindleberger, Charles P. (1973), *The World in Depression, 1929–1939* (Berkeley: University of California Press).
——— (1978) *Manias, Panics and Crashes* (New York: Basic Books).
Levy, Walter J. (1982), *Oil Strategy and Politics, 1941–1981* (edited by Melvin A. Conant) (Boulder: Westview Press).
Mishkin, Frederich A. (1978), 'The Household Balance Sheet and the Great Depression', *Journal of Economic History*, vol. 38, no. 4, pp. 918–37.
Moggridge, D.E. (1982), 'Policy in the Crises of 1920 and 1929', in C.P. Kindleberger and J.-P. Laffargue (eds), *Financial Crises: Theory, History and Policy* (Cambridge University Press).
Sachs, Jeffrey (1982), 'LDC Debt in the 1980s, Risks and Reforms', in Paul

Wachtel (ed.), *Crises in the Economic and Financial Structure* (Lexington, Mass.: D.C. Heath), pp. 197–243.
Sayers, R.S. (1976), *The Bank of England, 1891–1944* 3 vols. (Cambridge: Cambridge University Press).
Schumpeter, Joseph A. (1939), *Business Cycles* 2 vols. (New York: McGraw-Hill).
Temin, Peter (1976), *Did Monetary Forces Cause the Great Depression?* (New York: W.W. Norton.
Toniolo, Gianni (1978), 'Crisi economica e smobilizzo publicco dell banche miste (1930–1034)', in Gianni Toniolo (ed.), *Industria e banca nella grande crisi, 1919–1934* (Milan: Etas Libri).
Wicker, Elmus (1980), 'A Reconsideration of the Causes of the Banking Panic of 1930', *Journal of Economic History* vol. 40, no. 3, pp. 571–84.
Williamson, John (ed.) (1982), *IMF Conditionality* (Washington, DC: Institute of International Economics).

5 Bank Failures: The 1930s and The 1980s*

INTRODUCTION

The banking troubles of recent years have aroused new interest in those of the 1930s. The recent literature has emerged against the background of a debate between Friedman and Schwartz (1963, chap. 7) and Peter Temin (1976) over whether the Great Depression of the 1930s had been caused by the decline in the money supply in the United States—a monetarist position—or by exogenous Keynesian changes in spending—unexplained according to Temin—that reduced the demand for money and hence the supply. Neither view gives much attention to a more complex model in which money-supply and income changes are both connected with the stock-market boom and crash, the spread of a liquidity seizure from the stock market to commodities, which fell sharply in price, and later strong deflationary pressure from perverse capital flows in Europe and the United States, foreign-exchange crises and a 40 per cent appreciation of the dollar with deflationary effects (Kindleberger, 1973).

In the recent literature monetarism is represented by Anna Schwartz (1981) and Roland Vaubel (1984), with some support from Wicker (1980), who however, blames a major bank failure of 1930 on a record of bad loans and investments; Eugene White ascribes the 1930 failures to banking regulations that prohibited branch banking (1984); Ben Bernanke contends that the financial crisis of the 1930s worked to reduce national income less through its effect on the money supply than through inhibiting financial intermediation and thus reducing investment and other spending (1983).

* Paper presented to A Conference Sponsored by the Federal Reserve Bank of San Francisco, at Asilomar, California, 23–5 June 1985 and published in the Bank's *The Search for Financial Stability: The Past Fifty Years*, San Francisco: Federal Reserve Bank of San Francisco, no date (1986), pp. 7–34.

Most of these analyses dismiss other views with short shrift, although Gordon and Wilcox (1981) and Anderson and Butkiewicz (1982) find something to be said for both the monetarism and Keynesian (spending) viewpoints. Recently some slight attention has been paid to the international aspects of the depression of the 1930s by Meltzer, Schwartz and Gordon and Wilcox, limited for the most part to the alleged deflationary impact of the Hawley-Smoot tariff of June 1930 on farm income (in Brunner, (ed.), 1981). Vaubel, on the other hand, dismisses the suggestion that Europe had any share in the origins of the Great Depression, despite a German recession starting in 1928, and bank difficulties requiring rescues or mergers in Britain and Italy well before the first US banking panic of November 1930 (1984). Bernanke ignores the Minsky-Kindleberger hypothesis of banking instability on the ground that it is built on an assumption of irrationality (1984).[1]

Also missing from most of this recent analysis is any role for falling prices. These are dismissed because of a theoretical assumption that to admit prices into the model is to be guilty of money illusion. Leaving changed terms of trade out of account, it is held that while producers may lose from falling prices, consumers gain from them. True enough. It is not true, however, that the effects need be symmetrical and fully offsetting. Producers know that their profits have shrunk, certainly and immediately. Consumers may be slow to realize that they have gained. Moreover, the banks of producers may fail when producers default on their loans or mortgages. Consumers are unlikely to start new banks with their increased consumers' surpluses. Bernanke asserts that debtor insolvency is currently neglected by historians—one wonders what historians he has been reading—and admits it can occur from falling prices when debt is fixed. He cannot understand, however, why markets have not responded to this possibility by indexing all loans (1984, p. 260 and note 15). Again history is questioned for failing to conform to theory, rather than the other way around.

In what follows I choose to explore, qualitatively without mathematical models or econometrics—perhaps anecdotally—the contributions of various causes to bank failures in the 1930s, and in the 1980s. I hope to demonstrate that no parsimonious mono-causal theory is valid. For the earlier period, the emphasis is on 1929 and 1930. I distrust explanations that run from the middle of 1929 all the way to 1933, perhaps shifting back and forth from nominal to real variables, and from levels to rates of change, when it is my conviction that relevant models in history may change from one period to another and did change in this instance. The emphasis is on the 1930s, though there is a concluding section on the similarities and differences with the 1980s. First, however, a brief analysis of bank failure.

CAUSES OF BANK FAILURE

Bank failure can originate on the asset side of the balance sheet, on the liability side, or in shocks affecting both simultaneously or in rapid succession. Martin Mayer (1974) has described how banks that were concerned with asset management, in recent years have shifted to liability management. In the 1980s, years of syndicated bank lending to Third World countries, falling oil prices and falling farm and farm-land prices, attention is presumably shifting back to assets. Banks are interested in the default risk of borrowers, and in the decline in prices of investments, whether because of loss of profitability or of company bankruptcy. In addition, increases in interest rates knock down prices of long-term fixed obligations such as bonds and mortgages. This interest-rate risk has been reduced for commercial banks by their shifting from fixed to adjustable interest-rate loans. The slow turnover and growth of mortgage portfolios, and the fact that they have adopted adjustable mortgage rates only recently has meant that thrift institutions—savings banks and savings and loan associations—are unable to protect themselves against interest-rate risk to the same degree as commercial banks. Two risks also exist on the liability side, one of interest-rate increases leading depositors to shift their funds into higher-paying non-bank accounts—disintermediation—with the consequent necessity of the bank to liquidate assets, possibly at a loss, or to buy funds in the market with certificates of deposit at higher rates. This effect is felt slowly. The other is a run on deposits, or the liquidation of a bank's certificates of deposit when the holders of these liabilities become worried about the bank's solvency. Bank runs arise quickly. The danger of runs by depositors was sharply reduced in 1933, after the wholesale closing of banks in the bank holiday, by the establishment of the Federal Deposit Insurance Corporation. Limits to the amounts insured left a residual risk for large depositors. The limit was $5,000 from mid-1934 to 1950 and was raised gradually thereafter in the course of inflation. It was $20,000 at the time of the Franklin National failure in 1974, was quickly raised to $40,000, and most recently, at the time of the Continental Illinois run, was $100,000. This still leaves the large money-centre banks with huge deposit liabilities to major corporations and CDs in the millions at risk. The most recent troubles of Ohio savings and loan associations which lost heavily in the failure of E.S.M., a Florida financial house and were mostly insured in the weaker state system, moreover, shows that all danger of depositor runs is not past.

Default risk for a bank can be of several kinds. For the purpose of identifying risk for bank examiners, Flannery and Guttentag divide problem banks into 'Alphas' that have a high probability of failure in the existing environment because of internal weakness of one kind or another; inadequate capital, poor asset quality, weak management, low earnings, or illiquidity; and 'Betas' which are at risk because of the possibility of adverse external circumstances: tight money, sectoral depression, abusive practices of owners or managers (1980, pp. 176–8). The Comptroller of the Currency, the Federal Deposit Insurance Corporation, and state agencies from time to time have indicated the reasons for bank failures. In the *Annual Report* of the Comptroller for 1931 (1932, p. 232) setting out the causes of failure of national banks still in receivership on 31 October 1931, three causes were given: A, incompetent management; B, dishonesty; and C, local financial depression from unforeseen agricultural or financial disaster. A tabulation of the larger banks still in receivership on 31 October 1931 that failed before and after 1929 showed the following:

Table 5.1: Causes of failure of National Banks, 1929–31
(by numbers of banks with capital of $100,000 or more)

	A	AB	AC	B	BC	C	Total
Failed before 10/31/29	12	3	6	3	1	15	40
Failed 11/1/29–10/31/31	16	—	25	1	—	31	73

The Comptroller's *Annual Report* for 1935 has a table showing bank assets of national banks still in receivership on 31 October 1935, with book values of their assets divided into three categories: good, doubtful, and worthless. As an illustration bearing on the 'first banking panic' of November and December 1930, four national banks with capital of $500,000 or more can be shown from the list (1936, p. 286). The Bank of United States in New York is not among them as it was a state bank. In three of the four cases worthless assets exceeded the bank's capital. If half of the doubtful assets had been added to the worthless, bad assets would have exceeded the bank's capital by three to six times.

The *Annual Report* of the FDIC for the year ended 31 December 1937 reported that action had been taken in 1937 against 39 banks, national and state, for unsafe or unsound practices or violations of the law. It noted further that 75 banks had been declared insolvent in the year. Unsafe and unsound practices were enumerated, presumably

relating to both warned and failed banks, with some banks singled out
for more than one practice:

Table 5.2: Asset quality of failed banks

			Assets*		
Bank	Date Closed	Capital	Good	Doubtful	Worthless
Quincy-Ricker Nat'l Bank and Trust Co. Quincy, IL	10/11/30	0.5	0.7	3.5	0.5
Holston-Union Nat'l Bank Knoxville, KY	12/11/30	0.75	5.3	8.5	0.6
National Bank of Kentucky Louisville, KY	17/11/30	4.0	22.61	11.6	6.1
City National Bank of Miami Miami, FL	30/12/30	0.5	3.3	3.3	0.7

In millions of dollars

It is impossible from this material to form anything but the most
general impressions of the causes of bank failure. It is also evident
that the distinctions between incompetence and dishonesty, or wilful
and inadvertent violations of laws are vague and shadowy.

BANK FAILURES 1921–1933

Bank failures from 1921 to 1933 were studied by the Federal Reserve
Board in 1937. A large number of banks had been created between
1900 and 1921, the study stated, especially in agricultural areas, because
of rapidly rising farm prices and land prices during World War I (1937,
p. 1204). The run-up of farm prices at that time has been characterized
as a 'land-market mania' (Johnson, 1973–4). Decline of farm prices
from the 1920 peak was a major cause of the farm foreclosure crisis
of the early 1920s and responsible for the closing of unit banks in the
agricultural regions of the United States after 1925 (Alston, 1983). The
Federal Reserve Bulletin commented that bank losses were easily
avoided during the rising prices up to 1921 when bank judgments were
not challenged to the same extent as in periods of falling prices. Bank
numbers doubled from 1900, reaching more than 30,000 in 1925 at the
peak. Price declines and the steady drain of deposits from agricultural
areas through adverse regional balances of payments led to increasing

Table 5.3: Unsafe and unsound practices of banks, 1937

Practice	Number of banks
Capital	
Operation with impaired capital	18
Operation though insolvent	2
Operation with insufficient capital	2
Loans and Investment	
Lax credit and collection policies	18
Failure to maintain adequate credit file	16
Abnormal number of substandard loans and securities	14
Abnormal number of past-due loans	11
Failure to support real estate loans with appraisals, etc.	8
Excessive credit to officers or directors or their affiliates or interests	8
Excessive credit to other favoured borrowers or habitual overdrafts	7
Lax investment policies	5
Management	
Hazardous, untrustworthy or incompetent management	13
Failure of directors to manage properly	2
Bookkeeping and General Records	
Inclusion of losses in bank's assets	15
Violations	
Making and carrying loans in excess of legal limits	11
Violations of state banking laws	8
Violations of regulation IV of the FDIC or regulation Q of the Federal Reserve System	5
Others	scattered

bank suspensions after the 1921 shakeout had ended. It started at the end of 1923 in the West North Central wheat areas, and in 1924 spread to the East North Central corn regions, especially Iowa and Illinois. The study offered a table (as follows) comparing bank failures by specified states, that clearly shows the dominance of agricultural areas in bank failures, in numbers if not in the volume of deposit liabilities of failed banks.

While the collapse of the Florida land boom produced a wave of bank suspensions in the South East after 1925, the bulk of bank suspensions from 1921 to 1929 was recorded in farm country, as was also the case in seven of the ten top states in 1930–3. Friedman and Schwartz suggest that part of the reason for the bank failure in farm areas was the improvement in transportation, the spread of urbanization, both making possible economies of scale for the larger banks and closing down the smaller (1961, p. 308). White recognizes the delayed response to the land boom and crop expansion in World War I, noting that in 1929 the farm bank sector was said to be still licking old wounds (1984, p. 126). In general, however, he blames bank regulation which forebade branch and chain banking in most states, and kept the structure one of atomistic unit banks. In the 1920s and 1930s, it is true that the Far West had a much lower rate of bank failure than the central and southern states, attributable in part, no doubt, to the lack of strong Populist sentiment and the strength of its bank chains. As we shall see below, however, chain banking proved to be no guarantee against failure in Arkansas, Kentucky, and Tennessee.

The position changed in the last two months of 1930. Explanations vary. The *Federal Reserve Bulletin* notes that the first ten months of 1930 were similar in bank suspensions to the average of the previous nine years, though suspensions picked up in November and December (1937, p. 1205). Friedman and Schwartz seem to think that the farm-belt bank failures of these months were unusual, and led to bank runs

Table 5.4: Numbers of bank suspensions by states

1921–1929		1930–1933	
State	No.	State	No.
Iowa	452	Illinois	817
North Dakota	427	Iowa	785
Minnesota	419	Missouri	560
South Dakota	392	Wisconsin	505
Nebraska	366	Michigan	470
Georgia	322	Nebraska	409
Missouri	293	Indiana	407
Oklahoma	264	Pennsylvania	401
South Carolina	225	Ohio	334
Texas	219	Minnesota	306
Subtotal Ten States	3,379	Subtotal Ten States	4,994
All Other States		All Other States	
and D.C.	2,032	and D.C.	3,818
TOTAL	5,411	TOTAL	8,812

Source: *Federal Reserve Bulletin*, December 1937, p. 1211.

into currency and postal savings generally throughout the country, with no geographical limits (Friedman and Schwartz 1963, p. 308; White, 1984, p. 121). Temin attributes the failures up to December 1930, when the Bank of the United States in New York City failed, in considerable part to the decline in the prices of second-grade bonds held in bank portfolios. Interest rates had started to rise in mid-1928 when the stock-market boom attracted money-market funds into brokers' loans. The rise in interest rates generally lowered the market values of investments fixed in money terms, notably mortgages and bonds. While yields on government bonds recovered quickly after the October 1929 crash, a wedge developed between government and low-grade bonds (Friedman and Schwartz, 1963, chart p. 304) and between high and low-grade foreign bonds (Sachs, 1983, chart, p. 227). Both wedges were the consequence of changes in expectations. That in foreign bonds occurred first, about March of 1930, well before the discouraging German election of September when the Nazis recorded a big increase in Reichstag seats. The wedge in domestic securities first appeared in September 1930. Measurement by classes of bonds, with low-grade bonds in each case represented by the Baa rating, sharply understates the size of the wedge, as Temin has demonstrated, since deterioration of a given Baa bond that eliminated it from the class raised the average rather than lowered it. Temin uses regressions to suggest the role of the wedge, comparing failures with wheat, cotton and other farm income, and with previous suspensions as a proxy for poor investments. The test is a rough one at best. Previous suspensions were caused to a considerable extent by declines in farm income. The correlation explains less than half of the variation in bank failures by states, and is partly spurious, as well as employing a dubious proxy (Temin, 1976, p. 88).

A new element was introduced into the discussion in 1980 by Elmus Wicker who called attention to an old book by John Berry McFerrin, *Caldwell and Company* (1939, reissued, 1969). Rogers Caldwell had entered business in 1917 as an investment banker in Nashville, Tennessee, specializing in municipal bonds. He started slowly, picked up momentum in 1926 and moved into banking, insurance, and industrial securities, eventually owning even newspapers and a baseball team. In 1930 his financial empire spread from Tennessee into Kentucky, Missouri, Arkansas, Illinois and North Carolina. Its failure in November 1930 produced a wave of failures in those states, not only in banking but in insurance and in industry. The underlying McFerrin book gives a clear picture of the collapse of the empire, but does not undertake to relate it to the national banking scene. Wicker, however, asserts that the failure of Caldwell and Company accounts for the banking panic of November–December 1930 far more than did the Bank of the United States December failure on which Friedman and Schwartz dwell, and observes that it was unrelated to the decline in farm prices or the deterioration in the prices of second-grade bonds. In his view it was autonomous and unconnected with the depression, due in fact to factors that predated the depression. 'Questionable managerial and financial practices inaugurated in the twenties to foster rapid growth and expansion explain the firm's demise' (1980, p. 583). My judgment differs considerably. As I see it, the failures of both Caldwell and Company and the Bank of the United States in November and December 1930 were intimately related to the fragile structures of the two banks brought on by the stock-market boom and the aggressive tactics of Rogers Caldwell starting in 1926, and of Bernard Marcus of the Bank of the United States after his father's death in 1928. Both cases fit precisely the Minsky–Kindleberger hypothesis of credit stretched taut in a positive feedback process, akin to the chain drawings of bills of exchange by people of little capital described by Adam Smith (1776, pp. 293–7) and practised in Holland, Germany, Scotland and Britain (Kindleberger, 1978, pp. 59–63).

In the Caldwell case, credit was expanded on an exiguous capital base by selling municipal bonds under depository agreements that left the borrowed funds on deposit until disbursed in a bank set up for the purpose. The proceeds of these deposits were used to buy insurance companies, other banks, an investment trust, and industrial concerns, each of which kept its money with Caldwell's bank and bought securities that Caldwell could not sell to the public. Caldwell was careless or dishonest, substituting poor for good bonds, when these were required as collateral against government deposits, or substituting surety bonds of employees of the investment house or of the Bank of Tennessee for good bonds where the net worth of the surety depended on the ultimate success of the several highly-leveraged ventures (McFerrin, 1969).

In the case of the Bank of the United States, after the death of his father who founded the bank, the younger Marcus rapidly expanded the bank through mergers and acquisitions. From $6 million of capital and six branches in New York City in late 1928, he expanded it to $25 million of capital and 57 branches in April 1929, exchanging capital stock and swapping assets and claims back and forth (Temin, 1976, pp. 90–3). Temin dismisses the defence of the Bank of the United States by Friedman and Schwartz who rely on the fact that it paid out 83.5 per cent of claims, four-fifths within two years, by noting that over one fifth of the 60 per cent paid out in the two years was the result of offsets, i.e. the cancellation of liabilities among the merged banks and their security affiliate, a demonstration of the pyramiding that led to insolvency when the speculative real estate dealt in by the bank fell in price. Writing before Wicker had called attention to the Caldwell case, Temin thought that the November wave of bank failures in the St. Louis and Atlanta Federal Reserve districts were connected with the fall in cotton prices.

A reading of McFerrin's book, however, demonstrates that the Caldwell and Bank of the United States failures were closely parallel to one another, albeit in different locales. They were dissimilar to the ordinary failure of a unit bank with inept management that is surprised by a fall in farm prices or bought risky bonds and thus can be accused of poor judgment. Like the farm-land market mania in World War I and the Florida land bubble of 1925, the Caldwell and Company story has elements of typical euphoric expansion on a thin capital base. McFerrin's account is replete with elements of aggressive highly-leveraged bank expansion that do not appear in Wicker's summary: 'Napoleonic complex' (p. xv); 'expansion fever' (p. 50); 'a general trend toward the wholesale and disastrous relaxation of standards of safety and the underwriting of securities of the most speculative nature' (p. 124); 'securities in Caldwell and Company's inventory were not of a type in which a commercial banker could invest the funds of its depositors; but Caldwell and Company, as with many other institutions carrying on both types of banking . . . had seemingly . . . little regard for the safety of depositors' funds' (p. 142). In his conclusion, McFerrin states that external forces were more important than internal in the collapse of Caldwell, including among the external the 'runaway bull market of 1928 and 1929', and among the internal a 'mad rush to expand' (p. 246).

Caldwell and Company and the Bank of the United States were high flyers, with modern counterparts in the Franklin National Bank in New York and Jake Butcher in Nashville, Tennessee. Aggressive to make their way against solid and entrenched banks, they took the risky loans left to them by more conservative bankers, doing well so long as business flourished and the prices of real estate and securities were rising. When the turn came in October 1929, they were in serious trouble.

The Caldwell empire was a chain of sorts, but instead of their interrelationships strengthening the separate banks in the combine, it weakened them. The AB Banks string of 55 rural banks in Arkansas, the Banco Kentucky chain in that state, and separate banks owned by Caldwell and Company throughout the states of Tennessee and Kentucky and in Asheville, North Carolina all folded up after the collapse of the investment house. Their failure was a consequence of having been stripped of money to support the flagship, and having had unsaleable securities stuffed into their portfolios. The same was true of the insurance companies in the conglomerate. Branch or chain banks are helped where the separate units have occasional troubles that are unrelated. Where the chain has been organized as a method of expansion, however, and all are stretched taut, the component units are each worse off than if they had gone their own way.

Wicker claims that Caldwell and Company was not a casualty of the depression (1980, p. 583), and Friedman and Schwartz assert that the Bank of the United States could have been saved if the banker members of the New York City Clearing House had rallied to its aid with a guarantee of liabilities (as the London banks did in 1890 in the crisis of Baring Brothers) (1963, pp. 309 ff). It is difficult to agree. Caldwell, to be sure, had already lost some of its glow well before the crash because of its public association with dubious politicians. The stock in its investment trust, for example, was slipping badly, despite support by Caldwell in the summer of 1929. But 'the weakness of the company was brought to a head by the stock market crash' (McFerrin, 1969, p. 125). After the crash the investment house moved to support the shares of the banks it owned, a measure of desperation pursued by banks in Austria and Germany during 1930 and 1931 (Born, 1967, pp. 60–1), and one that weakened cash/capital and cash/deposit ratios. Caldwell, morever, found itself with several large issues of bonds that it had underwritten before the crash, but could not sell. This was the plight that undid Baring Brothers in 1890, when it had to make the third payment of Buenos Ayres Water Supply Company on bonds it had not been able to move. The period from the crash in October 1929 to 12 November 1930, Caldwell having waited to close down until a day after the gubernatorial election so as not to hurt the chances of its candidate, was characterized as a continuous 'scramble for cash' (Chapter XIV).

The wedge between the yields on Aaa and Baa corporate bonds opened up widely in 1930. Interest rates in general had been pulled up after 1927 by the stock-market boom and the resulting demand for brokers' loans. The brokers' loan rate rose from an average of 4.32 per cent in 1927 to 8.86 per cent in December 1928 from which it slipped to 8.25 in September 1929. Alexander Field has recently attributed the general start of the economic downturn in 1929 to the rise in interest rates generated by the stock markets's transactions demand for money, settling econometrically to his satisfaction whether the stock market can absorb money (1984), an issue listed by Samuelson in a popular article among 'Fossils from Old Debates' (1979, p. 9). But the liquidity squeeze was quickly over after the crash. By December

1929, the brokers' loan rate was down to 4.83 per cent, by January 1930 to 4.31 and by July 1930 to 2.18. With it short-term rates and the yield on US government securities generally declined.

Short-lived as it was, the acute liquidity squeeze put pressure on commodity prices, created concerns about the liquidity and profitability of poorer companies, and, in Bernanke's phrase, if one wants to put it that way, increased the cost of intermediation. (It seems to me clearer to say that the wedge reflected a change in expectations about the economic outlook.) Large corporations piled up cash and government securities, as did large banks; small companies and small banks were strapped for cash and for assets that could be sold without substantial loss or would qualify for discounting by those banks belonging to the Federal Reserve system (Hunter, 1982).

The wedge between good and poor bonds, understated as it was by the nature of the construction of the index, widened throughout 1931, from 3.09 per cent in March to 4.29 per cent in August, from which level it rose to 4.88, 5.41, 5.30 and 6.45. Numbers of bank failures for the last five months of the year were 78, 158, 305, 175 and 358. The October 1931 peak in this period is ascribable to two events, the sharp fall in commodity prices from the 40 per cent appreciation of the dollar (depreciation of sterling which left gold on 21 September), and the rise in the Federal Reserve discount rate from $1\frac{1}{2}$ per cent to $2\frac{1}{2}$ per cent on 9 October and $3\frac{1}{2}$ per cent on 16 October—called by Friedman and Schwartz the sharpest rise within so brief a period in the whole history of the system, before or since (1963, p. 317), and by Emile Despres 'perhaps the most disastrous policy decision of the Great Depression' (1973, p xii). Friedman and Schwartz go so far as to maintain that the existence of the Federal Reserve System, in place of the National Banking System established in 1863, made it impossible to adopt what they regard as the optimal remedy for a bank run verging on panic—restriction of currency payments by the banks (1963, p. 316 note).

Temin's argument that the monetarist version of the depression is inconsistent with the decline in interest rates is dismissed by Vaubel along with Temin's objection that real money balances increased from 1929 to 1930 and early 1931. The argument is complex and somewhat opaque. But Vaubel acknowledges the possibility that there could have been a dramatic demand shift from private long-term securities and real assets to cash and riskless short-term securities eligible for discounting. He goes on to say, 'Note that if this were the case, it would have been more appropriate for the government to issue money *and* [his italics] government securities [to finance a budget deficit] than to issue money in exchange for government securities [expansionary open market operations] or rediscounting' (1984, p. 253, note 4). This seems an oddly Keynesian position for a professed and positive monetarist—if indeed Vaubel takes it—the paragraph is written in hypothetical language. It makes the point, however, that the banks that were collapsing—small banks in small towns—could not have been saved by open-market operations or lowering of the discount rate as they lacked government securities and eligible paper. Only the large banks and corporations had government bonds to sell, and the shrinking volume of eligible paper was concentrated in the large banks too (Hunter, 1982).

White asserts that the Federal Reserve System had little interest in the small, state non-member banks and did not mind seeing them winnowed out (1984, p. 136). If it had wanted to act as a lender of last resort, however, it would have had to loosen its standards to a great extent. In crises, central banks have often found it necessary to cast aside their rules for the eligibility of assets discounted by banks in trouble. In the course of coming to the aid of the British banking system, the Bank of England has frequently gone beyond its rule of lending only on bills of exchange bearing two names of established London bankers, lending on occasion on country paper, mortgages, including a mortgage on a plantation in the West Indies, on unimproved land, railway debentures, notes of an iron works, Indian securities and the like (Kindleberger, 1978, pp.174–8). Similar breaches of rules have occurred in France, not always in emergency. In the United States, the Reconstruction Finance Corporation created at the end of 1931 presumably had wider latitude than the Federal Reserve System in the loans it would make, but could not create money. The Italian equivalent of the R.F.C,, the Istituto di Riconstruzione Italiana (IRI) was formed in 1933 out of a very mixed bag of loans and investments that the Bank of Italy had taken over from the Italian banks in crises of 1907, 1923, 1926 and 1930–31 (Toniolo, 1980, Chapter V).

The fall in commodity prices and company profitability seems to me more important in decreasing the demand for money than a rise in the cost of intermediation based on transactions and information costs. The Temin reasoning applies. The decline in demand came from a shift of the demand curve to the left and down, not from a reduction in the supply of finance owing to transactions cost and a movement upward along a fixed demand curve. The question follows why price declines led to bank failures in 1931 and 1932 when their effects had been limited in 1921 and 1922. The answer, I believe, rests on the difference between the collapse of a bubble, in which windfall profits are wiped out, and a price decline of the same magnitude from a position in which farm and industrial profits have been worn away over several years. Keynes made the point in December 1930 (1932, p. 136). More recently Vaubel distinguished between disinflation and deflation, both producing declines in prices, but the latter larger pressure on output (1984, p. 251).

In summary, the high rate of bank failure to November 1930 had one cause—a delayed response to the World War I boom in agriculture, as prices of farm products and farm land slid downward against the background of high farm debt, persistently from 1925 and precipitously after October 1929. Beginning in November 1930, a different phenomenon was encountered, the collapse of two large institutions that had grown aggressively on a limited capital base by dubious methods and could survive only as long as security and real estate prices kept rising. They got into trouble when the stock-market crash brought down the prices of stocks, second-grade bonds, real estate, mortgages and commodities. About the middle of 1931 a third source of deflation set in, starting with the foreign runs on Austria, Germany, Britain and at the end of the year, Japan. The uncontrolled depreciation of sterling, resulting in a 40 per cent appreciation of the dollar, applied strong deflationary pressure to commodity prices in the United States, especially in October 1931. Heavy pressure was also felt from still another direction as the European gold bloc, panicked by foreign-exchange losses on holdings of sterling, undertook wholesale conversion of dollars into gold. The Federal Reserve System responded in the traditional, but in the circumstances, mistaken manner of tightening interest rates.

It is thus simplistic to apply a single model, whether Keynesian or monetarist, to the 1929–33 period as if it were monolithic.

BANK FAILURES IN THE 1970s AND 1980s

The differences between the 1980s and the 1930s exceed the similarities. The analogy between the Butcher and the Caldwell empires has been mentioned, and that between the Franklin National Bank and the Bank of the United States. Farm incomes started falling in 1979 after a rapid rise in farm debt, and farmland has fallen in price by 30 per cent in many states, and by as much as 37 per cent in Iowa. Ten of the twenty-seven banks that failed between 1 June and 1 September 1984 were 'farm banks', that is, banks that made 25 per cent of more of their loans to farmers, while six more of the twenty-seven banks had made between 10 and 25 per cent of their loans to farmers (*The New York Times*, 21 October 1984). The percentage of farm banks among problem banks on the December 1983 list of the FDIC was 24, as compared with 26 per cent of the number of commercial banks. By June 1984, the proportion of farm banks among problem banks had risen to 34 per cent. In November 1984, Norwest, a bank holding company with a chain of eighty-two banks in Minnesota, Wisconsin, Iowa, Nebraska, South Dakota and Montana, announced its first quarterly loss ever for the 3rd quarter of 1984. The chairman admitted that the mortgage company of the chain had grown very fast and made some mistakes; hence the need to write off $50 million. Outside the bank it was estimated that the holding company had charged 8 per cent of its farm loans off completely and placed another 14 per cent on non-performing status (*The New York Times*, 21 November 1984). Farm debt is estimated to have climbed from $141 billion in 1978 to $214 billion at the end of 1983 as farmers borrowed to keep going. Some observers attribute the downturn in farm income to President Carter's embargo on wheat sales to the Soviet Union following its invasion of Afghanistan, but the more compelling reason was the appreciation of the dollar which priced US agricultural exports out of world markets. A potential casualty of the rapid run-up of debt and the turndown of income has been the farm machinery industry. A number of companies, including International Harvester and Massey-Ferguson, have been selling off parts of their holdings and negotiating with bankers in an effort to stave off bankruptcy.

The troubles of farm banks came after the 1979 recession. The earlier sharp setback of 1974–5 produced a crop of urban bank failures, mostly associated with real estate speculation of the years previous. An early and spectacular collapse was that of the Franklin National Bank of New York City that failed on 29 October 1974, nine months after climbing to the rank of 20th largest bank in the country. The managers of the Franklin National, Sinkey claims, were inept rather than dishonest (1979, p. 148). Oppositely to the Bank of the United States which started in New York City and moved to Long Island, the Franklin National began on Long Island and in 1964 transferred to New York, moving aggressively into consumer banking and business accounts; and taking on risky loans that established commercial banks shunned. Lack of an established backlog of depositors required it to borrow a substantial proportion of its money through the Federal funds market and by marketing certificates of deposits. With the purchase of control of the bank by the Italian financier, Michele Sindona, in 1972, and the inception of floating exchange rates in 1973, the bank moved into foreign-exchange trading in New York and London. The underlying structure of the bank remained weak and classified loans rose from 5.9 per cent of the total in 1972 to 7.7 per cent in June 1974. The *coup de grace* came from a foreign-exchange loss of $14 million, with Sindona betting against the lira when it proved to be the dollar that was weak (Sinkey, 1979, Chapter 6; and Spero, 1980). To blame the bank's losses solely on ineptitude is misleading. There was fraud as well as bad judgment. When the bank lost $8.3 million in foreign-exchange operations in the first quarter of 1974, it began doctoring its books, recording fictitious operations and fictitious profits (Spero, 1980, pp. 69, 83, and 86). Three of its employees were convicted of concealing losses. Michele Sindona, who owned a fifth of the bank, served a prison sentence in New York state and was later extradited to Italy on charges connected with the June 1982 failure of the Banco Ambrosiano in Milan (Cornwall, 1983).

The Franklin National failure is interesting because it exhibits another type of bank run than one by depositors, one, moreover, in which deposit insurance can have little effect. This is a 'run' by other banks. Something of the sort may have been involved in the 1930 instance of the Bank of the United States when the Clearing House refused to come to its assistance. But interbank connections were far denser 44 years later. As early as November 1973 a New York bank went to the Federal Reserve Bank of New York to complain of the risks being taken by the Franklin National, partly on domestic lending but primarily in foreign-exchange speculation. Subsequently the banks asserted that they would no longer lend Franklin National federal funds or trade with it in the forward market for foreign exchange. On interbank loans in the Euro-currency market, moreover, they added a penalty charge to LIBOR (the London Interbank Borrowing Rate) (Spero, 1980, pp. 66, 71, 85, 91). In this instance depositors may have been ignorant of the risks taken by Franklin National but the banking community was not; in effect, it produced an insiders' run. Continental Illinois' CD rate was raised by the banking community as the bank's troubles mounted in the summer of 1984, but its closing resulting from a regular 'run' by foreign holders of its CDs, mostly in excess of the FDIC $100,000 limit.

The economic recession coming from the sharp rise in OPEC oil prices after the Yom Kippur war had early origins in the boom of the 1960s. The $1 billion failure of the United States National Bank of San Diego in November 1973 came from a series of real-estate deals stretching over a dozen years that had been publicly criticized as early as 1969. C. Arnhold Smith, his family and associates had acquired land, small firms, and securities and sold them at high prices to a conglomerate, Westgate California, controlled by Smith and financed by the bank. The bank derived 20 per cent of its deposits from governmental units in the area. In the end Smith served time in prison for violations of laws limiting loans of a bank to single interests (Sinkey, 1979, pp. 218–33).

Other major failures in the mid-seventies were widely scattered, the Security National Bank of Long Island, which expanded in New York City, like the Franklin National, and the Hamilton National Bank of Chattanooga which was caught in 1974 in the setback to real-estate prices in the Atlanta area. Both had had recent changes in management that led to aggression expansion tactics. The lag between recession and failure was variable, depending on the capacity of the bank to get help. The Security National was taken over by the Chemical Bank in January 1975; the Hamilton National, which had financed the expansion of its Atlanta mortgage subsidiary with Federal funds and repos, hung on until 1976.

Recovery after 1975 slowed down the rate of failure until the new oil shock of 1979 which was combined with a shift to tight money by the Federal Reserve System. With the usual lags, the troubles began to surface in 1982. By the third quarter of 1984, a strong economic recovery seemed to portend, in the short run at least, a respite.

Many of the difficulties of the banks had roots going back a long way into the 1970s, in real estate and in syndicated bank loans to sovereign Third World countries. There were, however, a number of new elements, excessive expansion in financing oil exploration, and speculation in silver and in government securities.

The mixture of aggressive risk taking, ineptitude and violations of the law or fraudulent deals is difficult to disentangle. The Butcher bank chains in Tennessee and Kentucky which collapsed in 1983 were said to have been the victims of at least six years of abusive practices, essentially gaining control of small banks with excess deposits and limited loan outlets, and diverting the money to the Butcher business interest, and even to Swiss bank accounts. One of their accountants has confessed to bankruptcy fraud and has been sentenced to prison. Jake Butcher was indicted for fraud, confessed, and was sentenced to jail.

The Crocker National Bank of San Francisco, rescued in 1984 by a new infusion of capital from the Midland Bank of London that already owned 57 per cent of its shares, got into trouble in financing a boom in very expensive Los Angeles real estate which was found to be overpriced when tight money in 1979 slowed down the purchase of luxury condominia. It had taken a quantum jump in investments in Southern California when it absorbed the United States National Bank of San Diego in 1976.

The highly speculative area outside of real estate was oil, but first let me dispose of some near misses arising from the speculation of Bunker Hunt in silver, and of Drysdale, Lombard-Wall, and E.S.M. in government securities. Bunker Hunt had pyramiding profits from going long in silver until he became so extended that he could not accept delivery on his long contracts and had to settle with the shorts. It was said in the press that he lost perhaps $1 billion of his fortune of $3 billion. The bear squeeze threatened to catch him illiquid, if solvent, and unable to pay off loans to Bache securities that had financed a portion of his holdings. To stave off a market crisis, the Federal Reserve carried Bache over the bind. Two government security houses also ran into trouble in 1982 when they went long on US treasuries on a highly leveraged basis and lost heavily when interest rates tightened and bond prices fell. The Chase Manhattan Bank had extended long lines of credit to Drysdale, and the Dormitory Authority of the State of New York had made a major loan to Lombard-Wall. When the two security houses failed, their supporters were threatened with major losses.

The latest in this series of collapses of financial houses dealing in government securities on a highly-leveraged basis was that of E.S.M. Government Securities, Inc. of Fort Lauderdale, Florida, which was closed in early March 1985. Its officers and an outside auditor were charged with concealing losses of several hundred million dollars. The loss of $150 millions by the Home State Savings Bank in Cincinnati led to depositor runs on all the savings and loan associations insured by the Ohio state system, rather than the FSLIC (Federal Savings and Loan Insurance Corporation), and the closing of savings and loan associations by the governor, until federal assistance should be forthcoming. A month later, some thrift institutions, with only state insurance, were run in Maryland, and in June 1985, a largely Chinese bank in San Francisco, that had issued both insured and non-insured certificates of deposits. These were the only instances of small depositors' runs on banks in the 1980s. They stirred up political trouble and confusion, without, at this writing, lasting effect. They raise, however, profound questions concerning the regulation, examination and insurance of banking institutions by various federal and state systems with different standards.

The foremost difficulties of 1982 to 1984, however, came from oil and loans to Less Developed Countries (LDCs). It quickly became apparent that the OPEC price hike to $34 a barrel for high quality crude could not be sustained, and exploration companies formed to take advantage of the profit prospects at that price were in difficulty. So were their banks. The Penn Square Bank of Oklahoma City had undertaken very aggressive and apparently partly illegal lending to oil-exploration companies, some with insider connections with the bank. It sold off loans in excess of FDIC limits, when it did not disguise them, to other banks around the country, notably the Seafirst of Seattle, the Michigan National Bank and the Continental Illinois National Bank of Chicago, getting each of those banks into trouble when it, Penn Square, failed in July 1982. Seafirst was absorbed by the Bank of America in the summer of 1983. The Michigan National Bank's difficulties went beyond the $195 million of Penn Square loans they purchased, and included more than $100 million in loans to insider companies, and $50 millions in loans to companies going through bankruptcy proceedings (*The New York Times*, 6 August 1982). The troubles of the Continental Illinois Bank were not limited to Penn Square from which it bought $1 billion in loans. It was a heavy lender to many other companies in trouble, including International Harvester and Nucorp Energy, both in reorganization, and was weighed down by a large holding in syndicated bank loans to Third World countries. At the end of the third quarter of 1984 these amounted to half of its non-performing loans.

The literature on syndicated bank loans to Third World countries started as a trickle in 1977 with the publication of a symposium organized by Stephen Goodman of the Export–Import Bank (at that time), and has risen in 1985 as this is written, to a torrent. A recent survey notes two contrasting views of the role of the US banks: one, expressed especially by bankers, that they were passively responding to a vigorous demand from the country borrowers, much as 'wallflowers' waiting to be asked to dance, and a second, that the banks themselves, through a frequently expressed view that there was no risk involved (for example, in letters to *The New York Times* by officers of Citicorp) were loan pushers (Eaton and Taylor, 1986, forthcoming, citing articles by Irving Friedman of Citicorp and Darity, 1985). Too little attention had been paid, in my view, to the role of the Federal Reserve Board under the chairmanship of Arthur Burns, in trying to lower interest rates prior to the 1972 election, at a time when the Bundesbank in the Federal Republic of Germany was trying to raise them. Capital poured out of the United States into the Euro-currency market, where German companies, including multinationals located in that country, borrowed it to pay down their high-cost debt in Deutschemarks. Given the weakness of the dollar at the time, they were not loath to go short of dollars long term. The borrowed dollars were sold to the Bundesbank, redeposited in the Euro-currency market, and gave rise to a multiple expansion of dollars in that market. The 'deficit' in the balance of payments in the United States rose, on the unsatisfactory liquidity definition, from an average of $2–4 billions annually in the late 1960s and 1970 to $20 billion in 1971 and $30 billion in 1972. Awash with dollars, the Euro-currency market, including the European branches of American banks lowered interest rates and started an eager search for new lending outlets. Similar bursts of foreign lending had occurred in the nineteenth century from British debt conversion, once in 1822 after the Napoleonic war, and again when Goschen converted the consols in 1886. 'John Bull can stand many things, but he cannot stand 2 per cent.' The stimulus of the Fed failing to realize the necessity for coordinated monetary policy in the US and the Federal Republic was felt long before the oil price shock of November 1973 that is often singled out as the start of the foreign-ending surge. Successive reschedulings of the large debts of Mexico in August 1982, Brazil in the fall of 1983, and Argentina in the fall of 1984 threatened the banks with large loan classifications and/or writeoffs in a series of dramatic scenes reminiscent of the 1920s motion-picture serial, 'Perils of Pauline'.

The bank failures and rescue operations of 1974–76 and 1982–4, therefore, were brought on by booms in real estate, farm land, oil exploration and Third World lending that went to excess before they were cut short by recessions in 1974–5 (the oil shock) and in 1980–2 (tight money from October 1979). In the 1980s, tight money knocked down the prices of luxury housing, farm land, timber, farm machinery, and ultimately, because of the cobweb excess, of oil and some raw materials. Tight money and the consequent rise in the exchange rate of the dollar increased the service charges on Third World debt, and insofar as these were borrowed, the debt itself. Tight money further led to extensive disintermediation of thrift institutions, with the need for mergers and substantial governmental aid. The only serious run occurred in the case of Continental Illinois, started, according to press reports, by foreign holders of its certificates of deposits. Rumours that might have led to runs on the Manufacturers Hanover in New York, and the First Chicago in that city were quickly quashed.

The bank failures of the 1970s and 1980s thus seemed to arise from a historical pattern of displacement, euphoria, boom in which many bankers lost sight of conventional and conservative standards of asset management, and in some cases crossed the line into violations of the law. The relaxation of standards produced loan and investment portfolios vulnerable to recession, according to what might be called the 'quality theory of money and banking'. The sharpness of the rise of interest rates in 1979 in the effort to halt inflation started a process of bank loss that produced the troubles of 1982, 1983 and 1984.

The similarities between the 1930s and the 1980s reside then in farm banks—though the process was drawn out in the 1920s and 1930s, and precipitous in the later period, in the parallels between Butcher and

Caldwell on the one hand and Franklin National and the Bank of the United States on the other, and in the relaxation of standards of banking practice in boom.

The differences were perhaps more extensive than the similarities: in the 1980s it was the big banks that had trouble, in the 1930s the small; in the 1980s, the banks of Texas and California faced difficulty whereas in the 1930s they had barely been touched; real estate played a limited role in the 1930 troubles but the bubbles of the 1980s were more widespread, not only in real estate, but also in oil and in syndicated Third World bank loans (it is true that part of the euphoria of the 1920s after the Dawes loan success led to a burst of lending on foreign bonds, but this died away in mid-1928); stock-market credit plays only a limited role in the later 1970s as compared with 1928 and 1929, though speculation in silver and government bonds threatened serious trouble, thus far happily evaded.

The major difference, however, was that in the 1980s the FDIC and FSLIC were in place to rescue institutions in trouble by taking over bad loans and merging troubled banks with others, or paying off depositors in banks that closed. In other respects, too, the lender of last resort function was understood and evoked appropriate responses despite the uncharted nature of some of the waters being navigated. Lockheed, Chrysler Corporation and New York City seem to constitute the list of salvage of non-banking institutions aided in our period, although going further back one could add Penn-Central. Major borrowers among the Third World countries have been aided by the International Monetary Fund, by the lending syndicates headed by money-market banks, and by bridging loans from the Bank for International Settlements, and the US Government or the Federal Reserve System to avoid default. Debt service payments have been rescheduled and in recent months, problem loans have been written off at a faster rate.

The major bank rescue, and a dramatic one, was that of the Continental Illinois National Bank and Trust Company that received a $2 billion loan from the FDIC, along with a $5.5 billion credit from a syndicate of twenty-eight of the country's largest banks. The rescue was not without penalties for the bank: its officers and most of the directors were dismissed, and the bank stock sank to low levels. In other instances, moreover, the Comptroller of the Currency directed two major banks, the Bank of America in California and the First National Bank of Chicago, to enlarge their capital or buttress it with subordinated debentures, and to tighten credit standards by requiring dirctor approval of any loan or investment in excess of $10 million. IMF help to Third World countries in connection with rescheduling, moreover, has been accompanied by conditions guiding economic policies.

From a short-run perspective, the third quarter of 1984 may have been the low point. In that trimester bank write-offs were heavy and many banks recorded losses. Bank stocks declined to new low levels and low multiples of earnings from which they recovered sharply at the end of the year. The market was burdened by great uncertainty over the Continental rescue on the one hand and the renegotiation of Argentine debt on the other. In subsequent months a settlement with Argentina was reached, interest rates came down, bank shares recovered, but especially encouraging was the continued impressive recovery of the American economy. The sailing, however, is far from plain. Rough passages and umarked shoals lie ahead.

One further difference between then and now: the banking crisis of 1933 gave rise to a long list of reforms and institutional changes to forestall a recurrence: the Glass–Steagall act separating investment and commercial banking the FDIC, measures to strengthen farm and home mortgage finance with government intermediation, and the like (Minsky, 1984). The crisis of 1982–4, if one can put an end date to it, took place in a climate of bank deregulation. Some pressure has been felt for stricter bank examinations. The Comptroller's cutting off the heads of the officers and directors of the Continental Illinois 'to encourage the others' has been mentioned. There is even limited sentiment, as expressed for example, by Henry Kaufman of Salomon Brothers, for bank reregulation. On the whole, however, sentiment continues to run in favour of loosening up the guidance given to banks. Holding companies introduced to defeat unit banking are firmly established. Insurance companies, retail stores, stock brokers and banks are invading one another's businesses. Deregulation leading to national or regional banking across state lines is in process of enactment. A rising ultra-monetarist Austrian school of thought is advocating free banking and the abolition of central banks. Authors such as Friedman and Schwartz oppose the Federal Reserve System, to be sure, but in their support of control of the money supply and a role for a lender of last resort are beginning to appear old-fashioned. Even if the Congress were to wish for new legislation to strengthen the banking system, it would be hard to find a consensus on the direction that changes should take. Economists and economic historians interested in banking are constrained to recall the Chinese curse: 'May you live in interesting times.'

NOTES

1. It seems to me that the question whether banks were always or occasionally unstable should be settled by an appeal to history rather than to what such instability might imply as an assumption for economic behaviour. The monetary-theory requirement of rationality cannot mean that all persons in an economy are equally rational all the time, with the same intelligence, information and vantage point. If one concedes the existence of the fallacy of composition, moreover, each person can be rational but the collectivity can behave in irrational ways, e.g. running for the doors in a theatre fire. When history and theory clash on such a point, it is irrational to dismiss history in favour of strong prior assumptions. Note that Blanchard and Watson 'prove' that bubbles (instability) are possible with rationality (1981), feeling the need to lay aside any assumption of irrationality because the mathematics of the formal modelling of irrationality are difficult. Again, it is not self-evident that the historical record should be set aside in favour of easier mathematics.

REFERENCES

Alston, Lee J. (1983), 'Farm Foreclosures in the United States during the Interwar Period', *Journal of Economic History* 43, 4 (December), pp. 885–904.

Anderson, Barry L. and Butkiewicz, James L. (1982), 'The Causes of Bank Failures During the Great Depression', mimeographed.

Bernanke, Ben S. (1983), 'Nonmonetary Effects of the Financial Crisis in the Propagation of the Great Depression', *American Economic Review* 73, 3 (June), pp. 257–76.

Blanchard, Olivier J. and Watson, Mark W. (1982), 'Bubbles, Rational Expectations and Financial Markets', in Paul Wachtel (ed.), *Crises in the Economic and Financial Structure*, Lexington, Mass: D.C. Heath, pp. 295–316.

Born, Karl Erich (1967), *Die deutsche Bankenkrise: Finanzen und Politik*, Munich: Piper.

Brunner, Karl (1981), editor, *The Great Depression Revisited*, The Hague: Martinus Nijhoff.

Comptroller of the Currency (1932) (1936), *Annual Reports* for 1931, 1935, Washington, DC: U.S. Government Printing Office.

Cornwall, Rupert (1983), *God's Banker: The Life and Death of Roberto Calvi*, London, Gollancz.

Darity, William, Jr. (1985), 'Loan-Pushing: Doctrine and Theory', International Finance Discussion Paper, Federal Reserve Board, Washington, DC.

Despres, Emile (1973), *International Economic Reform: The Collected Papers of Emile Despres*, edited by Gerald M. Meier, New York: Oxford University Press.

Eaton, Jonathan and Taylor, Lance (1986), 'Developing Country Finance and Debt', paper prepared for a conference on 'New Directions in Development', forthcoming.

Federal Deposit Insurance Corporation (1938), *Annual Report* for the year ending December 31, 1937, Washington, DC: US Government Printing Office.

Federal Reserve System (1943), *Banking and Monetary Statistics*, Washington, DC: Board of Governors.

Federal Reserve Bulletin (1937).

Flannery, Mark J. and Guttentag, Jack M. (1980), 'Problem Banks: Examination, Identification and Supervision', in Leonard Lapidus and others, *State and Federal Regulation of Commercial Banks*, Washington, DC. Federal Deposit Insurance Corporation, vol. II, pp. 171–226.

Friedman, Irving (1978), 'Emerging Role of Private Banks', in Stephen H. Goodman (ed.), *Financing and Risk in Developing Countries*, New York: Praeger.

Friedman, Milton and Schwartz, Anna Jacobson (1963), *A Monetary History of the United States, 1867–1960*, Princeton: Princeton University Press.

Goodman, Stephen H. (1978) (ed.), *Financing and Risk in Developing Countries*, New York: Praeger.

Gordon, Robert J. and Wilcox, Jame A. (1981), 'Monetarist Interpretations of the Great Depression: An Evaluation and Critique', in Karl Brunner (ed.), *The Great Depression Revisited*, The Hague, Martinus Nijhoff.

Hunter, Helen Manning (1982), 'The Role of Business Liquidity During the Great Depression and Afterwards: Differences between Large and Small Firms', *Journal of Economic History*, 42, 4 (December) pp. 883–902.

Johnson, H. Thomas (1973–74), 'Postwar Optimism and the Rural Financial Crisis of the 1920s', *Explorations in Economic History*, 2, 2 (Winter).

Keynes, John Maynard (1930), 'The Great Slump of 1930', in J.M. Keynes, *Essays in Persuasion*, New York: Harcourt, Brace.

Kindleberger, Charles P. (1973), *The World in Depression*, Berkeley, California: University of California Press.

——— (1978), *Manias, Panics and Crashes: A History of Financial Crises*, New York: Basic Books.

Mayer, Martin (1974), *The Bankers*, New York: Ballantine.

McFerrin, John Berry (1939, 1969), *Caldwell and Company: A Southern Financial Empire*, 1969 reissue, Nashville: Vanderbilt University Press.

Minsky, H.P. (1984), 'Banking and Industry between the Two Wars: The United States', in *Journal of European Economic History*, 12, 2 (special issue), pp. 235–72.

The New York Times, various issues.

Sachs, Jeffrey (1982), 'LDC Debt in the 1980s: Risk and Reform', in Paul Wachtel (ed.), *Crises in the Economic and Financial Structure*, Lexington, MA: D.C. Heath.

Samuelson, Paul A. (1979), 'Myths and Realities about the Crash and Depression', in *Journal of Portfolio Management*, 6, 1 (Fall), pp. 7–10.

Schwartz, Anna (1981), 'Understanding 1929–1933', in Karl Brunner (ed.), *The Great Depression Revisited*, The Hague: Martinus Nijhoff.

Sinkey, Joseph F., Jr. (1979), *Problems of Failed Institutions in the Commercial Banking Industry*, Greenwich, Conn.: JAI Press.

Spero, Joan Edelman (1980), *The Failure of the Franklin National Bank: Challenge to the International Banking System*, New York: Columbia University Press (for the Council on Foreign Relations).

Temin, Peter (1976), *Did Monetary Forces Cause the Great Depression?*, New York: W.W. Norton.

Toniolo, Gianni (1980), *L'economia dell' Italia fascista*, Rome-Bari: Laterza.
Vaubel, Roland (1984), 'International Debt, Bank Failures, and the Money Supply', *Cato Journal*, 4, 1 (Spring/Summer), pp. 249–67.
White, Eugene Nelson (1984), 'A Reinterpretion of the Banking Crisis of 1930', *Journal of Economic History*, 44, 1 (March), pp. 119–38.
Wicker, Elmus (1980), 'A Reconsideration of the Causes of the Banking Panic of 1930', *Journal of Economic History*, 40, 3 (September), pp. 571–83.

6 Reversible and Irreversible Processes in Economics*

In his recently published *The Rhetoric of Economics*, Donald N. McCloskey claims that many apparently scientific views of the world are in fact matters of rhetoric. The author argues that they are based less on deduction or induction than on generalizations of more or less plausibility, derived from intuition and supported by appeals to metaphors, authority, symmetry, and the like. In economics, a basic metaphor turns on whether a process is reversible or not. Economists with a strong liberal or neo-classical view of the world use words such as equilibrium (which in theoretical discourse should be said to exist and be unique on the one hand and to be stable on the other), elasticity, and cycles to emphasize that departures of the economy from stasis if left alone will return to something approximating the earlier position or at least something recognizable as growing naturally out of it. They oppose government intervention of one kind or another—to redistribute income; to correct shortages or gluts; to relieve unemployment; to control prices, the exchange rate, foreign trade, etc. An ultraclassical or Austrian position even wants to get rid of central banks and give up control of the money supply.

Keynesian economists as a rule are ready to grant that capitalist economies behave much of the time, perhaps even most of the time, in ways that conform to this balancing, self-correcting servo-mechanism, but are more apt to concede the possibility of discontinuities and the threat of irreversibilities that may require government intervention. Wages rise more rapidly than they fall because of downward (but not upward) stickiness. Consumption is more likely to increase as income rises than to decrease as income falls, beause of the Duesenberry consumption

* Adapted from a lecture presented at the State University of Arts and Science, Geneseo, New York, 11 March 1986 and published in *Challenge*, vol. 29, no. 4, September–October 1986, pp. 4–10. Reprinted with permission of publisher M.E. Sharpe, Inc., 80 Business Park Drive, Armonk, NY 10504.

function that turns today's luxuries into tomorrow's necessities.

In financial crisis, it may be useful and even necessary to have a lender of last resort to prevent a rush out of real and illiquid financial assets into money that would depress the prices of those assets and result in debt deflation, business bankruptcies, and bank failures that proved to be irreversible in the short run. A sharp debate has arisen over whether or not it is desirable to require margin on the issuance of so-called junk bonds, with interventionists worried that the flurry, even mania, for issuing such debt to finance corporate takeovers may lead (through debt deflation in a future business turndown) to bankruptcies and deep depression. Liberal economists of the Chicago school object to such interference in market processes, and would push beyond halting this sort of regulation to further deregulation of financial and economic markets.

HUMPTY DUMPTY SYNDROME

Reversible and irreversible processes are complex in nature. Smash a pane of glass and this may properly be regarded as an irreversibility except by some archeologist years hence who painstakingly and at great cost reconstitutes it, as is done today for ancient pottery and sculpture. Birth and death are the big discontinuities and irreversibilities in the short run, although the words of the funeral service—'ashes to ashes, dust to dust'—reminds us that from a given perspective there is reversibility in the long run. Learning is irreversible (again, in the short run, and before the return to second childhood): learning to read, to ride a bicycle, to swim; or the first kiss, the loss of virginity—these natural changes are not reversible in the same way that much disease and wounds to the body are (short of crippling or pushing to the level of death). Thomas Wolfe's title, *You Can't Go Home Again*, is relevant. The current debate among doctors and moral philosophers about living wills turns primarily on the problem of recognizing when the approach of death under various circumstances is irreversible and when not. How much is illness like chess, in which expert players, far from the end game, see the conclusion as so inevitable and foregone that the player slightly behind gives up, pulls the plug so to speak, and resigns?

Like human bodies, physical objects are sometimes reparable, sometimes not. Working on intelligence in matériel during World War II, my O.S.S. colleagues and I learned that a military tank was immortal (so long as there were enough spare parts to hang on it or insert into it) unless it went over a cliff or caught fire. A direct hit by an armour-piercing shell that did not start a fire did not ruin it; the hole was merely papered over since the probability of a direct hit in the exact same place by a non-armour-piecing projectile was small. Eggs, milk, and tomatoes have an irreversible half-life measured in days; houses last virtually forever unless, as in the case of the tank, they are consumed by fire or tornado or earthquake, or slide down an eroded bank. 'On the brink' expresses the teetering possibilities of thousands of situations.

A friend to whom I mentioned my interest in reversibility and irreversibility loaned me a book on physics that deals with the subject. It is *From Being to Becoming: Time and Complexity in the Physical Sciences* by Ilya Prigogine (New York: W.H. Freeman, 1980). My comprehension of physics is limited and when I learn that Albert Einstein did not believe in irreversibility, while his physicist friend and correspondent, Michele Besso did (p. 202), I fear I am over my head. Besso maintained that time produced irreversibility, whereas Einstein held that the distinctions among past, present, and future are only an illusion. If I gain a glimmer of understanding from the book, celestial mechanics—*vide* the solar system and, as a current example, Halley's comet—rests on stability, and so does quantum mechanics for which I have no ready example. Both are tied to 'being'. But thermodynamics with the introduction of entropy produces a shift to 'becoming'. I have been further instructed by another friend that the analogy between reversibility and irreversibility in physics and in economics is not acceptable. Reversibility and irreversibility in physics are related to 'laws' of nature that are inexorable. The question in economics is probabalistic. But I hope I will be forgiven if I do not pursue the subject further along these lines.

Reversibility and irreversibility are found not only in the life sciences—the world of animate and inanimate objects—but also in politics. In a democracy under the two-party system with majority rule, the majority acts with restraint toward the minority because it is aware that the position is readily reversible. Marxist political philosophy sees revolutions as irreversible, leading (in the simplistic formulation) from feudalism to capitalism to the dictatorship of the proletariat to socialism. Revolutions are discontinuities, although counterrevolutions are not completely excluded and recent years have produced the salubrious spectacle of military revolutions in Latin America giving way peacefully to a return to democratic regimes.

PARALLEL IN ECONOMICS

My study of reversibility and irreversibility in economics has emerged as an extension of my interest in economic and financial history, fluctuating exchange rates, and financial crisis. Especially as we approach the fortieth anniversary of Secretary of State George C. Marshall's speech at Harvard proposing the European Recovery Program, I am fascinated by the revisionist proposition that the help offered by the United States and accepted by Europe was not really needed.

But first let me digress to consider a recent case concerning the Kodak Company in Rochester, New York. It was reported in the *New York Times* of 9 January 1986 that Kodak had lost a plea for a stay of an injunction barring it from the instant-camera industry because it violated Polaroid patents. Kodak had asked for a stay while it was preparing an appeal on the patent violation. When the request was rejected, the company decided to withdraw permanently from the production of instant cameras, stating 'that it would not be economically feasible to comply with the injunction and then open again if it wins the appeal. Thus, the injunction has the effect of putting Kodak out of the business permanently.'

This kind of economic irreversibility is often the result of dumping in international trade. Dumping—selling goods in a distant market for what they will bring above the cost of getting them there—is something detested by local business in the market where the goods are dumped, unless the institution is old and hallowed like Filene's basement in Boston, January white sales, or postseason clearances. Economists typically tolerate it. In the wave of exchange dumping that occurred after World War I, Jacob Viner analyzed the subject (*Dumping*, University of Chicago Press, 1923) and distinguished sporadic, persistant, and predatory types.

Sporadic dumping earns little opprobrium. The producer makes a mistake, such as overestimating the popularity of a book, and remainders it. Persistent dumping is thought of as beneficial to the market where the goods are sold, but harmful to the home market which has to bear a disproportionate share of the overhead costs. Predatory dumping used to be condemned: low prices to drive competitors out of business, permitting then the establishment of a monopoly. But the late international economist Harry Johnson defended even predatory dumping on the ground that if the dumper established a monopoly and raised prices the companies driven out of the trade could re-enter. This is a neo-classical view, assuming easy entry and exit and disregarding what economists later called 'transactions costs'—the costs of leaving, waiting in the wings, and then making new investments.

MONETARY INTERVENTION

The question also arises in macroeconomics. When should monetary authorities stay out of a foreign-exchange market and when should they intervene, and in each case, why? I cite the case of the Italian lira in 1963. There was a short, sharp capital outflow of funds as Italian capitalists went on strike so to speak, to protest the nationalization of the electric power industry. Would a flexible exchange-rate system have been helpful in this case? Or should the Italians (as they did) have undertaken swaps with the leading financial centres, in effect borrowing foreign exchange—to use to hold the rate steady—to be repaid later? The proper course depends upon whether Italian prices would have returned to the original level, rising during the depreciation of the lira, and falling later when the capital returned and the lira appreciated. But prices and wages in such a country as Italy are not smoothly reversible. The capital flows may be judged to be reversible, but the price changes, if the exchange rate moves, would not be. This makes a strong case for intervention. It happened, however, that the short-run case for intervention did not exclude long-run depreciation under the impact of domestic inflation and the rate proved to be indefensible at 900 lira per dollar.

A particular aspect of irreversibility in the short run is the ratchet sometimes set in motion under flexible exchange rates. In a world of deflation, as in the 1930s, a flexible exchange rate working through a sine wave pattern lowers prices continuously. Conversely, it raises them in a world of inflation. When an exchange rate changes between two countries, prices in the depreciating country may fall, those in the appreciating country may rise or the changes can be shared between them. In any event, the old relation between the two sets of prices must change. Which way it changes depends (the answer to most questions in economics is 'it depends') on the elasticities.

In a world of deflation with supply and demand inelastic with respect to price decreases, depreciation is likely to leave prices unchanged whereas appreciation will lower them. If a given currency follows a sine wave—first down, then up—prices will remain unchanged in the first phase, then decline, hold steady on the second depreciation, then decline again. The effect is a ratchet that depresses prices as was the case from 1930 to 1932. In a period of world inflation, on the other hand, such as that of the 1960s and 1970s, the ratchet works the other way, raising prices during depreciation and leaving them unchanged in periods of appreciation. The world seems to have emerged from that pattern in the 1980s, and whether the ratchet will turn and work downward is unclear at the moment, though raw material prices are slipping badly. In a balanced world of neither inflation or deflation, a sine wave of exchange rates is likely to produce a reversible process of price changes, partway down in depreciation, partway up in appreciation.

The structural inflation of less developed countries is of course the interaction of repeated depreciations accompanied by higher domestic prices.

THE MONEY CHASE

Gresham's law evokes another historical asymmetry or irreversibility. The subject is too vast to do more than offer a brief sketch. Assume two monies: gold and silver, or perhaps gold and foreign exchange, or two reserve currencies such as dollars and sterling that third countries may want to hold. It can happen that money-holders value them in some relationship that makes economic sense or conforms to rational expectations—for example, in proportion to a country's trade, or with short-term balances in foreign exchange, long-term reserves in gold. But the portfolio of such liquid assets can follow the mechanics of a see-saw, rather than a weighing balance, with one money judged overvalued, intrinsically weak, and likely to depreciate in value so that it is sold off and the other is hoarded. In a sellers' market it is possible that good money will drive out bad, as sellers insist on getting good money for their wares; some advocates of free banking rely on that possibility. In buyers' markets, however, buyers insist on spending the 'bad money', and in portfolios switching out of overvalued money into the undervalued. In this, the usual circumstance, bad money drives out good.

Gresham's law seems to me more general than in its applications to money. It applies to money of all kinds on the one hand and to commodities—real assets such as land and buildings, capital equipment, etc.—and illiquid financial assets on the other. Classical economists assert that markets are stable. I agree that this is true as a rule. It can happen, however, that expectations of a rise in price for a given class of assets will lead to a continuous flow out of money and unutilized credit into such assets that overshoots and is likely to be followed later by a revulsion and a movement out of assets into money. Where this is convulsive, it may lead to a panic or crash, widespread bankruptcy, bank failure, and the like; in other words, to economic irreversibility judged from a fairly short-term time perspective. The model in my book, *Manias, Panics and Crashes*, I claim, is not universal nor unavoidable; it is one, however, that is met from time to time and it rests on a mechanism of irreversibility.

The employment of a lender of last resort to resist such crashes and to keep the economy stable, balanced, in equilibrium, and reversible seems to me wise. To be sure, it poses a moral hazard, as does insurance, when the person saved from his folly by an outside force loses incentive to be cautious. Therefore, some reckless actors must be allowed to go under 'to encourage the others'. It is the presence of the ambiguity that is important. There should be ambiguity whether the reckless borrower and/or the reckless lender will be saved. But the masochism of an Andrew Mellon: 'Liquidate labour; liquidate stocks; liquidate the farmers; liquidate real estate' (Hoover, p. 30) which he considered essential to long-run revival is thought by most—though not all—observers today to hasten an irreversible process unnecessarily.

It is easy to exaggerate the gloom and doom of cataclysm. I collected a list of hyperbolic statements in *Manias* (p 216): Halting the conversion of bank notes into gold by the Bank of England gives rise to 'horror'. 'If the Bank of England refused to lend on the securities of the government, the game is up, no saying what would happen to anyone.' The US bank holiday of 4 March 1933 was anticipated as the end of the world by many but in actuality lightened the spirits of Americans, as if a weight had been lifted. The remark of Lewis Douglas to James Warburg as they walked most of the night through Washington on 18 April 1933 after the White House meeting in which President Roosevelt said he was accepting the Thomas amendment that permitted taking the dollar off the gold standard seems extravagant: 'This is the end of Western civilization' (Warburg, p. 120). Nonetheless, and despite Alfred Marshall's epigraph *Natura non facit saltum* (there are no discontinuities in nature) in *Principles of Economics* (Macmillan, 1930) there can be critical turning points, although classical economists and others may not agree in their identification.

A CASE IN POINT

Such an historical corner was approaching, in my view, when Secretary of State George C. Marshall offered a plan for European recovery in his Harvard commencement address on 5 June 1947. The Marshall Plan was conceived as a means of preventing economic collapse in Europe that might lead to irreversible political collapse.

World War II had left Europe reeling. Following the freezing and floods of the winter of 1946–7 and the drought of the previous summer, a disastrous harvest was anticipated for 1947. Food was scarce and economic prospects were dim, especially in Germany, France, and Italy. While Germany was occupied, there was fear of Communist political victories in France and Italy that might prove irreversible. The literature of the time emphasized the nearly unanimous view held by the American press, governmental leaders and some Europeans that economic collapse was imminent unless new steps were taken. Substantial aid had been given by the United States to Europe, and emergency loans, in contravention of the articles of agreement, had been furnished to France by the International Monetary Fund and the International Bank. More aid was thought to be needed to avert crisis. Joseph M. Jones in *The Fifteen Weeks* (Viking Press, 1955) characterized the period from the British revelation that they could no longer help Greece and Turkey (1 February 1947) to the Marshall speech (5 June 1947) as momentous in producing an overdue assertion of US responsibility for world economic stability.

There was a minority view at the time expressed by economists Frank D. Graham, Gottfried Haberler, Henry Hazlitt, Friederich Lutz and Senator Joseph Ball of Minnesota that the position in Europe could have been corrected by proper economic policy on the part of local governments. All they had to do was control the money supply, balance their budgets, and depreciate the exchange rate to some equilibrium level, or more generally, halt the inflation and adjust the exchange rate to correct for overvaluation.

FORTY YEARS LATER . . .

More recently, revisionist literature has tended to regard the dangers as seen in 1947 as exaggerated, to argue that the economic difficulties of the time would have been met automatically if there had been no Marshall Plan, or could have been solved in other ways. It is held that the risk of revolution in France and Italy through Communist political victory in elections was declining and would have been overcome without outside economic help.

One such view has come from Harold van Buren Cleveland, who in the Department of State in 1947 had been a strong proponent of a comprehensive plan of US aid to Europe for reconstruction (Jones, pp. 242–3). On the 35th anniversary in 1982, in an essay entitled 'If there had been no Marshall Plan . . .' Cleveland held that with devaluation of the pound and the French franc, private lending from

the United States would have restored those countries to economic
health. However, he maintained, bureaucrats—a group to which he
had once belonged—would not have wanted to give up their role in
providing relief to the Bizone area in West Germany. Italy was a more
difficult problem which he did not attempt to second-guess in a short
paper. But he held, in accordance with the classical position expressed
in 1947 and 1948, that the dollar shortage of the period was largely
the result of internal European mismanagement (see Hoffmann and
Maier, Chapter VIII). In the discussion that followed, largely among
other participants in the Marshall Plan, doubt was expressed that open
societies would have been maintained, especially in France, Italy, and
Germany, had there been no Marshall Plan. There was no discussion
of the plausibility of Cleveland's counterfactual suggestion that in the
absence of government assistance there would have been a substantial
private flow of lending from the United States to France, Britain, and
Germany, despite the dismal record of US private lending to Germany
and Latin America in the 1920s.

A scholarly assessment of the Marshall Plan's accomplishments
comes from a non-Establishment younger British economic historian,
Alan S. Milward. He argues that the dangers of economic collapse in
1947 were wildly exaggerated. While conceding that the level of
nutrition in West Germany was low, Milward maintains that the United
States would have had to feed the Germans in all circumstances. The
fear of Undersecretary of State William L. Clayton that interdependence
of city and countryside was breaking down elsewhere in Europe is
dismissed out of hand. The balance-of-payments crisis is attributed to
no more than technical difficulties in making international payments,
with the 'timing attributable overwhelmingly to domestic policies that
could have been postponed or avoided.' Most of the structural changes
in Europe thought of as severe were 'only short-lived consequences of
the war', an emphatic assertion that they were readily reversible.
Milward's conclusions seem to this perhaps biased participant in State
Department preparation for the Marshall Plan to stem in part from
his will to revise (exhibited in somewhat disdainful characterizations
of most of the leading participants) and from a study of archival
material in Europe as well as in the United States. Such material is
so abundant, of course (largely in justification of decisions taken, but
with some expression of divergent viewpoints), that it is possible to
select from it evidence that supports almost any proposition. Milward
pays almost no attention to the contemporary evidence from the
press—noted at length by Jones, whose book Milward dismisses as a
panegyric in praise of the Department of State.

There are a few concessions to the dominant 1947 point of view. It was 'most improbable' that social conditions were worse in the summer of 1947 than in 1946, 'except in Belgium, France and Italy'. 'In Austria, Germany and Italy calorific intake would not sustain health for long.' In France, 'there were difficulties in obtaining sufficient wheat from farmers through the summer and from August bread in Paris was made out of mixture with maize', but in the next sentence this is 'related to errors in pricing policy as well as to the catastrophic harvest whose baleful influence was felt mostly in 1948'.

Other revisionist points of view are not lacking. Charles S. Maier is ready to credit the bad weather of 1947 as the catalyst of the Marshall Plan. He concedes that ideological and economic threats appeared potentially catastrophic in 1947–8, but he argues that 'in any event Europe would probably not have "gone Communist" or collectivist if the United States had not intervened with the same resolution'. In a 1984 working paper for the European University Institute, Giorgio Fodor admits that Europe needed the Marshall Plan in 1947, but only because the United States permitted prices to rise, taking off controls in June 1946, though this may have been inevitable. Walton regards the Milward case that the economic crisis that produced the Marshall Plan was not caused by deteriorating economic conditions as 'convincing'. Perhaps of most interest is a debate between two German points of view: One is voiced by a macroeconomic theorist, Werner Abelshauser, who asserts that Germany had enough capital and labour to grow at a rapid rate without outside assistance; the other comes from a pair of microeconomic historians, Knut Borchardt and Christian Buckheim, who maintain that German industry, especially textiles, was able to use its limited stocks of raw materials only because it knew they would be replenished (*Germany and the Marshall Plan*).

HISTORY REVISITED

The issue then is what would have happened if there had been no Marshall Plan? This sort of speculation used to be mocked as belonging to the school of history that wondered what would have been the outcome if Cleopatra's nose had been one-quarter inch longer. In the case of European recovery, one can hypothesize a flow of private capital to Europe in response to higher interest rates—a market solution; or altered governmental policies in Europe to restrain capital investment, although that calls for governmental action that most classical economists believing in reversible processes think unlikely since government is mostly a source of muddle. Maier concedes the economic difficulties but assumes they would not have led to a political discontinuity.

That European governments thought themselves in crisis is attested by the fact that they were spending their reserves freely, rather than seeking loans in the United States or going through traumatic reconsideration of policies. Milward states that the 'British and French governments went ahead fatalistically based on an unspoken, perhaps unutterable assumption that the United States would have to act' (p. 50).

It will not surprise you to learn that my counterfactual to the Marshall Plan in 1947 was an irreversible breakdown, short-run perhaps in economics, longer-lasting politically. I claim that this choice is based not solely on a predilection for intervention. In an earlier historical episode—the Great Depression of 1929–33—I have argued that if there had been an international lender of last resort to prop up the Austrian schilling after the failure of the Creditanstalt, the deflationary spiral that ran for the next two years might have been averted through the recuperative forces of the market. In other words, one timely and modest intervention was needed to stave off an irreversible disaster in the longer term. This position is not accepted by D.E. Moggridge, who contends that a more thoroughgoing intervention was needed, something on the order of the Marshall Plan. Implicitly he believes that the Marshall Plan averted a major breakdown in Europe after World War II. We differ, however, over whether the structural maladjustments after World War I and its tangle of reparations, war debts, commercial debts, and disequilibrium exchange rates were too far-reaching to be reversible by market forces if panicky collapse could have been avoided.

HISTORY LESSONS

There is an issue of relevance to the world today. Is the proliferation of debt—US government debt, credit-card and instalment debt of consumers, mortgages, corporate junk-bond debt that has gone some distance in replacing equities, and Third World syndicated bank loans—so great that the world is headed for a crash that could be regarded as an irreversible outcome? Or if these particular problems are handled one at a time as limited crises appear, can the world economy be stabilized through market forces? Thus far, the world has made it past the difficulties of Lockheed, Chrysler, New York City, Continental Illinois, Mexico, Brazil, and Argentina. Are we asserting like the man falling off the Empire State building as he passes the

40th floor: 'It's OK so far'? I think muddling through is the right way to cope with the present-day mountain of debt, but I am prepared to admit that this is a question to which no definitive, scientific answer can be given and on which answers may differ.

There are in economics, as in the physical and biological worlds, difficulties that correct themselves in reversible fashion and those that prove irreversible. In all cases they are judged in some time perspective. If the problem will solve itself without intervention, it is a mistake to intervene. For example, in the nineteenth century, medicine found that many diseases like typhoid and typhus had a natural rhythm of running a course to recovery without the application of bizarre herbs, heavy metals, and fomentations that were popular at the time. In other cases, swift and proper treatment determined life or death. The trick is to apply the appropriate adage: 'If it ain't broke, don't fix it' or 'A stitch in time saves nine'.

Before the event and again afterward, serious people of intelligence will differ as to whether a given process is reversible and should be left alone or is likely to deteriorate further to some breaking point and on that account needs therapy. Temperament makes a difference in determining judgments, and so do political attitudes. Intelligence is an important ingredient; for persons of equal intelligence, however, and an equal sense of history, the outcome may be determined by one's strong prior belief on the one hand, or pragmatic approach on the other. Closeness to the scene of the action along with responsibility for the outcome may overwhelm strongly held beliefs—witness President Hoover in 1929; or it may not—President Hoover after the middle of 1930. In the case of the Marshall Plan I find myself voting on the side of the pragmatists with responsibility and against those with strong beliefs on the sidelines. Among historians, finally, I sympathize more with those who try to explain why people did what they did, than with the revisionists who, safely above the battle, see only the myopia or stupidity of those wrestling with the unfolding problems of the world.

The choices that those in authority must make are based on economic science, but also come in part from temperament, an artistic feel for the given situation, intuition, and a sense of responsibility. This will not satisfy those who believe that the world must be conducted by rules and not by men. It does satisfy (though it does not completely reassure) me.

REFERENCES

Abelshauser, Werner, 'The Economic Role of the ERP in German Recovery and Growth after the War: A Macroeconomic Perspective' and Borchardt, Knut and Buchheim, Christian, 'The Marshall Plan and Economic Key Sectors: A Microeconomic Perspective' in *Germany and the Marshall Plan*, Charles S. Maier (ed.), forthcoming 1988.

Graham, Frank D. 'The Cause and Cure of "Dollar Shortage"', in *Essays in International Finance*, Princeton, NJ, 1949.

Haberler, Gottfried, 'Dollar Shortage', in *Foreign Economic Policy for the United States*, S.E. Harris (ed.), Harvard University Press, 1948.

Hazlitt, Henry, 'Will Dollars Save the World?', Foundation for Economic Education. Irvington-on-Hudson, NY, 1947.

Hoffmann, Stanley and Maier, Charles (eds.) *The Marshall Plan: A Retrospective*, Westview Press, 1984.

Hoover, Herbert, 'The Great Depression, 1929–41', in *Memoirs of Herbert Hoover, Vol. III*, Macmillan, 1952.

Lutz, Friedrich A. 'The Marshall Plan and European Economic Policy', in *Essays in International Finance*, Princeton International Finance Section. Princeton, NJ, 1948.

Kindleberger, Charles P. *International Economics*, Richard D. Irwin, 1963.
——— *The World in Depression, 1929–1930*, University of California Press, 1973.

McCloskey, Donald N. *The Rhetoric of Economics*, The University of Wisconsin Press, 1985.

Maier, Charles S. 'The Two Postwar Eras and the Conditions for Stability in Twentieth-Century Western Europe', in *American Historical Review*, vol. 86, no. 2, April 1981.

Milward, Alan S. *The Reconstruction of Western Europe, 1945–51*, Methuen, 1984.

Moggridge, D. E. 'Policy in the Crises of 1920 and 1929' in *Financial Crises: Theory, History and Policy*. C. P. Kindleberger and J. P. Laffarque (eds). Cambridge University Press, 1982.

Thomas, Lewis, 'Biomedical Science and Human Health: The Long-range Prospect' in *Daedalus*, vol. 106, no. 3, Summer 1977.

Walton, Gary, 'Review of Milward, The Reconstruction of Western Europe' in *Journal of Economic History*, vol. 45, no. 4, 1985.

Warburg, James P. *The Long Road Home: The Autobiography of a Maverick*, Doubleday, 1964.

7 A View from Experience*

I believe in international money. The arguments for international money are the same as those for national money. As a unit of account money makes goods and asset price comparisons possible, and facilitates making contracts. As a medium of exchange it multilateralizes transactions and makes it possible safely, provided prices are relatively stable, to separate earning and spending in time. It is a public good. ·

I believe in fixed exchange rates. Flexible exchange rates are the antithesis of international money. Separate transactions can be accomplished by separate exchange transactions between national monies, but not flows of receipts and payments. A system of fixed exchange rates among national monies is equivalent to international money by Hicks's theorem that states that two goods with a single fixed price between them are the same as a single good.

Gold is a commodity like copper. Its Midas mystique lingers on in some quarters, but it is finished. One cannot put Humpty-Dumpty back together again. Artificial monies such as the SDR and in Europe the Ecu won't do. They interpose an additional transaction between earning and spending that business instinctively avoids, just as households demand cheque-writing privileges on Super-Now accounts. From the times of the Florentine florin, the Venetian ducat, Amsterdam guilder, pound sterling and dollar, international monies have been the national money of the dominant financial power. The sterling standard wore the happy disguise of the gold standard; the dollar standard masqueraded as the Bretton Woods system.

Maintaining a national money as international money calls for a division of function, as Mundell pointed out some years ago. The

* A five-minute talk to the so-called Congressional Summit (Kemp–Bradley) on Exchange Rates, 13 November 1985, held at the National Academy of Science, Washington, DC. Unpublished.

country issuing the international money must be committed to maintaining stability of prices; the rest of the world must balance its international payments. The issuer can ignore its balance of payments because it is the reciprocal of those of the rest of the world. The difference is that between a bank and a firm. Different standards apply to each. A bank typically has a reserve-to-deposit ratio of 1:5; a firm in good shape has a quick asset ratio of 2 or 3 to 1.

The Bretton Woods system broke down for several reasons. The United States inflated at home because of the Vietnam war which could not be financed by taxes without opening up President Johnson's policies to Congressional attack. Later, in 1970, the Federal Reserve System flooded the world with dollars to help insure President Nixon's election—more than a year before the first OPEC price hike,—at a time when the Bundesbank was tightening interest rates. Macroeconomic policies were not coordinated as they must be to sustain fixed exchange rates.

Flexible exchange rates, thought by some economists to be a first-best system, are better than protection and exchange controls, but far worse than fixed rates with coordinated policies.

In addition to the Johnson and Nixon blunders, the dollar suffers from some loss of United States innovative capacity in an ageing economy, and a dramatic decline in rates of personal savings.

While the dollar has lost much of its credibility as an international money, there is no new currency waiting in the wings to take its place. Transitions are tricky: the shift from sterling to the dollar lasted from 1913 to 1945 and produced the Great Depression as a by-product. At the moment, the monetary world is waiting for the other shoe to drop.

Many voices call for a new Bretton Woods. It is a mistake, however, to have a meeting of bodies before there is a meeting of minds. The attempt to do so at the World Economic Conference of 1933 proved a fiasco. The solution must be evolutionary. It is not enough to announce an intention by the world financial powers of working toward fixed rates; it must be demonstrated. As Armand Van Dormel's account shows, Bretton Woods was imposed in wartime by the United States, not negotiated by a wide number of equally-participating countries. A similar imposition today is neither possible nor desirable. Constitution-writing should be postponed until practice evolves in a satisfactory way.

There is no need for all countries to agree. Some advocate a system of regionally fixed rates floating against one another; this has it backward. The major financial powers should gradually fix key currencies in relation to one another, and let the smaller countries adapt—fix or flex—as they see fit. Secretary James Baker's initiative on 22 September 1985 among the five leading finance ministers, holding out the possibility of renewed American leadership in policy coordination and moving toward international monetary stability is the way to go. It should be the first of a series of informal negotiating steps over the coming months and years.

8 Distress in International Financial Markets*

The subject of financial crises goes back at least to Adam Smith who discussed it in terms of 'overtrading, followed by revulsion and discredit'. These three stages were expanded to nine in a taxonomy developed by Lord Overstone, the distinguished monetarist of the middle of the nineteenth century, to wit: quiescence, confidence, prosperity, excitement, overtrading, CONVULSION [his capital letters], pressure, stagnation, ending again in quiescence. Today's organization of stages of a financial crisis, worked out by Hyman Minsky with a small assist from me, runs in terms of displacement or shock, followed by euphoria, which after a time turns into distress, that may or may not develop into a financial crisis, which may or may not be relieved by a lender of last resort. Distress is the period between overtrading and revulsion in Adam Smith's formulation. In Overstone's I would reverse the order of convulsion and pressure, and call pressure distress.

Displacement is an exogenous shock that changes profit opportunities. It can be war, the end of war, an unexpected revolution or anti-revolution, a sudden rise in a price such as oil in 1973 or 1979, an innovation such as led to the canal mania in the 1790s, the railway mania in England in the 1840s, or the heavy investment in automobiles in the 1920s, virtually any massive change that has not been discounted long in advance. Investment rushes to take advantage of the new opportunities, and in the course of rushing may overshoot the equilibrium level. The object of investment and/or speculation can be virtually anything, domestic or foreign shares or bonds, commodities, land, houses, factories, office buildings, shopping centres, Real Estate Investment Trusts (REITs), shipping, tankers, airplanes, syndicated

---

* A talk to the Stockholm Economics Club, Stockholm, Sweden, 15 December 1982. Unpublished.

110

bank loans to less developed countries, more or less any sort of real or financial asset (other than money).

It may be asked why control of the money supply does not prevent overshooting. The answer is that under euphoric conditions with a rush out of money into real or other financial assets, the markets monetize credit and create new money (or give rise to higher velocity if the definition of money is restricted). If money is limited to specie, the market will expand the use of banknotes and bills of exchange; if banknotes are included in money, add bank deposits; if currency and bank deposits, the market will use CDs, repos, NOW accounts, credit cards, instalment loans, and in a particularly ingenious market in Kuwait this last year, post-dated cheques. Bills of exchange may be drawn in chains, A on B, B on C, C on D and so on back to A, as observed by Adam Smith and practised in Germany, Amsterdam and London. Credit expanded wondrously in this fashion. Sir Francis Baring in 1808 knew of clerks not worth £100 who were allowed discounts of £5,000 to 10,000. In 1857, the accountant John Ball noted the existence of firms with less than £10,000 in capital and obligations of £900,000 and claimed it was a fair illustration. In Hamburg there was said in the same financial crisis to have been a man with £100 of capital and acceptances outstanding in the amount of £400,000. How evocative these statements are of Drysdale Securities in New York which borrowed $4 to 5 billion in government bonds, passed along by the Chase Manhatten Bank from its customers' portfolios, when Drysdale had a capital of only $100 million. The postdated cheques in Kuwait now in liquidation amounted at the peak to 20 billion Kuwaiti dinars, or close to $90 billion.

The term distress is borrowed from the field of corporate finance, where Myron Gordon uses it to describe the position of a firm which can contemplate the possibility, as it looks into the future, that it may not be able to meet its obligations and will be forced to seek receivership or bankruptcy. Distress is not based on certainty. Business is not like chess where in a game between players of a certain class a small disadvantage will cause a player to resign because the end can be predicted with virtual certainty. In business and in banking, the flow of receipts and of payments is fraught with great uncertainty. There is great variance in the anticipated cash flows in and out, including new loans, repayments on old loans, and old loans that can or cannot be rolled over. Assets planned for sale to meet debts may rise or fall in price. A company, and by extension a financial market is in distress when it considers the probability of acute cash squeeze high, and how high and how to measure height in this instance, I would not want to be precise about.

The essence of distress is that the expectations on which the period of euphoria was based are beginning to erode. Crisis occurs when such expectations are thoroughly reversed, and the rush is changed from getting out of cash into real or other financial assets to getting out of real and other financial assets into money. But while distress does not inevitably lead to crisis, it is inevitably nerve-wracking.

In the usual case, distress arrives slowly as expectations erode gradually. The chain-letter syndrome of euphoria gradually leads to the realization that everyone cannot win unless the process proceeds to infinity, and this it seldom if ever does. Expansion or investment slows down, and with a sideways or slightly downward movement it becomes clear that some highly-leveraged decisions of the past are going to turn out to be wrong. The multiplier–accelerator model of the ordinary business cycle which has been working on the upside looks as though it has a chance of working on the downside, leaving ebullient companies like Dome Petroleum in oil (or banks such as Penn Square lending to oil) in difficulty.

Distress may be the result of a straightforward decline in demand as an extended group tries to cut back. Farmers worldwide after expanding steadily over decades began to worry about their debt and cut their purchases of equipment from International Harvester and Massey-Ferguson, with repercussions for the banks on which they leaned for support.

Or fear of inflation on the part of monetary authorities may lead to tight money, inducing banks to shorten loans, charge higher rates, lower debt limits. A particularly general precipitator of financial crisis is a sudden halt to long-term lending, such as took place in June 1928 when New York investors shifted away from German and Latin American long-term bonds to plunge in the New York stock market, and Germany and the periphery had to borrow short term to keep going while they tried to adjust their expenditure downward. The cut-off of international capital flows was responsible for much of the trouble in 1825, 1836, 1866, 1890 and 1928. When it occurs, the former borrowers have to scramble to meet their obligations.

Distress is not a condition that can be described precisely or put into an econometric model. Financial crisis itself is something for which the econometricians have to resort to dummy variables, breaking the series into periods first with expectations of rising profits and asset prices, second with the reverse. The area of distress between, which may last a long time, is often described in the economic history literature, but never expressed as a quantifiable variable.

For description, let me borrow from my 1978 book on *Manias,*

Panics and Crashes where I have gathered a collection of metaphors used to describe distress:

uneasiness, apprehension, tension, stringency, pressure (the same word as used by Lord Overstone), uncertainty, ominous conditions, fragility. More colourful expressions include an ugly drop in the market or a thundery atmosphere. A French writer notes the presentiment of disaster. A German metaphor speaks of the bow being bent so in the fall of 1782 that it threatened to snap.

Since then I have collected still further expressions. In 1845, a good two years before the financial crisis of 1847, Lord Overstone wrote 'We have no crash at present, but only a slight premonitory movement under our feet.' This evokes the statement of Joseph Schumpeter about the first half of 1930—between the stock-market crash of October 1929 and the deepening of the depression beginning in 1931: 'People felt the ground give way under their feet.' M.M. Warburg of the Hamburg banking house wrote to his brother Paul Warburg of Kuhn, Loeb in New York after the assassination of Walther Rathenau in June 1922: 'One feels again the oppressive atmosphere that precedes a storm.'

One can inflate the excitement of metaphors if one chooses: distress occurs when one has a bear by the tail, or is riding a tiger, or is a passenger with no flying experience trying to bring the light plane to earth on radioed instruction after the pilot has had a heart attack. If these are too exciting, try 'waiting for the other shoe to drop'.

In short distress is not disaster, but the realization that disaster is well within the range of possibilities and that one should prepare to evade it or meet it.

For the sailors among you, the metaphor of a storm raises a spectrum of possible courses of action to be taken: 1) batten down the hatches, shorten sail and hold course; 2) maintain full sail and head for shelter; 3) run out to sea clear of all rocks and shoals and ride the storm out; and perhaps 4) heave to where one is when the storm strikes. But this menu of courses of action is appropriate only to the single boat with no responsibility to anyone but itself. For monetary authorities and leading banks the position is more complicated, as if one were the commander of a large flotilla, whose members' actions had to be coordinated in some way. In actual financial practice the choice is among 1) backing out. This is possible perhaps for individual banks but not for all. It is a tempting course to, say, the regional banks in the United States but one which the responsible money-market institutions will seek to prevent; 2) lending more, hanging on, hoping for the world economy to recover and rescue the borrowers bit by bit;

or 3) some intermediate course such as lending the interest, stretching out loans as they come due, but gradually slowing down a bit, to change the metaphor, rather than tramping on either the brake or the accelerator.

What of the possibility that distress will end in financial crisis? History is full of the variety of incidents that precipitate the rush out of other assets into money that constitutes the crisis. It may be a failure of a leading house, such as Overend, Gurney in London in 1866 or the Ohio Life and Trust Company in Ohio and New York in 1857. In 1929 it was the Wall Street crash, caused in my judgment by the tightening of interest rates in London because of the Hatry failure and revealed swindle, which pulled call money out of New York back to London and started a process of liquidation that fed on itself because of the high leverage in the market. I do not subscribe to the Jude Wanniski view, based on rational expectations that the New York stock market when it went into a nose dive on 24 and 29 October, was responding to a decision taken in a Senate subcommittee in favour of raising tariffs on carbides, which signalled to the market that the Hawley–Smoot tariff would be passed in May 1930, signed into law by President Hoover over the objections of more than 1,000 American economists, and elicit retaliation from thirty-plus countries.

The mention of swindlers is interesting because history reveals two types: one, who is always ready and willing to fleece the innocent, and the second who is led into sin in an effort to get out of the trouble that his excesses have led to. The first might be called demand-led, the second supply-led. In the upswing and the euphoria, nothing is so exciting to many people than seeing their friends get rich. When this happens their appetite for risky adventures increases, and the infinite supply of swindlers lurking in waiting takes advantage of them. Supply-led swindling picks up in distress when various financial actors are brought face to face with the prospect of bankruptcy. Bleichroeder said of Baron Bethel Henry Strousberg: 'He's clever, but his undertaking of new ventures to mend old holes is dangerous, and if he should encounter a sudden obstacle his whole structure may collapse and under its ruin bury millions of gullible shareholders.' Much the same metaphor was used by Baron James de Rothschild of Paris about his ancient enemy, Emile Pereire:

A man who is in constant monetary straits, stops up one hole while making another and who is compelled to execute a perpetual egg dance among more or less dangerous debt balances, will, in the end, after every fresh success in averting catastrophe, think himself a financial genius.'

1982 has not been without its candidates for this sort of immortality,

Robert Calvi, leader of the Banco Ambrosiano who was found hanging under the Tower Bridge in London, with the bank itself well stripped, or allegedly James Posgate of the Lloyds insurance syndicate who sold his firm to an American conglomerate, but minus tens of millions of dollars of assets.

Bunker Hunt's failure at cornering the world's silver market might have precipitated trouble had it not been that with $2 or 3 billions in wealth he was in a position to lose $1 billion in an ill-advised speculation, and that the banking system rescued the brokerage house that he had temporarily embarrassed.

One course of action, tried by Italian, German and Austrian banks during the early years of the depression before the acute liquidity squeeze of 1931, was to support their shares in the capital market in order to raise their prices, restore confidence, and if possible attract more capital. The manoeuvre weakened the banks by reducing both their capital/deposit and their cash/deposit ratio. Instead of attracting capital, it probably merely let some insider escape the devastation to follow.

The world today is not in crisis; it is in distress, waiting, if you will, to see if the other shoe drops or not. There has been a series of minor crises, in the fringe banks in London in 1974–5; in the Herstatt and Franklin National banks of 1974; in bank failures that have spread through Latin America in Argentina, Chile, Colombia and Mexico—failures that some economist specialists on the area believe had their origin in a too literal following of advice to improve capital markets by stopping their repression and ended up in encouraging them in wildcat practices; in Paris club operations to reschedule the debts of Rumania, Zaire and Turkey, a B.I.S. bridging loan for Hungary, IMF bailout for Mexico and the start of negotiations by that institution with Argentina and Brazil; a special arrangement of the banks for Poland.

In the outstanding financial crises of the past, there have as a rule been two markets in trouble at the same time, for example wheat and railroads in 1847 and cotton and Egypt in 1866. The natural resilience of financial markets can cope with one market in trouble at a time: the Florida land boom in 1925, or the California land and housing boom of 1982. The troubles in REITs, tankers, 747s and the first countries requiring Paris rescheduling all came fairly well spaced and one at a time. Unhappily today distress is widespread, in the disintermediation of thrift institutions in the United States under the impact of high interest rates they must pay for their money while they earn far less on their old mortgage loans; the slowdown and glut in oil leaving in trouble Mexico, Dome Petroleum, a number of OPEC countries and the banks that loaned to them and to oil drillers in trouble financed directly by Penn Square Bank of Oklahoma and indirectly by a host of banks such as First Securities of Seattle, Continental Illinois of Chicago, and the Chase Manhattan Bank of New York; in many corporations, especially those in farm machinery, as noted earlier, but also more widely spread Poclain in France, AEG-Telefunken in Germany, Johns Manville in the United States and Grupo Alfa in Mexico; the sovereign-risk loans of Argentina, Brazil and Mexico in Latin America and Rumania, Poland, Yugoslavia in Eastern Europe.

Despite the excellent start in providing lender of last resort support for these sovereign-risk loans, on top of the marked steadiness of money-market banks in continuing to lend to these countries, I see the greatest danger here. I have no special insight, and perhaps I should have greater confidence in the confidence of such bankers as Walter Wriston, G.A. Costanza, Irving Friedman and the like. It is hardly necessary to observe the big differences in Latin America between 1929 and the present day. In 1929 the Latin American banks stood up in the depression despite the collapse of commodity prices, and the widespread default on foreign borrowing had relatively mild repercussions on the world economy since the money was owed to individual bond-holders. Today the Latin American banks have experienced a series of convulsive failures, but much more serious, foreign debt on which they might default, but have not yet defaulted, consists largely of syndicated bank loans, default on which would put in jeopardy the stability of the world banking system. It is reassuring to observe that the various debtor countries—in Eastern Europe as well as Latin America, though perhaps less so elsewhere—are striving with great zeal to avoid default. The reason is not universally apparent but lies, in my judgment, in the experience of the last 150 years which shows that default takes on the average about 30 years to overcome and to enable a country to approach the world capital market again. Waves of Latin American borrowing followed by default occurred in 1826, 1857, 1890, 1925–28 and the new wave of borrowing from 1971 to the present. Between 1890 and 1925 there was a boom in foreign borrowing that peaked in 1913 and might well have led to convulsion had not the great war intervened.

Banking troubles exist outside the United States and Latin America, notably in the Banco Ambrosiano in Italy, the Banca Catalana in Spain, the major banks with problems lending to Dome Petroleum and Massey-Ferguson in Canada, the Dresdener Bank with its involvement in AEG-Telefunken in West Germany, and doubtless others of less prominence. The IMF is struggling with the debt problems of Mexico and Argentina and getting ready to contemplate the tangle presented by Brazil. All this is well short of a crash, but falls squarely in my definition of distress.

Will pressure be followed by convulsion, overshooting by revulsion and distress by a crash? In the present state of economic science I see no way of making a confident prediction one way or the other. Moreover, I doubt that our science will make sufficient progress in the years immediately ahead to throw light on a dynamic problem of this complexity. Many factors are involved: critical distances, such as the spacing of rescheduling operations or defaults, and their size; a loss of nerve on the part of a few major banks or a large number of smaller banks who tried to escape ahead of the others, leading to a route as in a battle suddenly turning against one side or a panic as in a fire in a theatre where the exits are seen not to be numerous or large; the intrusion into the question of financial stability of extraneous considerations of international politics or politico-economic ideology, such as prevented France pitching in to help Austria and Germany on an adequate scale in 1931; the quick recognition or failure to recognize in approaching crisis who is responsible for what.

If the expectations that drive the euphoric movement out of money into real or other financial assets erode and then are sharply reversed and threaten a convulsive movement out of real and other financial assets into money, the therapy to be administered, as recognized notably by Walter Bagehot but as early as 1802 in Henry Thornton's *Paper Credit* is for a lender of last resort to make money freely available, albeit at a penalty rate. Limits distort behaviour, and fear that the money supply is limited when liquidity is short leads to panic. In the classic panics of 1847, 1857 and 1866, the markets were calmed by suspension of the Bank Act of 1844 that set a limit to the issue of Bank of England notes. Other devices used from time to time have been the issuance of exchequer bills that merchants in trouble could discount to get cash, or guarantees of the liabilities of banks or firms. The lender of last resort does not cure the trouble but alleviates the threat of financial collapse and gives time for the longer-run adjustments to be worked out.

There are to be sure a long list of problems to be solved in applying this therapy. Among the most troublesome is the question of moral hazard, also met in insurance. If people are guaranteed that they will be saved from the consequences of irresponsible behaviour they will behave less responsibly. A former director and governor of the Bank of England, Mr Hankey, called Bagehot's formulation of the theory of the lender of last resort 'the most mischievous doctrine ever broached in the monetary or banking world'. There is a further question as to who is the lender of last resort. This was critical at the national level in the nineteenth century when treasury and central bank would occasionally bow to each other in the Gaston-and-Alphonse tradition, urging the other to take the lead. Today the issue is thoroughly settled for domestic banking difficulties. Responsibility lies with the central bank. Some ambiguity remains, however, in the international field. When the Bundesbank was slow in taking care of the foreign liabilities of the Herstatt Bank in 1974, it was agreed among the central banks at the Bank for International Settlements that each central bank would take care of the obligations of the banks of its nationals anywhere in the world. This protocol failed to solve a few issues, such as who was responsible for banks owned by international consortia, but the issue was thrown into some confusion this year when the Bank of Italy was unwilling to make good the liabilities of the Banco Ambrosiano in Luxemburg on the ground that they belonged to a subsidiary, not to a branch.

When troubles threatened among the financially more important countries, starting with the sterling crisis of 1961, the lender of last resort internationally proved to be the swap network. The International Monetary Fund could not be used in the front lines because it was too slow, decisions had to be referred back by executive directors to national governments, and for most directors to many governments. Three weeks were necessary at a minimum, and three weeks waiting for a decision might see the financial system to be saved well lost as the three-week debate over the Hoover moratorium because of French questions in 1931 amply demonstrated. The swap network took decisions in hours, perhaps in the early days with decisive leadership from the United States. If the swaps could not be reversed entirely in six months, the unresolved portion could then be passed along to the IMF. But the swap network could not be used for the developing countries which lay outside the system. For them there was the Paris Club for debt rescheduling, recourse to the International Monetary Fund, and if time were pressing, a bridging loan from the Bank for International Settlements, such as that provided to Hungary last summer [1982], and again to Mexico this fall [1982].

A serious problem is who should be saved. The Bagehot doctrine says that only solvent houses should be rescued, houses that are illiquid but possessed of good assets. The difficulty is that the liquidation of insolvent houses lowers the prices of the assets jettisoned and makes more houses insolvent. There is a further question of the insider–outsider sort, taking care of banks that belong to the club or the Establishment but not of others thought to be overly aggressive, pushy, not belonging. It has been stated that the Bank of the United States was allowed to fail in December 1930 because it had offended the inner circle by its business methods. The Catholic Union Générale failed in 1882 while the Protestant insider Comptoir d'Escompte, which might have failed with the suicide of its director Denfert-Rocherau in 1888 after the collapse of the corner in world copper, was rescued.

In an earlier book I ascribed the depth, width and length of the world depression of the 1930s to the fact that there was no lender of last resort. Britain which had played that role with help from France in the period from 1873 to 1914 could not, and the United States and France, for somewhat different reasons, would not. The transition between *Pax Britannica* and *Pax Americana*, Britain and later the United States as responsible for world economic stability, was not the only transition that paralyzed timely action. There were also the transitions in the United States from the locus of financial power in the Federal Reserve Bank of New York led by Benjamin Strong to the Board of Governors in Washington (with divided leadership), and in 1932–3 from the presidency of Herbert Hoover to that of Franklin D. Roosevelt.

This view that the troubles of the period may be laid at the door of financial instability does not go uncontested. Donald E. Moggridge, the Canadian economic historian and editor of the magnificent set of volumes on the works of Keynes, insists that while correcting the financial instability of the period was perhaps necessary, it was far from sufficient. What was needed after World War I was a far-reaching programme of adjustment, perhaps on the order of the European Recovery Program (the Marshall plan) after World War II. The point is relevant to the question of what ought to be done in the present period of distress in international financial markets besides girding up the world's loins to meet the possible need for a lender of last resort (including adding resources to the IMF's quotas), keeping our powder dry, watchful waiting and the like.

In a fascinating book on his experiences in charge of the Federal Reserve Bank of New York's foreign-exchange operations, Charles Coombs makes a contrast between economic fundamentals on the one hand and a feel for the market on the other. He is rather derisive about the former, speaks highly of the latter. People who bet on fundamentals lose their shirts, and so on. But Coombs's only reaction to each foreign-exchange crisis among the developed countries was to expand the size of the swap lines. It hardly seemed enough.

The view that stabilizing the financial system in 1929 would not have been sufficient rests on recognition of the world's excess capacity in a number of commodities, notably wheat and sugar, where European recovery ran against the wartime expansion outside Europe, of the overvaluation of the pound, undervaluation of the French franc, the troubles caused by war debts, reparations. Perhaps these problems were incapable of correction without the purging fires of deep depression. I would argue, however, that the economic system has considerable capacity to correct such misallocations as those inherent in the world's excess capacity in a number of commodity lines so long as world income is maintained more or less stable. The microeconomic problems are to a considerable extent capable of solving themselves. Given macroeconomic stability the micro problems of resource allocation can most (all?) be left to themselves.

The macroeconomic problems, to be sure, go well beyond those of forestalling the development of periods of distress into financial crisis. There are macroeconomic fundamentals of great and grave importance, Coombs to the contrary notwithstanding, and the period of distress is one when they should be addressed. Countries suffering from balance-of-payments deficits, budget deficits, inflation, declining productivity, excessive rent-seeking, strangling distributional coalitions such as cartels, too powerful trade unions, strong vested interests seeking tariff protection, should work to correct such fundamentals, helped in these endeavours by avoidance of financial crisis. There is always a temptation to relieve the tension by precipitating crisis. It should be resisted. I characterize Heinrich Brüning, the German Chancellor who sought to free Germany of reparations by advancing the collapse of the economy as belonging to the Charles Lamb school of economics. Charles Lamb, you recall, was the English essayist who wrote a 'Dissertation on Roast Pig', in which the pig was roasted by burning down the house around it.

I would argue that there should be no early attempt to cope with the present distress by cosmic methods, by a worldwide rescheduling of debts, a new world economic conference, a new Bretton Woods, world Reconstruction Finance Corporation, or the like. Add to the resources of the International Monetary Fund, to be sure, work hard on the fundamentals and with luck inch our way back through distress to the near side of financial crisis. It is not a heroic programme, but distress is not a time for heroics. Shorten sail and steady as she goes. Keep lending, rescheduling, preparing for eventualities. The outlook improved substantially in the early part of November when the stock market in New York rose sharply and when interest rates declined. The bear we have by the tail is beginning to tire. Perhaps in time we can let go without trouble, and let it shuffle away.

Part II
International Public Goods

9 International Public Goods without International Government*1

When the word of my prospective elevation to this exalted position first circulated at MIT at the end of March 1983, I happened to encounter Peter Temin in the library. He offered congratulations, and added, 'In your presidential address, skip the methodology. Tell them a story.' This is the technique that he and Paul David used to great effect in the session on economic history at Dallas a year ago. I choose, however, to follow the lead of another historian, Donald McCloskey, who maintains that economics should be a conversation (1983).

In a recent paper, unpublished I believe, George Stigler discussed 'the imperialism of economics', which, he claims, is invading and colonizing political science—through public choice theory and the economic theory of democracy—law, and perhaps especially sociology, where our soon-to-be president-elect, Gary Becker (1981), has extended the reach of economics into questions of the family, marriage, procreation, crime, and other subjects usually dealt with by the sociologist. 'Imperialism' suggests super- and subordination, with economics on top, and raises the question whether as a profession we are not flirting with vainglory.

My interest has long been in trade, and I observe that economics imports from, as well as exports to, its sister social sciences. In public choice, we can perhaps explain after the event whose interest was served by a particular decision, but we need political science to be able to forecast which interest is likely to be served, whether that of the executive, the legislature, the bureaucracy, some pressure group—and which pressure group—or, in the odd instance, the voters. Individuals act in their own interest, let us grant, but a more general motive of

* Presidential address delivered to the ninety-eighth annual meeting of the American Economic Association, 29 December 1985, New York, NY and published in the *American Economic Review* vol. 76, no. 1 (March 1986), pp. 1–13.

emulation may be drawn from sociology as Adam Smith was aware in *The Wealth of Nations* (1776, p. 717), as well as in *The Theory of Moral Sentiments* (1759 (1808), I,p. 113). I want today to borrow one or two ideas from political philosophy, and to conduct a conversation with a new, impressive, and growing breed of political scientists working on international economic questions. The discussion falls into two loosely connected halves—the first dealing with what economists can, perhaps should and to some extent do, import from political philosophy and sociology; the second dealing more especially with international public goods.

I

That sharp and sometimes angry theorist, Frank Graham (1948), thought it a mistake to think of trade between nations. Trade took place between firms, he insisted. The fact that they were in different states was irrelevant so long as economic policy was appropriately minimal, consisting perhaps of free trade, annually balanced budgets, and the gold standard. But states may differentiate between firms, through such measures as tariffs, embargos, monetary, fiscal, and exchange rate policy which affect all firms within a given space, and this adds a political dimension (see my 1978 study). The essence may go deeper. In an early graduate quiz, I asked for the difference between domestic and international trade, expecting a Ricardian answer on factor mobility. One paper, however, held that domestic trade was among 'us', whereas international trade was between 'us' and 'them'. The student who wrote this (now escaped from economics and teaching international law at a leading university) had come from Cambridge University and a course with Harry Johnson. We go beyond this simple statement today in saying that nations are groups of people with common tastes in public goods (Richard Cooper, 1977). Geography discriminates between countries, as a hypothetical customs union beween Iceland and New Zealand would demonstrate, and so do governments. Behind and alongside of governments, people discriminate.

Public goods, let me remind you, are that class of goods like public works where exclusion of consumers may be impossible, but in any event consumption of the good by one consuming unit—short of some level approaching congestion—does not exhaust its availability for others. They are typically underproduced—not, I believe, for the Galbraithian reason that private goods are advertized and public goods are not—but because the consumer who has access to the good anyhow has little reason to vote the taxes, or pay his or her appropriate share. Unless the consumer is a highly moral person, following the Kantian Categorical Imperative of acting in ways which can be generalized, he or she is apt to be a 'free rider'. The tendency for public goods to be underproduced is serious enough within a nation bound by some sort of social contract, and directed in public matters by a government with the power to impose and collect taxes. It is, I propose to argue in due course, a more serious problem in international political and economic relations in the absence of international government.

Adam Smith's list of public goods was limited to national defence, law and order, and public works that it would not pay individuals to produce for themselves. Most economists are prepared now to extend the list to include stabilization, regulation, and income redistribution (Cooper, 1977), even nationalism (Albert Breton, 1964), and standards that reduce transaction costs, including weights and measures, language, and money. Public goods were popular a decade ago. There is something of a tendency today, at least in political science, to draw back and claim that such institutions as open world markets are not public goods because countries can be excluded from them by discrimination. One monetarist goes so far as to maintain that money is not a public good, arguing, I believe, from the store-of-value function where possession by one individual denies possession by others, rather than from the unit-of-account function in which exclusion is impossible and exhaustion does not hold (Roland Vaubel, 1984).

II

Before addressing international public goods, I want to digress to suggest that there are other limits to the imperialist claims of economics. Social goods are not traded in markets, for example—honour, respect, dignity, love. In his address to the Columbia University Bicentennial Assembly, Sir Dennis Robertson asserted that what economists economize is love (1955, pp. 5–6). Michael Walzer (1983, pp. 101–2) has compiled a list of 'things' that contemporary moral philosophy will not tolerate being bought and sold: human beings, political power, criminal justice, freedom of expression, marriage and procreation rights (*pace* Becker), the right to leave the political community, exemptions from military service and jury duty, political office, basic services like police protection, desperate exchanges such as permission for women and children to work fourteen hours a day, prizes and honours, love and friendship, criminally noxious substances such as heroin. The inclusion of a number of items on the list is debatable, and history reveals that most of them have been traded on occasion in some cultures. The market, moreover, strikes two lawyers as a dubious device for making 'tragic choices', like those in which scarcity confronts humanistic moral values, for example, allocating food in famine, children available for adoption, or organ transplants (Guido Calabrese and Philip Bobbit, 1978). It is difficult to dissent from Walzer's conclusion that a radically *laissez-faire* economy would be like a totalitarian state, treating every social good as if it were a commodity (1983, p. 119). There is, moreover, a similar remark from a founder of the Chicago school, Frank Knight, who said that the extreme economic man, maximizing every material interest, and the extreme Christian, loving his neighbour as himself, were alike in that neither had any friends.[2]

To admit social goods, not traded in markets, into our economic calculus does not call for altruism. Economists are reluctant to depend on self-denial to any degree (Kenneth Arrow, 1975, p. 22), and moral philosophers are not far behind. To a modern student of ethics, James Fishkin (1982, Chapter 2), obligations to others fall into three categories: minimal altruism, where the benefit to the receiver is substantial and the cost to the altruist low—the acts of a cheap Samaritan; acts of heroic sacrifice that are not called for; and a robust zone of indifference where one has no cause to be concerned over the effects of one's acts on others. This is for positive actions. Acts that harm others are proscribed by the Golden Rule. Adam Smith expressed the same viewpoint forcefully: 'Every man is, no doubt, by nature first and principally recommended to his own care' (1759 (1808), I, p. 193), but goes on: 'Although the ruin of our neighbour may affect us less than a very small misfortune of our own, we must not ruin him to prevent that small misfortune, or even to prevent our own ruin' (*ibid.*, p. 194). Does this prohibit us from playing zero-sum games or negative non-zero-sum games? In international trade, must we refrain from levying the optimum tariff? The optimum tariff works to self-interest mainly in the absence of retaliation, and if Adam Smith excludes hurting our neighbour, he recognizes that 'as every man doth, so shall it be done to him, and retaliation seems to be the great law of nature' (*ibid.*, p. 191).

Note parenthetically that today's moral philosophers cover a wide territory either side of Fishkin, from Peter Singer (1972) at one extreme whose criterion of justice requires successive acts of altruism until the welfare of the recipient has risen to that of the giver which has fallen, to Robert Nozick (1974) at the other who believes that self-interest rules out altruism almost altogether.

III

Self-interest then is legitimate over a large zone of indifference provided that justice is served by our not hurting others. But the robust zone of indifference applies to strangers, and not to those with whom we have a special relationship, sharing collective goods. It does not apply in the family, the neighbourhood, in clubs, in the tribe, racial or religious group, or in the nation. There is some uncertainty whether it applies in regions within a country—New England, the West, the South—or to arrangements between countries short of the world level such as North America or the European Common Market. Collective goods involved here are distributed by mechanisms different from the market: gifts, grants, unequal exchange, sharing through a budget according to need, interest-free loans, inheritance, dowries, alimony, and the like all have a place. Membership in these groups is decided in various ways: by birth, by choice—as in moving into a certain neighbourhood or migrating between countries, by application for admission and acceptance. Walzer defends the right of countries to keep out would-be immigrants motivated by economic self-interest, but not those subjected to persecution: 'The primary good that we distribute to one another is membership in some community' (1981; 1983, Chapter 2, p. 1). He argues, however, that states lack the right to keep members from emigrating if there is some other community ready to take them in. Clubs discriminate against outsiders. Neighbourhoods are more complex, being presumably open to anyone able to afford and find a place to live, but, in sociological reality, often exhibiting tendencies to attract their own kind and repel others, including harassment or unwritten or even legal restrictions against property ownership. The groupings are amorphous, but they exist.

The nature of the positive bonds that link families, neighbourhoods, tribes, regions, and nations is usually taken for granted and left unexplored, but the consequences are not. Albert Hirschman (1970), for example, makes a distinction between voice and exit: voice—speaking up and trying to persuade—being the appropriate action when one disagrees with the course followed by a group to which one belongs; and exit—resigning or refusal to buy the good or service—as a response to what one dislikes in the market. Adam Smith minimizes the difference between families and strangers, suggesting that affection is little more than habitual sympathy produced by propinquity; despite the greater thickness of blood than water, he claims that siblings educated at distances from one another experience a diminution of affection (1759 (1808) II, pp. 68–70). In arguing against Walzer's view that countries owe immigrants the right to become citizens, Judith Lichtenberg (1981) echoes Smith's view in saying that the crucial difference between members and strangers lies between those with whom one has face-to-face contact and those with whom one does not. An accident that kills someone in one's town or a neighbouring community is likely to be more moving than a catastrophe at the other end of the world in which hundreds or thousands die. Adam Smith goes further, comparing the loss of a little finger with a catastrophe that swallowed up China: '. . . if he lost his little finger he could not sleep, but for China he can snore . . . provided he has never seen them' (*ibid.*, I, p. 317).

Some years ago in a book on the brain drain, Harry Johnson (1968) argued in favour of a cosmopolitan solution, encouraging emigration, and Don Patinkin (1968) for a national one. In discussing the Bhagwati scheme for taxing professional emigrants earning more abroad than at home, for the benefit of the poor sending country—saying this was akin to paying alimony in a divorce case for breaking a social taboo—I suggested (1977) that the Johnson position was equivalent to saying that a person should go where he or she could earn the highest return, while Patinkin said that people should stay where they belonged. Patinkin chided me privately for this interpretation, and it is admittedly oversimplified. But the difference between the Johnson and Patinkin positions, both emanating from Chicago, suggests the line between market and non-market areas in economics is shadowy.

In writing about the multinational corporation, I have from time to time suggested that host countries resist the intrusion of strangers because '. . . man in his elemental state is a peasant with a possessive love of his own turf; a mercantilist who favours exports over imports; a populist who distrusts banks, especially foreign banks; a monopolist who abhors competition; a xenophobe who feels threatened by strangers and foreigners' (1984, p. 39), usually adding that it is the task of international economics to extirpate these primitive instincts and to teach cosmopolitanism. The fact that some of these reactions remain at a late stage in the educational process can be tested by the device of asking students on examinations, *seriatim*, a series of questions:

Do you advocate free trade, or at least is there a strong presumption in its favour?

Do you advocate the free international movement of portfolio capital?

. . . of corporate capital in foreign direct investment?

. . . free migration of students and professional labour?

. . . immigration of relatives of persons permanently resident in this country?

. . . free migration for all?

(It is desirable to feed these questions to the victims one at a time without revealing the whole list before the first answer is given and to take up the replies to the first questions so that there is no chance to go back and amend early answers.) There will be sophisticated answers expatiating on the second, third, and fourth-best if the marginal conditions for a Pareto optimal solution are not met, and I would particularly excuse a James Meade (1955) solution that would limit immigration from countries that have not accomplished their Malthusian revolution, on the ground that their emigrants will be replaced, so that free immigration will reduce world income per capita, if not world income as a whole. Most economists and non-economists alike would agree, however, that goods are less intrusive than money, money less so than corporations with control over *our* economic decisions.[3] Intellectuals with whom we identify are hardly intrusive at all. Most of us grant that relatives must be permitted to come together. On the other hand, free migration of labour in general poses a threat to the national identity. The Swiss cut off immigration, despite the appeals of business for more labour, when immigrants constituted one-third of the labour force. In Germany, separate localities felt threatened and stopped inward migration when immigrants reached 12 per cent of the resident population. Feelings differed, of course, depending upon the origin of the migrants and their appearance, language, and religion.

One early venture of international economics into this line of investigation was Robert Mundell's 'optimum currency area' (1961), initiating a discussion of how large the area for a single currency should be, that can readily be extended to economics in general and to other social sciences. Mundell defined an optimum currency area as one where labour moved freely within the area, but not between it and other areas, taking us back to the Ricardian criterion distinguishing domestic from foreign trade: factor mobility within but not between countries. In neither case is the discontinuity in mobility explained. Perhaps something is owed to low transport costs, but additionally, factor mobility requires a group with such strong social cohesion that those moving are willing to shift, and those at the receiving end are content to receive them.

Ronald McKinnon (1963) offered a different criterion: an optimum currency area was one that traded intensively at home, but only to a limited extent abroad. This implied that tastes within a country are homogeneous for traded goods (as well as for public goods), and that regionally specialized production had grown up to serve those tastes. The Mundell and McKinnon criteria do not necessarily converge: on Mundell's standard, Canada is too big to be an optimum currency area, because of limited movement between Quebec and the English-speaking parts of Canada, and the comparative isolation of the Maritimes and Vancouver. On McKinnon's criterion, however, it was too small because so much of its trade is with the United States.

If one broadens the issue from the optimum currency area to economics more generally and to the other social sciences, anomalies arise from the divergence between the optimum economic area, which on efficiency grounds I take to be the world, and the optimum social unit, one that gives the individual a sense of belonging and counting—which is much smaller. In shifting to the optimum political unit, at least two problems arise, one related to the nature of the ties, the other to the ambitions of its members. To take the second point first, for a nation bent on glory—led by a Bismarck or a de Gaulle—bigger is better; whereas if one is merely trying to get along without trouble, like, say, Denmark, small is beautiful enough.

On the first issue, political ties vary widely. There are leagues, alliances, commonwealths, confederations, federations, provinces, states, principalities, kingdoms. Some lesser units are 'united' in varying degrees, as in the United Provinces of the Netherlands, the United States of America, the United Kingdom of Great Britain, and Northern Ireland. The North in the American Civil War was a union, as the Union of Socialist Soviet Republics asserts it is. The small amount of literature I have explored in examining the differences among these forms is not very conclusive, but perhaps the main distinction is between the single state that is centralized, and federations that are loosely joined, with greater powers at the local level. Designations are not always congruent with reality: the Federal German Republic is highly unified, despite the efforts of the occupation powers after World War II to spread political power widely; the Federal Reserve System was created as a loose agglomeration of twelve regional money markets but quickly fused into a single system in World War I. Centralization and federalization have reflections in demography and in finance. City populations in unified states follow a Pareto-skewed distribution with a single dominant city like London, Paris or Vienna, and no close rival among the tail of smaller cities and towns. In federations the distribution of cities is log normal (Brian Berry, 1961). Parallel to the demographic division is the financial. Paris has 91.3 per cent of French bank clearings; London 87 per cent of those for Britain. The contrast is with Canada: Toronto, 37.3 per cent; Montreal, 25.5 per cent; Vancouver, 6.5 per cent. Between these extremes lies Japan with Tokyo 51.2 per cent and Osaka 19.7 per cent (Jean Labasse, 1974, pp.144–5).

One explanation for differences between centralized and federal states is historical: where larger states were formed later from unification of lesser units, administrative and financial functions were already being discharged at the local level, reducing the need for centralized services. This hypothesis faces the difficult counterexamples of Italy and Germany, unified out of smaller units in the second half of the nineteenth century, that quickly centralized administrative and financial functions, in Rome and Milan for Italy, and in Berlin for Germany. Another explanation runs in terms of size, with larger states necessarily federal because of the difficulty of providing administration to local units over long distances. This fits Canada, Australia, the United States, perhaps India, but fails to account for Switzerland, unless size is a proxy for maintaining a dense network of communication, and division of valleys by high mountains produces barriers equivalent to those of continental states. If the mathematically minded reader needs an analogue, think of federal states as decomposable matrices.

The difference between a single state and a federation may be illustrated with two examples. Some years ago, Seymour Harris (1952) wrote a book on New England in which he claimed that the area got a raw deal from the rest of the country because it paid more in taxes to the federal government than it received in federal expenditure. This thesis implicitly violated the distinction between a budget and a market: in a market equal values are exchanged. A budget, on the other hand, is a device expressing the cohesion of a sharing group with monies raised according to one standard, perhaps ability to pay, and expenditure distributed according to another, some combination of efficiency and need. The other example, equally shocking to an international trade economist, was the notion of the *juste retour*, or fair return, propounded by France in connection with expenditure for joint projects in Europe. France insisted that all monies contributed by her be spent in France. Tied sales are a third- or fourth-best device to limit balance-of-payments deficits for a given contribution to joint efforts, or to maximize the contribution for a given deficit. They are inefficient rather than fair.

IV

But I want to move on to the geopolitical unit that produces public goods. It is a cliché that these have increased in size as costs of transport and communication have declined. Under the eighteenth-century Poor Law in England, the parish resisted immigration from neighbouring parishes because of reluctance to share with outsiders. Fernand Braudel (1982) and Sir John Hicks (1969) have each expatiated on the rise of the size of the economic unit from the city-state to the nation-state. National and international markets for goods and money grew slowly, with entrepot centres that intermediated between buyers and sellers surviving in money—cheap to move in space—and largely disappearing for goods where costs of transport were high and could be saved by direct selling, rather than relaying goods through fairs in the Middle Ages and later through cities such as Amsterdam, Hamburg, Frankfurt, and London. The hub-and-spoke system recently discovered in airplane travel and still in place for money has long been superceded in goods. Caroline Isard and Walter Isard's (1945) point that the most pervasive changes in the economy came from innovations in transport and communications remains valid: contemplate the rudder (in place of the steering oar), fore-and-aft sails; the turnpike; canal; railroad (despite Robert Fogel, 1964); the steamship; iron-clad ship; telegraph; telephone; refrigerator ship; radio; airplane; bulk carrier; jet airplane; satellite television. The numbers of people brought into face-to-face contact across continents and hemispheres has increased exponentially. It is true, to be sure, as was said about a well-known governor and presidential candidate, that it was impossible to dislike him until one got to know him, and increases in mobility and communications have been accompanied by separatism: of the Walloons from the Flemish in Belgium, of Scotland and Wales in the United Kingdom (to pass over the troubled Irish question), and of the *Québecois* in Canada.[4] But it is easier than in Adam Smith's day to imagine ourselves in the circumstances of the Chinese, the inhabitants of the Sahelian desert in Africa, or the tornado-struck islands of Bangladesh as we see them nightly on our television screens via satellite. Do wider communication and transport change the production and distribution of public goods?

Conflicts between economics and political science abound, and many arise from the fact that goods, money, corporations, and people are mobile, whereas the state is fixed. The increase in mobility produced by innovations in transport and communication during and after World War II led some of us to conclude that the nation-state was in difficulty. A reaction occurred in the 1970s.

It is significant that Raymond Vernon's influential book *Sovereignty at Bay* (1971), showing the multinational corporation ascendant over the state, was followed by his *Storm over Multinationals* (1977) in which the position is reversed. Cooper's *The Economics of Interdependence* (1968) was followed by an upsurge of interest in national autonomy, decoupling, and pluralism among political scientists, most of whom approve the nation-state and have as heroes, if they will forgive me, not Adam Smith and Woodrow Wilson, but Otto von Bismarck and perhaps even Charles de Gaulle. The tension remains, however. Mobility limits the state's capacity to enforce its writ in taxation, in foreign policy, in standards on such matters as antitrust, pure food and drugs, insider trading in securities, and the like. Mobility undermines social cohesion through the easy intrusion of different nationalities, races, religions, and traditions into the body politic.

V

I come at long last to international public goods. The primary one is peace. Economists are poorly qualified to discuss how, after war, peace is restored and maintained. Most of us reject the Marxian view that war grows directly out of capitalism, and as ordinary citizens and amateur students of history are prepared to agree that peace may be provided by a dominant world power—Pax Romana or Pax Britannica—or by balance-of-power manoeuvring, although that seems accident prone. Among the more audacious economists producing an economic theory or set of theories on war is Walt Rostow (1960, pp. 108 ff.). There are views that ascribe war to population pressure, to ambitious rulers aggressively seeking power, and to complex miscalculation. How these are to be avoided or contained is a question primarily for political science.

In the economic sphere, various international public goods have been identified: an open trading system, including freedom of the seas, well-defined property rights, standards of weights and measures that may include international money, or fixed exchange rates, and the like. Those that have interested me especially in a study of the 1929 depression and other financial and economic crises have been trading systems, international money, capital flows, consistent macroeconomic policies in periods of tranquillity, and as a source of crisis management when needed. By the last I mean the maintenance of open markets in glut and a source of supplies in acute shortage, plus a lender of last resort in acute financial crisis (see my 1973 book, revised 1986).

Public goods are produced domestically by government, unless the government agenda is blocked in stalemate among competing distributional coalitions as described by Mancur Olson (1982). Voluntary provision of public goods is plagued by the free rider. In the international sphere where there is no world government, the question remains how public goods are produced. Ralph Bryant is one of the few economists who has discussed the public good element in international cooperation. His vocabulary is different from that of the political scientists: their 'regimes' are his 'supranational traffic regulations' (1980, p. 470), and he expects leadership in cooperation in monetary and fiscal policy from supranational institutions such as the International Monetary Fund (p. 481). I find this doubtful on the basis of the interwar record of such institutions as the League of Nations.

Political science in this field has produced two schools: the realists who hold to a national-interest theory of international politics, and the moralists, whom Robert Keohane prefers to call 'institutionalists' (1984, p. 7). Realists maintain that international public goods are produced, if at all, by the leading power, a so-called 'hegemon', that is willing to bear an undue part of the short-run costs of these goods, either because it regards itself as gaining in the long run, because it is paid in a different coin such as prestige, glory, immortality, or some combination of the two. Institutionalists recognize that hegemonic leaders emerge from time to time in the world economy and typically set in motion habits of international cooperation, called 'regimes', which consist of 'principles, norms, rules and decision-making procedures around which the expectations of international actors converge in given issue areas' (Stephen Krasner, 1983, p. 1). Under British hegemony, the regimes of free trade and the gold standard developed more or less unconsciously. With subsequent American hegemony, a more purposeful process of institution making was undertaken, with agreement at Bretton Woods, on tariffs and trade, the Organization for Economic Cooperation and Development, and the like. Political scientists recognize that regimes are more readily maintained than established since marginal costs are below average costs; as hegemonic periods come to an end with the waning of the leading country's economic vitality, new regimes needed to meet new problems are difficult to create. Cooper (1985) has written of the eighty years it took to create and get functioning the World Health Organization despite the clear benefits to all countries from controlling the spread of disease. And it takes work to maintain regimes; in the absence of infusions of attention and money, they tend in the long run to decay.

I originally suggested that the 1929 depression was allowed to run unchecked because there was no leading country able and willing to take responsibility for crisis management, halting beggar-thy-neighbour policies from 1930, and especially acting as a lender of last resort to prevent the serious run on the Creditanstalt in May 1931 spreading, as it did, to Germany, Britain, Japan, the United States, and ultimately to the gold bloc. Britain, the leading economic power of the nineteenth century, was unable to halt the run; the United States, which might have had the ability, possibly assisted by France, was unwilling. This view has been rejected by one economic historian who holds that the troubles of the interwar period were more deep-seated, and that what was needed was more fundamental therapy than maintaining open markets and providing a lender of last resort, something, that is, akin to the heroic public good after World War II, the Marshall Plan (D.E. Moggridge, 1982). That may have been true, though there is no way I see that the issue can be settled. Leadership at an earlier stage in the 1920s, presumably furnished by the United States with some cost in foregone receipts on war-debt account, might have resolved the war-debt-reparations-commercial-debt tangle that proved so destabilizing after the 1929 stock market crash. I conclude that the existence of an international lender of last resort made the financial crises of 1825, 1836, 1847, 1866, and 1907 more or less ephemeral, like summer storms, whereas its absence in 1873, 1890, and 1929 produced deep depressions—shortened in the 1890 case by the *deus ex machina* of gold production from the Rand. Again there is room for disagreement.

The point of all this is that after about 1971, the United States, like Britain from about 1890, has shrunk in economic might relative to the world as a whole, and more importantly, has lost the appetite for providing international economic public goods—open markets in times of glut, supplies in times of acute shortage, steady flows of capital to developing countries, international money, coordination of macroeconomic policy and last-resort lending. The contraction of concern from the world to the nation is general, and applies to economists as well as to politicians and the public. In reading recent books on macroeconomic policy by leading governmental economists under both Democratic and Republican administrations, the late Arthur Okun (1981) and Herbert Stein (1984), I have been struck by how little attention the authors paid to international repercussions. The same observation has been made by Ralph Bryant (1980, p. *xviii*) and by the British economist R.C.O. Matthews, reviewing Arjo Klamer's *Conversations with Economists . . .* (1985, p. 621). There has been a recent upsurge of interest in the international dimension because of the connections among the federal deficit, the exchange rate for the dollar, and the balance-of-payments deficit, but the focus of this interest is almost exclusively on what the connections mean for US interest rates, industrial policy, growth, and wealth. The international impact is largely ignored, bearing out the truth in former German Chancellor Helmut Schmidt's statement that 'the United States seems completely unconscious of the economic effects of its policies on the Alliance' (1984, p. 27).

Some of the discussion of international regimes by political scientists verges on what my teacher, Wesley Clair Mitchell, used to call 'implicit theorizing', that is, convenient *ad hoc* theoretical explanations to fit given facts that lack generality. Charles Lipson (1985), for example, suggested that the slippage in US hegemony in the 1970s resulted in a loss of the international public good of secure property rights and therefore in the widespread nationalization of foreign direct investment. He went on to say that the reason less developed countries (*LDC*s) did not default on their debts to bank syndicates was that bank lending was 'better institutionalized', 'a smaller group', 'better protected by legal remedies' (pp. 136, 158, 170). He was surprised that the decline of British hegemony in the interwar period did not result in more *LDC* aggression against foreign property (p. 191), but failed to observe the widespread default on foreign bonds in the 1930s, despite the organization of international finance. In my judgment Keohane exaggerates the efficacy and importance of the international regime in oil that was formed after the first OPEC oil shock of 1973 (see his Chapter 10). The crisis caused by the Yom Kippur embargo of the Netherlands was to my mind shockingly mishandled by governments, and the public good of crisis management was left to the private multinational oil companies. The formation of the International Energy Agency was a classic operation in locking the barn door after the horse had been stolen.

Between national self-interest and the provision of international public goods, there is an intermediate position: indifference to both. An interesting contrast has been observed in the 1930s between Britain which forced Argentina into a bilateral payments agreement (the Roca–Runciman Agreement of 1933) in order to take advantage of its monopsony position, and the United States that had a similar opportunity *vis-à-vis* Brazil but ignored it (Marcelo de Paiva Abreu, 1984).

It is fairly clear from the historical record that economic hegemony runs down in decay—in the British case after 1913 and the United States about 1971—leading Felix Rohatyn (1984) to say that the American century lasted only twenty years. The Nixon shock of 1973 in cutting off soya bean exports to Japan—a significant harm to an ally for a small gain to this country—was the act of a bad Samaritan. The import surcharge of the same year may have been required to move the dollar out from the position of the nth currency when only $n - 1$ countries are free to fix their exchange rates, but it would have been possible to start with the later attempt at cooperation that resulted in the Smithsonian agreement. This is especially true when so much of the case against the 1971 exchange rate was the result of the easy-money policy of the Federal Reserve System under Chairman Arthur Burns, at a time when the Bundesbank was tightening its money market/go-it-alone policies of both banks that flooded the world with dollars.

The present US administration claims to be working for open trade and does fairly well in resisting appeals for protection. The positive push for a Reagan round of trade liberalization in services and agriculture, however, is in pursuit of a national and not an international public good. The regime in capital movements—the World Bank, the regional development banks and that in last-resort lending orchestrated by the IMF—seems to be working, with bridging loans and an *ad hoc* purchase of oil from Mexico for the US stockpile in 1982 when the IMF finds itself unable to move fast enough. But there are signs of dissension that may spell trouble. The June 1985 bridging loan for Argentina was declined by Germany and Switzerland on the grounds that Argentina had not been sufficiently austere and that its problems were not a threat to the world financial system (*New York Times*, 15 June 1985, p. 1). The Japanese contribution, moreover, was said to have been small, although no figures were given.

What I worry about mostly is exchange policy and macroeconomic coordination. The US Treasury under Donald Regan was committed to the policy of neglect, presumably benign, but in any event ideological. And the commitment to consultative macroeconomic policies in annual summit meetings of seven heads of state has become a shadow play, a dog-and-pony show, a series of photo opportunities—whatever you choose to call them—with ceremony substituted for substance. The 1950s and 1960s, when serious discussions were held at the lowly level of Working Party No. 3 of the OECD, were superior because the United States and other countries took them seriously.

I am a realist when it comes to regimes. It seems to me that the momentum set in motion by a hegemonic power—if we must use that expression, I prefer to think of leadership or responsibility—runs down pretty quickly unless it is sustained by powerful commitment. The IMF and World Bank were agreed at Bretton Woods largely as a result of the US Treasury: the forms were international, the substance was dictated by a single country (Armand van Dormel, 1978). In the early days of the IMF, Frank Southard told me, if the United States made no proposal, nothing happened. Today the same is true of the European Economic Community: unless Germany and France see eye-to-eye, which is infrequent, nothing happens. Proposals of great technical appeal from individuals or small countries are not welcomed as the preparatory phases of the World Economic Conference of 1933 demonstrated (see my 1973 book, pp. 210–14). There needs to be positive leadership, backed by resources and a readiness to make some sacrifice in the international interest.

The leadership role is not applauded. When the United States accused the rest of the world of being free riders, Andrew Shonfield countercharged the United States of being a 'hard rider', 'hustling and bullying the Europeans', 'kicking over chairs when it did not get its way' (1976, pp. 86, 88, 102). Furnishing the dollar to the world as international money has brought the United States an accusation of extracting seignorage, although the facts that the dollar is not a monopoly currency and that foreign holdings earn market rates of interest deflect that criticism in sophisticated quarters.

Neglect can verge on sabotage. When the European central banks collaborated to hold the dollar down at the end of February 1985, the conspicuous failure of the United States to participate on a significant scale encouraged speculators not to cover long positions. A former trader for the Federal Reserve Bank of New York has expressed concern that the habits of central bank cooperation and US official intimacy with the workings of the foreign-exchange market that have been built up over thirty years are being squandered for ideological reasons (Scott Pardee, 1964, p. 2).

Regimes are clearly more attractive in political terms than hegemony, or even than leadership with its overtones of the German *Führerprinzip* of of Italy's *Il Duce*, if not necessarily more so than responsibility. Polycentralism, pluralism, cooperation, equality, partnership, decoupling, self-reliance, and autonomy all have resonance. But it is hard to accept the view, so appealing to the political right, that the path to achieve cooperation is a tit-for-tat strategy, applied in a repetitive game, that teaches the other player or players to cooperate (Robert Axelrod, 1984). As Tibor Scitovsky demonstrated years ago (1937), this path can readily end by wiping out trade altogether. Hierarchical arrangements are being examined by economic theorists studying the organization of firms, but for less cosmic purposes than would be served by political and economic organization of the production of international public goods (Raj Sah and Joseph Stiglitz, 1985).

Minding one's own business—operating in the robust zone of indifference—is a sound rule on trend when macroeconomic variables are more or less stable. To the economist it means reliance on the market to the extent that the conditions for a Pareto optimum solution are broadly met. But the fallacy of composition remains a threat, and one cannot count on the Categorical Imperative. Markets work most of the time, as a positive-sum game in which the gain for one does not imply a loss for another. Experience teaches, however, that crises may arise. When they do, the rule changes from government and public indifference to the production of public goods by leadership or by a standby regime.

Leadership or responsibility limited to crises encounters another problem: how to keep the machinery for handling crises from obsolescence. In crisis one needs forceful and intelligent people, capable of making decisions with speed under pressure. It is sometimes said that the Japanese practice of decision by consensus with ideas coming up from below, makes it hard for that country to discharge in timely fashion the responsibilities of world leadership. In Marcus Goodrich's *Delilah* (1941), the amiable practice of fraternization between a watch officer and enlisted men on the bridge of the destroyer proved dangerous in a typhoon since the men had fallen into the habit of discussing the officer's orders. The paradox is that the attributes needed in crisis tend to atrophy in quiet times; for example in the control room of a Three Mile Island nuclear power plant.

Let me conclude by emphasizing once again my concern that politicians, economists, and political scientists may come to believe that the system should be run at all times by rules, including regimes, not people. Rules are desirable on trend. In crisis the need is for decision. I quote once more the letter of Sir Robert Peel of June 1844 a propos of the Bank Charter Act of that year:

My Confidence is unshaken that we have taken all the Precautions which Legislation can prudently take against the Recurrence of a pecuniary Crisis. It may occur in spite of our Precautions; and if it be necessary to assume a grave Responsibility, I dare say men will be found willing to assume such a Responsibility.

Parliamentary Papers, 1857, 1969, p. *xxix*

NOTES

1. I have benefited from comments and suggestions on an earlier draft from Susan Okin, Walt W. Rostow, Walter S. Salant, and Robert M. Solow. A paper with the same title before translation, but with a different coverage was written in 1980, and has appeared in French (1980).
2. This at least is oral tradition. I have been unable to find a specific reference in Knight (1936), or Knight and Thornton Merriam (1947).
3. If the intrusiveness of goods is less than that of corporations from abroad, it is perhaps anomalous that the standard of friendly international dealings exemplified in treaties of Friendship, Commerce, and Navigation is less hospitable for goods than for corporations. Foreign corporations in theory are given national treatment; goods only that of the most-favoured nation. In practice, many countries ignore the commitment to national treatment and discriminate both against foreign corporations as a class, and among those of different nationality.
4. Tastes in public goods can of course differ within countries. A striking comparison is furnished in E. Digby Baltzell's *Puritan Boston and Quaker Philadelphia* (1979). Boston is characterized as intolerant, extremely homogeneous, ascetic, philanthropic, and devoted to social and political responsibility. Philadelphia, on the other hand, was an ethnic and religious melting pot, materialistic, believing in money making, and shunning power

and responsibility. Boston produced four presidents of the United States, including one non-Puritan affected by the values of the city, Philadelphia none. Social scientists are wary of ascribing social responses to national (or urban) character. There may nonetheless be occasions when it is inescapable.

REFERENCES

Arrow, Kenneth J., 'Gift and Exchanges', in Edmund S. Phelps (ed.), *Altruism, Morality and Economic Theory*, New York: Russell Sage Foundation, 1975.

Axelrod, Robert, *The Evolution of Cooperation*, New York: Basic Books, 1984.

Baltzell, E. Digby, *Puritan Boston and Quaker Philadelphia: Two Protestant Ethics and the Spirit of Class Authority and Leadership*, New York: Free Press 1979.

Becker, Gary, *A Treatise on the Family*, Cambridge: Harvard University Press, 1981.

Berry, Brian J.L., 'City-Size Distribution and Economic Development', *Economic Development and Cultural Change*, July 1961, 9, pp. 573–88.

Braudel, Fernand, *Civilization and Capitalism* (15th–18th Century), vol. 2, *The Wheels of Commerce*, translated from the French by Sian Reynolds, New York: Harper and Row, 1982.

Breton, Albert, 'The Economics of Nationalism', *Journal of Political Economy*, August 1964, 72, pp. 376–86.

Bryant, Ralph C., *Money and Monetary Policy in Independent Nations*, Washington: The Brookings Institution, 1980.

Calabrese, Guido and Bobbitt, Philip, *Tragic Choices*, New York: W.W. Norton, 1978.

Cooper, Richard N., *The Economics of Interdependence: Economic Policy in the Atlantic Community*, New York: McGraw-Hill, 1968.

———, 'World-Wide vs Regional Integration: Is There an Optimal Size of the Integrated Area?', in Fritz Machlup (ed.), *Economic Integration: Worldwide, Regional, Sectoral*, New York: Halstead, 1977.

———, 'International Economic Cooperation: Is it Desirable? Is it Likely?', *Bulletin*, American Academy of Arts and Sciences, November 1985, 39, pp. 11–35.

de Paiva Abreu, Marcelo, 'Argentina and Brazil During the 1930s: The Impact of British and American Economic Policies', in Rosemary Thorp (ed.), *Latin America in the 1930s: The Role of the Periphery in World Crisis*, London: Macmillan, 1984.

Fishkin, James S., *The Limits of Obligation*, New Haven: Yale University Press 1982.

Fogel, Robert W., *Railroads and American Economic Growth: Essays in Econometric History*, Baltimore: Johns Hopkins Press, 1964.

Goodrich, Marcus, *Delilah*, New York: Farrar & Rinehart, 1941.

Graham, Frank D., *The Theory of International Values*, Princeton: Princeton University Press, 1948.

Harris, Seymour E., *The Economics of New England: Case Study of an Older Area*, Cambridge: Harvard University Press, 1965.

Hicks, John R., *A Theory of Economic History*, London: Oxford University Press, 1969.

Hirschman, Albert O., *Exit, Voice and Loyalty*, Cambridge: Harvard University Press, 1970.

Isard, Caroline and Isard, Walter, 'Economic Implications of Aircraft', *Quarterly Journal of Economics*, February 1945, 59, pp. 145–69.

Johnson, Harry G., 'An "Internationalist" Model', in Walter Adams, (ed.), *The Brain Drain*, New York: Macmillan, 1968.

Keohane, Robert O., *After Hegemony: Cooperation and Discord in the World Political Economy*, Princeton: Princeton University Press, 1984.

Kindleberger, Charles P., *The World in Depression 1929–1939*, Berkeley: University of California Press, 1973.

———, 'Internationalist and Nationalist Models in the Analysis of the Brain Drain: Progress and Unsolved Problems', *Minerva*, Winter 1977, 15, pp. 553–61.

———, 'Government and International Trade', *Essays in International Finance*, No. 129, International Finance Section, Princeton University, 1978.

———, *Multinational Excursions*, Cambridge, MIT Press, 1984.

———, 'Des biens public internationaux en l'absence d'un gouvernment international', in *Croissance, échange et monnaie en économie international Mélange en l'honneur de Monsieur le Professeur Jean Weiller*, Paris: Economica, 1985.

Knight, Frank H., *The Ethics of Competition and Other Essays*, London: George Allen & Unwin, 1936.

——— and Merriam, Thornton, W., *The Economic Order and Religion*, London: Kegan Paul, Trend, Trubner, 1947.

Krasner, Stephen D., *International Regimes*, Ithaca: Cornell University Press, 1983.

Labasse, Jean, *L'espace financier: analyze géographique*, Paris; Colin, 1974.

Lichtenberg, Judith, 'National Boundaries and Moral Boundaries', in Peter G. Brown and Henry Shue (eds), *Boundaries: National Autonomy and Its Limits*, Totowa: Rowman and Littlefield, 1981.

Lipson, Charles, *Standing Guard: Protecting Foreign Capital in the Nineteenth and Twentieth Centuries*, Berkeley: University of California Press, 1985.

McCloskey, Donald N., 'The Rhetoric of Economics', *Journal of Economic Literature*, June 1983, 21, pp. 481–517.

McKinnon, Ronald I., 'Optimum Currency Areas', *American Economic Review*, September 1963, 53, pp. 717–25.

Matthews, R.C.O., Review of Arjo Klamer, *Conversations with Economists . . . , 1983*, *Journal of Economic Literature*, June 1985, 23, pp. 621–22.

Meade, James E., *The Theory of International Economic Policy*, Vol. II, *Trade and Welfare*, New York: Oxford University Press, 1955.

Moggridge, D.E., 'Policy in the Crises of 1920 and 1929', in C.P. Kindleberger and J.-P. Laffargue (eds), *Financial Crises: Theory, History and Policy*, Cambridge: Cambridge University Press, 1982.

Mundell, Robert A., 'A Theory of Optimum Currency Areas', *American Economic Review*, September 1961, 51, pp. 657–65.

Nozick, Robert, *Anarchy, State and Utopia*, New York: Basic Books, 1974.

Ohlin, Bertil, *Interregional and International Trade*, Cambridge: Harvard University Press, 1933.

Okun, Arthur M., *Prices and Quantities*, Washington: Brookings Institution, 1981.

Olson, Mancur, *The Rise and Decline of Nations: Economic Growth, Stagflation and Social Rigidities*, New Haven: Yale University Press, 1982.

Pardee, Scott, 'The Dollar', address before the Georgetown University Bankers Forum, Washington, DC, September 22, 1964.

Parliamentary Papers: Monetary Policy, Commercial Distress, Shannon: Irish University Press, 1957, 1969.

Patinkin, Don, 'A "Nationalist" Model', in Walter Adams (ed.), *The Brain Drain*, New York: Macmillan, 1968.

Robertson, Sir Dennis, 'What Do Economists Economize?' in R. Leckachman (ed.), *National Policy for Economic Welfare at Home and Abroad*, New York: Doubleday, 1955.

Rohatyn, Felix G., *The Twenty-Year Century: Essays on Economics and Public Finance*, New York: Random House, 1984.

Rostow, Walt W., *The Stages of Economic Growth: A Non-Communist Manifesto*, Cambridge: Cambridge University Press 1960.

Sah, Raaj Kumar and Stiglitz, Joseph E., 'Human Fallibilty and Economic Organization', *American Economic Review Proceedings*, May 1985, 75, pp. 292–7.

Scitovsky, Tibor, 'A Reconsideration of the Theory of Tariffs', reprinted in AEA *Readings in the Theory of International Trade*, Homewood: Richard D. Irwin, 1949.

Shonfield, Andrew, *International Economic Relations of the Western World*, vol. I, *Politics and Trade* New York: Oxford University Press, 1976.

Singer, Peter, 'Famine, Affluence and Morality', *Philosophy and Public Affairs*, Spring 1972, 1, pp. 229–43.

Smith, Adam, *The Theory of Moral Sentiments, or An Essay Toward an Analysis of the Principles by which Men Naturally Judge Concerning the Conduct and Character First of their Neighbours and then of Themselves*, 11th ed., Edinburgh: Bell and Bradfute, 1759; 1808.

———, *An Inquiry Into the Nature and Causes of the Wealth of Nations*, Canaan (ed.), New York: Modern Library, 1776; 1937.

Schmidt, Helmut, 'Saving Western Europe', *New York Review of Books*, 31 May 1984, 31, pp. 25–7.

Stigler, George J., 'Economics—The Imperial Science?', mimeo., 1984.

Stein, Herbert, *Presidential Economics: The Making of Economic Policy from Roosevelt to Reagan and Beyond*, New York: Simon and Schuster 1984.

Van Dormel, Armand, *Bretton Woods: Birth of a Monetary System*, New York: Holmes and Meier, 1978.

Vaubel, Roland, 'The Government's Money Monopoly: Externalities or Natural Monopoly?', *Kyklos*, 1984, 27, pp. 27–57.

Vernon, Raymond, *Sovereignty at Bay*, Cambridge: Harvard University Press, 1971.

———, *Storm over Multinationals*, Cambridge: Harvard University Press, 1977.

Walzer, Michael, 'The Distribution of Membership', in Peter G. Brown and Henry Shue (eds), *Boundaries: National Autonomy and Its Limits*, Totowa: Rowman and Littlefield, 1981.

———, *Spheres of Justice*, New York: Basic Book, 1983.

10 Economic Development and International Responsibility*

Hiroshi Kitamura has experienced life in the entire spectrum of countries at different stages of economic development: receiving his higher degrees in Europe and Japan, spending time on economic research in Europe and the USA, teaching in Japan and promoting economic development in the Economic Commission for Asia and the Far East (ECAFE) in Bangkok. It may therefore be fitting, in honouring him for a long and distinguished career, to analyse the question of when a country should, in a normative sense, take on some appropriate (substantial?) share of responsibility for the world economic system. A similar problem presents itself in peace-keeping. Indeed the parallel between peace-keeping and international economic stability is a close one, both being international public goods that have to be provided in the absence of international government that could use coercion, and both goods that are plagued with 'free-riders', i.e. countries that hang back from paying the costs on the grounds that others will do so.

This is sometimes called the 'graduation problem': when does a nation cease to be a less developed country (LDC), entitled to exemptions, exceptions or preferences under the rules that developed countries follow in trade, investment, exchange policy and the like? I hope it will not be thought arrogant or patronizing if I draw an analogy between the family of nations and the family of man. I want to concentrate not on the complex set of rights (and perhaps a few duties) of children *vis-à-vis* their parents, but on the middle range. In the international sphere, this concerns countries with enough power to upset arrangements worked out by leading countries for the international

* Published in Ali M. El-Agraa (ed.), *Protection, Cooperation, Integration and Development, Essays in Honour of Professor Hiroshi Kitamura*, London: Macmillan, 1987, pp. 89–98.

order, but not strong enough to impose order on the system, or even to carry much weight in decision-making circles. To return to the metaphor of the family, the nations I have in mind are the equivalent of adolescents or young adults. I hope I am not chauvinistic if I think particularly of males. There is agitation in the USA at the moment for raising the drinking age from 18, 19 or 20 to 21, because of the large number of automobile accidents involving young men. Graduating from childhood to adult status takes place at different ages for different functions, to be sure: 14 for work permits, often 16 for driving an automobile, 18 for serving in the armed forces and increasingly 21 for public drinking. It is easy to empathise with the frustrations of youth, a period of heavy capital investment and limited consumption. As graduate registration officer at the Massachusetts Institute of Technology (MIT) I used to commiserate with the candidates for higher degrees who had the 'appetites of men, but the incomes of boys'. Similarly, many countries in the interval between being an LDC and becoming a developed country (DC) have the political ambition to be taken seriously as a sovereign among equals without the economic size—measured in gross domestic product (GDP) or perhaps GDP per capita—to wield much clout. In what follows, I do not address the interesting question of national physiology as the criteria for determining the readiness of a country to be admitted into the ranks of DCs.

DCs are organized in the Organization of Economic Cooperation and Development (OECD) whereas LDCs belong to the United Nations Conference on Trade and Development (UNCTAD) or to the 'Committee of 77' which claims a much larger and shifting number of adherents. In trade, some LDCs belong to the General Agreement on Tariffs and Trade (GATT) but mostly push their initiatives such as Generalized System of Preferences (GSP) in UNCTAD. LDCs have sought to legislate on the multinational corporation in the UN assembly where their large numbers, plus the one-country, one-vote system of scoring, increases their nominal victories over other countries, as compared with organizations such as the International Bank for Reconstruction and Development (IBRD or World Bank) or the International Monetary Fund (IMF) with voting weighted by economic size. The LDCs pushed a series of resolutions through the UN on the subject of international business with such titles as the Resolution on Permanent Sovereignty over Domestic Resources or the UN Charter of Economic Rights and Duties of States. That states might not be sovereign over their domestic resources has never been called into question, of course, so that the UN resolution affirming the obvious had another and covert purpose: it became interpreted as a demand for the right to nationalize concessions previously granted to foreign companies with nominal compensation, if any. The UN Charter of Economic Rights and Duties referred primarily to the rights of LDCs and the duties of DCs and multinational corporations. Among the rights was that to nationalize foreign property with 'appropriate compensation . . . provided all relevant circumstances called for it', the latter phrase carrying the implication that particular circumstances might negate such a call.

The same article in the UN Charter of Economic Rights and Duties went on to state that disputes over expropriation and compensation had to be determined under the domestic law of the nationalizing country. This follows the Calvo doctrine, developed by a distinguished Argentine jurist and not accepted by the USA. In advanced countries that are understood to hand out justice impartially, it goes without saying that disputes between the residents of a country and foreigners are to be settled in local courts, with any evident miscarriage of justice to be the subject of diplomatic representations by foreigners or appeal to an international tribunal. Where such impartiality is not an established tradition and the possibility exists that foreign petitioners will be discriminated against in local courts, developed countries are unwilling to renounce the right of diplomatic appeal or recourse to international law. The issue is analogous to states' rights in the USA: a generation ago, Mississippi and other Southern states claimed the right as sovereign states to discriminate against black people in various ways. The Federal government, however, was prepared to accept states' rights without question only when it could count on the state administering the affairs of its citizens impartially under the US constitution. Without knowing about it in detail, I judge that the Southern states have now 'graduated' to the point where they can be counted upon to behave in general as other states, and the question of 'states' rights' drops out of contention. The questions remain when and how such graduation will occur among LDCs.

Japan is an interesting case of this transition. Not an LDC, like many countries in Asia, Africa, the Middle East and Latin America, it remained, like Western Germany under the tutelage of the USA for an extended period after the Second World War. It was relieved of expenditure for national defence—forcibly as a consequence of defeat. Long before Europe was prepared to admit Japanese goods except in restricted quantities, the USA admitted them without requiring similar receptivity to American products in Japan. Japanese growth proceeded apace, and in due course US firms sought to find places in that rapidly expanding market through direct investments. Japan kept promising liberalization, and actually undertook a series of steps, starting with the Foreign Exchange Control Law of 1949 and the Foreign Investment

Law of 1950. The steps were limited, however, and by the mid-1960s, despite a series of deregulating measures, the Japanese market was not open to foreign direct investment unless a particular project could pass an imposing series of requirements.

One major reason for relaxing restrictions directed against foreigners is the desire to get favourable treatment for one's own industry abroad. It is universally recognized that reciprocity is called for among equals. Consistency may be the 'hobgoblin of little minds', as Ralph Waldo Emerson stated, but inconsistency is a hard line to follow in bargaining, wanting it both ways, to keep others out at home while getting in abroad. It is often tried. Josiah Wedgwood (the eighteenth-century English porcelain-manufacturer) wanted markets for his china in France, but wanted Sèvres and Meissen china kept out of England. Manchester cotton-textile manufacturers were free-traders as far as textile exports were concerned, but tried to limit exports of textile machinery so as to keep it plentiful and cheap at home. They were unable to sustain this inconsistent attitude for long. When Japan was growing to world industrial status in the 1960s, it reorganized the Foreign Investment Council in early 1967 and recommended a policy of capital liberalization. Fifty industries were to be opened for foreign investment; 33 per cent to 50 per cent ownership provided that control remained Japanese and no veto was left in foreign hands. 100 per cent ownership was permitted in the other seventeen industries. But this was disingenuous or a joke, as the industries designated were either those in which Japan had a strong comparative advantage and large export markets—such as steel, motor-cycles, shipbuilding, cotton textiles and synthetic fibre-spinning—or small, domestic and intrinsically Japanese—such as cement, beer, pianos, hotels, sake parlours, barber shops, beauty shops, sausage made from fish and the like. This was shadow with little or no substance, the form of reciprocity, but in fact the asymmetric acceptance of concessions from others without yielding an effective *quid pro quo*. It was in fact rather childish.

The early regulations, moreover, required that each investment should contribute to the Japanese balance of payments. Such a requirement is clearly second-, third- or fourth-best: using microeconomic measures to deal with a macroeconomic problem. The argument is used by LDCs in many other parts of the world, along with other second-best arguments, such as, that the consumer cannot be trusted to know what he or she wants: consumer sovereignty is set aside in favour of planning, and specified goods—notably soft drinks, breakfast foods, and in some instances, though not in Japan, fast foods, are kept out. Second-best reasoning can be generalized into the acceptable statement that if markets do not work they should not be used. First-best policy, of course, is to improve the performance of markets to the point where they produce consumer satisfaction at least cost. In balance-of-payments troubles, first-best policy is to adjust exchange, monetary and fiscal policies to correct the payments situation without distorting the efficient allocation of resources.

In his *International Political Economics,* Frey (1984) states that in tariffs, bargaining is the rule and that tariffs are reduced only with reciprocity. There is some doubt whether this is a valid historical generalization. DCs trading with LDCs do not insist on reciprocity, and even in trade among DCs, unilateral action to lower tariffs is sometimes taken in belief that Hume's law (that imports generate exports) will ensure that tariff reduction will be followed by export expansion. Such was the impact, indeed, of the British repeal of the Corn Laws, the Timber Duties, and the Navigation Acts in the late 1840s and 1850s, and of the German tariff reduction of 1956. US concessions to Japanese exports, however, seemed not to produce a surge of US exports to Japan. The USA set limits to imports in certain fields—cotton textiles, synthetic fibres, and more recently, automobiles. Despite these measures, the Japanese current trade account surplus *vis-à-vis* the USA continues to mount. With floating exchange rates, the yen did not appreciate against the dollar because of the current-account surplus, since financial deregulation and abundant savings in Japan, plus the US budget deficit and high interest rates in the USA, encouraged capital outflows that kept the yen rate down and the dollar up.

It is worth underlining from both sides that the trade account surplus in Japan and deficit in the USA should be separated from the question of openness of markets in goods and foreign direct investment. The first is a macroeconomic issue, the second a micro one. To link them is to indulge in second-best reasoning. Japan indeed has moved in the direction of perfecting world financial markets in freeing the inter-national flow of capital. But instead of Japan out-growing the second-best reasoning of the post-war period to the 1960s in trade and foreign direct investment, the USA is slipping back from a responsible attitude, based on well-functioning markets and effective policies, into second-best reasoning. With Japan having a personal savings rate above 20 per cent of personal income, and the US rate nearer 7 per cent with rates of investment and government net surpluses and deficits more nearly matched, Japan can expect to have a current-account surplus, the USA a deficit, on Keynesian or 'absorption' reasoning, to use Alexander's (1952) terminology. With a smaller capital outflow, the yen would appreciate and the surplus on absorption account would be reduced by an offsetting deficit because of the elasticities, with Japanese goods more expensive in the USA, and American goods cheaper in Japan. If, however, in mercantilistic fashion, Japan continues to guard certain import-competing interests—farmers, the telecommunication industry, electronics, wood products and medical and pharmaceutical industries—adjustment in the balance of payments is rendered that much more difficult.

Hierarchical organization in the world economy is ethically unattractive to the extent that the country at the apex seeks its national advantage, and to the extent that that country works for the international interest, free-riding countries abroad take advantage of the leader's restraint to push their own parochial interests. 'Beggar-thy-neighbour' policies by LDCs are probably of little consequence for world stability since their weight is not great. The exception, of course, was oil and the Organisation of Petroleum-Exporting Countries' (OPEC) price rises of 1973 and 1979. These price increases produced over-reaction in the panic in some DCs that they might lose access to raw materials of all kinds, and in the effort in non-oil LDCs to cartelize other raw materials, most of them with high elasticities of demand. In addition the OPEC price rise called for a New International Economic Order (NIEO), much like the non-negotiable demands of students in the tumultuous 1960s.

The demands under the NIEO for higher commodity prices, abandonment of restrictive business practices, free LDC access to patents and other technology, foreign aid, generalized preferences in DC markets as against other DCs, proved to be a vast disappointment. The generalized preferences were limited in quantity. More foreign aid should have been provided, but most DC electorates had become tired. Higher commodity prices for goods in inelastic demand could be achieved only by restricting supply, a difficult task which the LDCs wanted to turn over for execution to the DCs.

My reaction to the list of requests was that the DCs should have said to the LDCs, 'do anything you like: we will not participate or retaliate'. The DCs did not retaliate to the dramatic OPEC price increase, possibly because of fear. OPEC has ultimately learned, as producers of other demand-elastic commodities would learn more quickly, that to charge a price higher than the optimum export tax is dysfunctional. Quantity is cut more than price is raised, and total income is reduced. The LDCs must learn from experimenting on their own, without guidance or interference from the DCs which would harm learning; failure in these circumstances is blamed on the DCs rather than on the foolish policy. But retaliation—an unattractive policy at best—should be reserved exclusively for DCs. Only when LDCs graduate into the status of DCs and are prepared to moderate infant-industry and optimum tariffs in the interest of expanding trade generally, will retaliation be called for when and if they, with power, pursue narrow nationalistic advantages.

Japan would have seemed to have graduated long ago. If it continues with mercantilistic and nationalistic policies in trade, investment and payments, the difficulty is that it will goad the USA into slipping back into a retaliatory, tit-for-tat mode. Tariffs are low, to be sure, but American negotiators claim that Japan uses regulatory, testing, product certification and other non-tariff barriers to limit imports. There is doubtless a Japanese side to the story, and it is well known that Japan has suffered from such devices as the French designation of Poitiers, an inland city, with a small customs staff, as the only port of entry for video-cassette recorders. The ingenuity of man in devising replacements for simple tariffs is lamentably substantial.

In *The World in Depression, 1929–1939* (1973), I held that the Great Depression of the 1930s was so wide so deep and so prolonged because the world was in a transition stage between the economic leadership of the British, who had kept their markets open, run the world capital market, maintained an international currency and acted as a lender of last resort, and that of the USA. The transition was long. By 1931 the British could not and the USA would not act as a stabilizer in an unstable world economy that needed one. Japan recovered quickly after December 1931 with a 'beggar-thy-neighbour' policy of savage exchange-depreciation. This would probably have been tolerable had others leaned sufficiently against the wind. Britain quickly dropped any attempt at world responsibility for world interests: first uncontrolled depreciation of sterling, on top of that import tariffs, and when sterling started to recover in 1932, an Exchange Equalisation Fund to hold it down. The combination, with interest-rate reduction, was sufficient to make the rest of the decade after 1932 fairly satisfactory for Britain, largely at the expense of the gold and dollar blocs where prices and depression were forced deeper. The USA moved slowly into the forefront after its own devaluation, with the Reciprocal Trade Agreement Act in 1934, the Tripartite Monetary Agreement of 1936 and especially Lend–Lease, the Atlantic Charter, Bretton Woods, GATT and the Marshall Plan, not to mention relief for defeated areas and the Anglo–American Financial Agreement. It encouraged the European Community to form a great economic entity between the USA and the Soviet Union, launched programmes of aid for economic development in the LDCs after decolonization, and made room for surging Japanese exports well before Europe.

It would be fatuous to claim that US economic foreign policies were entirely selfless. As early as 1955, the USA brusquely excepted internal

American markets in farm products from tariff and quota reductions in GATT. It used diplomacy to support American business interests in trade and investment. The Export–Import Bank subsidized the export of heavy machinery, notably aeroplanes and nuclear reactors. When it perceived the dollar as weak in the early 1960s, it imposed the Interest Equalization Tax (IET) on foreign new issues of securities in American markets, extended it through the Gore amendment to bank lending, imposed first voluntary and then mandatory restraints on capital flows through direct investment, all the while urging American business to invest abroad without bringing dollars. And it tried, unsuccessfully, to bargain down Japanese barriers against US products and investment by US firms.

In the 1970s, the USA appeared to be an ageing economy. Savings kept declining: other countries caught up with and then overtook the country in a number of industrial lines: steel, shipbuilding, automobiles and machine tools. Smokestack industries seemed doomed. US capacity and willingness to provide economic stability in a world of greater or lesser free-riding declined. In peace-keeping, there were calls to bring troops home from abroad, and for Europe and Japan to take a larger share of the cost of their defence. There was little prospect of a new world economic order on which agreement could be reached. The Conference on the issues raised by the UNCTAD demand for a NIEO that met in Paris in the spring of 1978 was a quieter failure than the World Economic Conference of June–July 1933, but a failure nonetheless. With the economic leadership of the USA slipping in the 1970s, and no potential successor standing in the wings ready to take over, the world ran the risk of another vacuum of the 1929 variety, with no country possessing the vision, the determination and the power to propose and promote acceptance of national policies that were consistent in the aggregate and calculated to produce international stabilization.

Ideas do not sell themselves. During the months and years before the World Economic Conference of June 1933, a variety of proposals was put forward for an international credit institution, for international public works ideas of the sort that resulted after the war in the IMF and the World Bank. They were put forward by the International Labour Office, by Francqui of Belgium, and by Henderson and Keynes in England. Japan and Poland solicitously asked about them on preparatory visits to the USA. All were turned down by the USA and/ or France. Without strong backing, these good ideas failed lamentably when they were most needed (Kindleberger 1973, pp. 204–14).

In the 1970s, when US leadership was seen to be slipping, proposals were put forward for a 'bigemony' of the USA and Germany, or a

'trigemony' of the USA, Germany and Japan, to coordinate economic
policies, particularly in the fields of exchange rates, macroeconomic
policies and trade, and to form a nucleus of stability around which the
rest of the world could adhere. The one concrete proposal for the
three countries to act was for each to serve as locomotives to pull the
world out of the depression of 1974–5. It failed. The USA expanded
fiscally; Germany and Japan did not. In the early 1970s, it had been
said of Germany (and Japan) that they exhibited 'a very moderate
nationalism . . . but without the desire for prestige or a clear will to
influence directly the evolution of the national system' (Grosser, 1975).
With the US economy ageing, the possibility appeared that the world
might again find itself in the position of 1929 with no country able and
willing to discharge the responsibilities of world economic leadership.

Political scientists seem unworried. The passage of *Pax Americana*
was thought by some to be a blessing since the USA was *An Imperious
Economy* (title of a 1982 book by Calleo). A substantial group of
political scientists thought that the functions of a 'hegemony' could be
taken over by 'international regimes', that they defined as 'principles,
norms, rules and decision-making procedures around which actor
expectations converge in a given issue-area' (Krasner, 1983). In an
influential book, Keohane (1984) asserted that the habits of cooperation
developed during the world leadership of the USA produced enough
inertia to guarantee their continuance for an extended period after the
time that the USA was unwilling any longer to provide costly leadership.

There is, of course, much to worry about in hegemony. (I dislike
this word used by political scientists for its implication of Greek tyrants,
although its etymology is innocent, coming from the Greek word for
leader.) British political scientists have attacked the USA as a 'bully-
hustler', 'kicking over chairs when it does not get its way', 'an iron
fist in a velvet glove' and 'powerful and ruthless' (Shonfield *et al.*
1976). If others were free riders, the USA was said to be a 'heavy
rider'. In the same book (Vol. II, p. 301) Susan Strange characterizes
France as a 'free-rider' . . . 'negative, critical non-cooperative and
obstructive—but never actually destructive.' France is unlike Japan in
that it lacks managerial capacity over its economy which is needed to
strike out in positive directions. Both countries seem to elevate the
national interest far above the international and to disregard the latter
in any conflict. France resists attempts of others to provide the
leadership that I think necessary and political scientists do not. Japan
ignores them.

In the mid-1980s, the US economy and the US dollar recovered to
a degree while the economies of Europe languished. The USA and
Japan seem to be pulling ahead of Europe technically in such important

fields as computers, electronics, space and aircraft. The pattern changes rapidly and is hard to follow. Whether the USA will reacquire the capacity and taste for leadership is unclear, as is the likely course of Japanese involvement in world responsibilities.

To recur to our metaphor of a family and adolescents, like an ageing parent, the USA had been slipping into irresponsibility, giving up autonomy for passivity, but seems to be making a comeback. There remains a danger that the budget deficit, the trade deficit and the overvalued dollar—though the dollar bounces about from day to day—will produce a crisis as foreign funds are withdrawn, the dollar bubble collapses, prices soar and the exuberance of the US economy is lost.

Like so many young adults, havng sown their wild oats, it is time for Japan to settle down and take on world responsibilities. At the least it should eschew the role of free rider and conform to the Kantian Categorical Imperative, which calls for people and countries to act in ways which can be generalized. It should no longer depend on the forebearance of others to escape the fallacy of composition.

A danger for the world is that the USA may perceive Japan as moving by herself in directions inconsistent with world economic coherence and stability and set out to discipline her. Retaliation, trade war, monetary restrictions, more industrial competition extending even to bribery and espionage may follow. The picture is unattractive.

REFERENCES

Calleo, D. (1982) *An Imperious Economy* (Cambridge, Massachusetts: MIT Press).
Frey, B. (1984) *International Political Economics* (Oxford: Oxford University Press).
Grosser, A. (1975) unpublished paper for a Nelson Rockefeller symposium.
Keohane, R.O. (1984) *After Hegemony: Cooperation and Discord in the World Political Economy* (Princeton: Princeton University Press).
Kindleberger, C.P. (1973) *The World in Depression, 1929–1939* (Berkeley: University of California Press).
Krasner, S.D. (ed.) (1983) *International Regimes* (Ithaca: Cornell University Press).
Shonfield, A. *et al.* (1976) *International Economic Relations in the Western World* (Oxford: Oxford University Press for the Royal Institute of International Affairs).

11 Hierarchy versus Inertial Cooperation*

ROBERT O. KEOHANE, *AFTER HEGEMONY:
COOPERATION AND DISCORD IN THE WORLD
POLITICAL ECONOMY.* Princeton: Princeton University
Press, 1984.

It is somewhat embarrassing for an economist and economic historian with the usual strong sense of turf and a need to be identified with his own to find his name cropping up from time to time in the 'foreign' field of political science. True, the conclusion of my book on the Depression borrowed the concept of leadership from political scientists Norman Froelich and Joe A. Oppenheimer, who put forth the notion that public goods would be underproduced (because of free riders), unless a leader agreed to bear a disproportionate share of their costs.[1] My conclusion stated that the 1929 Depression was so wide, so deep and so long because no leading country was able and willing to discharge the role of a stabilizer. The United Kingdom could not; the United States (with or without the help of France) would not.[2] The responsibilities of a stabilizer, as I originally detailed them, were to furnish an outlet for distress goods (or in periods of acute shortage, to share its supplies with highly dependent countries); to maintain the flow of capital to would-be borrowers; and to serve as a lender of last resort in financial crisis.[3] (Since that book appeared in 1973, I have added two other responsibilities to the role of a would-be stabilizer of the world economy: to maintain a structure of exchange rates and to coordinate macroeconomic policies.)[4]

Political science has now transmuted the concept of leadership into 'hegemony', a word that makes me uncomfortable because of its overtones of force, threat, pressure. I think it is possible to lead

---

* Published in *International Organization*, vol. 40, no. 4 (Autumn, 1986), pp. 841-7.

without arm-twisting, to act responsibly without pushing and shoving other countries. The father of a family, for example, usually has important responsibilities and is often a leader, but he is not frequently thought of as a hegemon. The word *hegemon* means leadership in Greek, to be sure, but my *Columbia Encyclopedia* associates it with the Peloponnesian Wars and the struggle for dominance between Athens and Sparta.

Semantic quibbles aside, is hegemony needed for stability or can cooperation among nation-states be provided in the economic arena by functional cooperation among nation-states—called 'regimes' by political scientists? Stephen Krasner defines regimes as 'principles, norms, rules and decision-making procedures around which actor expectations converge in a given issue area.'[5]

The relevance of the issue to present circumstances is evident. The world economy was relatively stable from 1850 to 1914 when Great Britain provided leadership with free trade, the gold standard, and the British navy. The transition from British to American leadership after World War I was drawn out and fateful. Now, forty years after World War II, the economic strength and resolve of the United States are faltering. Will there be a similar disturbed and disturbing interregnum? Economics raises the question but has no answer. Political science has two: the realistic answer which holds that self-interest determines states' actions and that it is probably not in the interest—in the short run at least—of any country to follow the example of the United States and try to stabilize the world economy; and the perhaps romantic, perhaps optimistic, but in any case institutional answer, which holds that international regimes that grew up during the period of American hegemony may produce enough inertia in the form of forward motion to hold entropy at bay.

The study of international regimes is currently a growth industry. However, the profession is not united in enthusiasm for regimes. Stephen Krasner has edited a special issue of *International Organization* on international regimes which contains a dissenting article by Susan Strange.[6] I live in a town with limited services and asked a political scientist at the sanitary landfill, formerly known as the town dump, what he thought of regimes (I do not mention his name because he was not speaking for attribution). 'I do not believe in regimes,' he said, 'I believe in strong states.'

The research moves ahead. Joanne Gowa has produced a monograph on the collapsing regime in monetary gold. Charles Lipson observes the changed attitude toward property rights in the international economy, subsequent to the decline in American hegemony. Young and Krasner deal with regimes in resources. But the broadest synthesis, widely noted and universally praised by critics, is *After Hegemony*, by Robert Keohane, which holds that the end to American economic leadership in the international economy has not led to a repetition of the disintegration of the 1930s because of the operation of a series of international regimes, created during the period of American hegemony.[7]

Keohane's book explores the theory of hegemony, including hegemonic cooperation and the establishment of regimes that continued after the supporting scaffolding of the hegemon has been dismantled. The illustrations that provide the basis for the theory are drawn from the worlds of money, in which the central institution is the International Monetary Fund (IMF); of trade, where a weakened General Agreement on Tariffs and Trade (GATT) still stands with its finger in the dike; and of oil. His discussion of oil is far more extensive and detailed than his discussions of money and trade—it runs to fifty-five pages in all, extending over three chapters—and to my mind is not very persuasive. For the period before 1973—the period of 'hegemonic stability' or 'hegemonic cooperation'—Keohane focuses on four separate episodes: the modification of the Red Line Agreement in the Middle East, covering 1943–49; the collapse of the Anglo–Iranian Oil company, 1951–64 and its replacement by a new company embracing new US interests; the emergency oil lift in 1956–57 following the closing of the Suez Canal; and the oil-importing quotas in the United States from 1959 to 1973. Keohane has reservations about the appropriateness of calling this unfolding history—well told to be sure—a hegemonic regime (p. 185), but he manages to suppress them (p. 185, note). Moreover, he admits that the 1973 crisis was badly handled by all governments, including that of the United States, and would have been much worse had not the private oil companies carried out the public function of distributing a vital resource equitably in a crisis (p. 223). He dwells at length on the International Energy Agency, created at the initiative of Henry Kissinger, which did no more than lock the barn door after the horse had been stolen; his account stops at 1981 (p. 221, note) after which, following a short and ineffective history, it sank without a trace. The accounts of money and trade are shorter and include both damaging admissions, such as that the GATT started to unravel in the 1960s when American hegemony was in full flower, and positive points, such as that cooperation under the IMF monetary regime spilled over into regime cooperation in the Third World debt crisis.

Overall, however, the theme of *After Hegemony* is not positive but conditional, bringing to mind the remark of Paul Streeten that if Soviet planning was imperative, and French planning indicative, British planning was subjunctive. The position *may* not be as bad as the realists think. Page 183 is a treasure trove of guarded statements:

> Decline of hegemony is likely to put hegemonic regimes under stress.

> It would be a mistake to infer . . . that cooperation is impossible without hegemony.

> . . . there are strong theoretical reasons for believing that hegemonic cooperation . . . does not constitute the only possible form of international cooperation.

> . . . that important elements of monetary and trade regimes persisted as hegemony waned suggests that international regimes may be adaptable to a post-hegemonic era rather than be doomed to complete collapse.

> . . . theory of hegemonic stability provides some insights into changes . . . but it is not entirely adequate to explain . . .

> . . . contention of this chapter is that the theory is partially valid . . .

Not on the same page, but in an optimistic aside elsewhere, Keohane follows the lead of Robert Axelrod, whom he cites five times, observing that a Tit-for-Tat strategy may teach players to cooperate.[8] But it may not. Economics can produce theories[9] and historical episodes[10] in which retaliation may ultimately destroy trade almost completely.

This leads me back to my aforementioned semantic quibble. It seems to me that the differences between hegemony and leadership or responsibility go considerably deeper than semantics. I do not know well the literature in political science (should I delete the word *science* and replace it with *politics?* or *government?*), but I was educated to believe that the principal difference betwen foreign policy makers was between those who believed exclusively in self-interest and those who allowed ethics—morality, principle, justice, obligation—to inform their judgments. Political *science* may be positive, and in weighing the likelihood that regimes will emerge from hegemonic cooperation Keohane is seeking to forecast the future. But there is a normative element in politics and/or government. Along with political science there is political philosophy. Machievelli's purposeful, self-interested Prince is paralleled by Plato's philosopher-king. Political philosophers explore the limits to obligation, the spheres of justice, the justification (if one exists) for lying, the degree to which we are bound by the Categorical Imperative to act only in ways that are acceptable if all do the same. In addition to the interest of self, there is the general interest. The national interest may be congruent or in conflict with the international interest. Leadership may be motivated by narrow interests as the examples of *der Fuhrer* and *il Duce* remind us. But unless specifically bounded, responsibility extends beyond the individual actor or group and implies concern for the system and even for humanity.

A similar issue arises in economics in what has lately been called 'the agency problem'.[11] A principal hires an agent to perform a task that is in the interest of the principal. But the agent has his own interest. In the absence of restraints the agent will serve his interest rather than that of the principal when the two conflict, or so it is alleged by economists who believe that people are motivated solely by self-interest. The agent will compare the gain to be had from violating his contractual obligation with the chance of being caught and convicted multipled by the penalty and will violate or not depending on the benefit–cost comparison. The principal, in deciding whether or not to hire an agent, will add to the wage bill the expense of monitoring the agent's actions and of bonding him to cover the possible loss from malfeasance. All this assumes a world of narrow self-interest in which the public good of 'magistracy', as Adam Smith calls it—law and order, and police and courts to enforce contracts, government, and the public good of orderly and dependable economic relationships – is either missing or expensive to provide. Ironically, while one group of economists is exploring the agency problem, having assumed that agents strain to violate commitments they entered into freely, another is trying to explain certain macroeconomic behaviour such as the stickiness of wages with the concept of 'implicit contracts' between employer and workers which go beyond the explicit terms of the hire.[12]

Froelich and Young are realists who believe that a leader is prepared to bear more than a proportionate share of maintaining the cost of the system because he is paid in another coin than material reward—prestige, or glory, or anticipated immortality. In international relations, Keohane assumes that whether the hegemon is concerned with long- rather than short-run interests, the interests are always his own. The hegemon presumably has what we in economics call a low rate of interest for calculating the present discounted value of future benefits (as compared with the present cost). Neither leaves room for conscience, duty, obligation, or such old-fashioned notions as *noblesse oblige*. My Presbyterian mother-in-law used to put it simply: 'You have it to do.' A hegemon presumbly wants to do it in his own behalf. A leader, one who is responsible or responds to need, who is answerable or answers the demands of others, is forced to 'do it' by ethical training and by the circumstance of position.

There are similar propositions in politics. I was struck once on hearing a political scientist—Karl Deutsch, if my memory serves—say that the essence of democracy was not that the majority rules but, rather, that the majority and the minority both understood—because their positions might one day be reversed—that the majority acts with restraint toward the minority. This view may imply strong self-interest on the part of political parties and a low rate of interest for future benefits, but it also contains substantial ethical concern for the larger polity. Perhaps the two views converge in the long run. There are, however, enough political actors with high rates of interest to merit distinguishing between self-interest and moral standards.

The restraint of the majority towards the minority is an implicit contract necessary to democracy. In international relations, the equivalent would be an implicit contract that leadership will be met with followership. What Keohane seems to be saying is that when the implicit contract between leader and followers breaks down or lapses, a new contract may (not will) emerge among a group including the former leader and former followers which holds that all will cooperate. To be sure, *anything* may happen in a contingent world. The question for social science is *what* will happen.

Keohane is writing to a particular situation in the world economy, and he is fully justified in writing his own book rather than one I should like to read. Nonetheless, it seems to me that political scientists with some sense of the past and present might usefully speculate on a series of questions in this field, such as:

1. While anything may happen, what is the likelihood that regimes will hold up after the dominance of a single country has broken down?
2. Do economic hegemony and political–military hegemony go hand in hand, and if so, which starts earlier and which ends later? I have in mind that US leadership, though faltering, generally holds up better in foreign-policy areas than in economic areas, for example, in NATO, SEATO, and the Middle East.
3. Does the absence of economic hegemony doom steps toward economic cooperation? The tariff truce agreed to at the World Economic Conference held in 1927 under the auspices of the League of Nations, to which no country paid attention, comes to mind, as does the inordinate time—approaching eighty years—it took to establish cooperation in the field of international epidemiology, where the self-interest of all countries, large and small, has been overwhelmingly evident.[13]
4. Are other 'creative' steps in world policy and economy barred

in the absence of a leader willing to bear a disproportionate share of the cost, on the one hand, and to 'crack the whip' over followers, on the other? Can real economic integration arrive in Europe without the effective leadership that the Federal Republic of Germany is unwilling to provide and that France and Britain are incapable of providing? The paradigm here is Prussian leadership in the formation of the Zollverein that led to the German Reich,[14] and the role of the Kingdom of Sardinia (largely Piedmont) and Count Cavour in uniting the Italian states.

5. Is it useful to distinguish trends from crises? Perhaps the market and regimes are capable of performing adequately in general, but stronger medicine, namely the assumption of responsibility by a leader, is required in crises. My initial discussion of leadership concerned a crisis, a time when there was a need for more open markets, continued capital flows, and a lender of last resort. Maintenance of a system of stable exchange rates and coordination of national macroeconomic policies, the functions I have added to my 1973 list, are required both for trends and in crises. The function of maintaining open markets for distress goods should be extended to sharing supplies of goods in acute scarcity (keeping in mind the notable failure of the United States in 1973 to share either oil or soy beans).

6. How large is the responsibility of the several classes of powers for regimes when there is no hegemony? William Diebold, Jr., has asserted that it is 'a fallacy to believe that the loss of power means that the United States has no responsibility for the repair of the international economic system.'[15] Keohane suggests that institutions are most helpful when a few like-minded countries are responsible for both making the rules and maintaining them (p. 246). Does he refer to a duumvirate? a troika? How stable are such coalitions? What is the responsibility of small countries, which, when they act in concert—like panicky people in a theatre or nightclub fire, or depositors drawing money from a bank—may have sizable consequences?

Keohane and his fellow researchers in international political economy have opened up a rich field for investigation. I permit myself to doubt, however, that *After Hegemony* will constitute the last word.

NOTES

1. Norman Froelich and Joe A. Oppenheimer, 'I Get Along with a Little Help from My Friends', *World Politics* 23 (October 1970), pp. 104, 20.
2. Charles P. Kindleberger, *The World in Depression, 1929–1939* (Berkeley: University of California Press, 1973), Chapter 14.
3. *Ibid.*, p. 293.
4. *Ibid.*, rev. and enlarged edition 1986.
5. Stephen D. Krasner, 'Structural Causes and Regime Consequences: Regimes as Intervening Variables', in Krasner (ed.), *International Regimes* (Ithaca: Cornell University Press, 1983), p. 1.
6. Susan Strange, 'Cave, hic dragones: A Critique of Regime Analysis,' in Krasner (ed.), *International Regimes* pp. 337–54.
7. Joanne Gowa, *Closing the Gold Window: Domestic Politics and the End of Bretton Woods* (Ithaca: Cornell University Press, 1983); Charles Lipson, *Standing Guard: Protecting Foreign Capital in the Nineteenth and Twentieth Centuries* (Berkeley: University of California Press, 1985); Oran R. Young, *Compliance and Public Authority* (Baltimore: Resources for the Future, Johns Hopkins University Press, 1979); Stephen D. Krasner, *Defending the National Interest: Raw Materials Investments and United States Foreign Policy* (Princeton: Princeton University Press, 1978); Robert O. Keohane, *After Hegemony: Cooperation and Discord in the World Political Economy* (Princeton: Princeton University Press, 1984).
8. Robert Axelrod, *The Evolution of Cooperation* (New York: Basic, 1984).
9. Tibor Scitovsky, 'A Reconsideration of the Theory of Tariffs', in American Economic Association, *Readings in the Theory of International Trade* (Homewood, Ill.: Irwin, 1949).
10. Joseph M. Jones, Jr., *Tariff Retaliation: Repercussions of the Hawley–Smoot Bill* (Philadelphia: University of Pennsylvania Press, 1934).
11. Michael C. Jensen and W.H. Meckling, 'Theory of the Firm, Agency Costs and Ownership Structure', *Journal of Financial Economics* 3 (1976). pp. 305–60.
12. Sherwin Rosen, 'Implicit Contracts', *Journal of Economic Literature* 23 (September 1985), pp. 1144–75.
13. Richard N. Cooper, 'International Economic Cooperation: Is It Desirable? Is It Likely? *Bulletin of the American Academy of Arts and Sciences* 39 (November 1985).
14. Hans-Werner Hahn, 'Hegemonie und Integration: Voraussetzungen und Folgen der preussischen Führungsrolle in Deutsche Zollverein', in Helmut Berding (ed.), *Wirtschaftliche und politische Integration in Europe in 19, und 20, Jahrhundert* (Gottingen: Vandenboeck & Ruprecht, 1984), pp. 45–70.
15. William Diebold, Jr., 'The United States in the World Economy: A Fifty-Year Perspective', *Foreign Affairs* 61 (Fall 1983), pp. 81–104.

12 The European Community: Hierarchy or Federation?*

Some years ago, I wrote an essay on the rise of financial centres and was struck how rapidly the process of their formation took place in some states, such as Germany and Italy after unification, and how slowly in others, such as Canada and Australia.[1] S.J. Butlin, the Australian economic historian, suggested to me in a letter that this might be because Canada and Australia were federations, not unitary states. It is of course evident that another federal state, Switzerland, has three financial centres, Geneva, oriented to France, Basle to Alsace and Baden-Wurtemburg, and Zurich a national and world centre. It occurred to me that there might be something to it.

Another distinction turns on the size of cities in a country. B.J.L. Berry has observed that city-size distribution follows two patterns: one primate, that follows a Pareto-distribution in which one city dominates a stratum of small cities and towns, and the truncated 'log-normal' in which the number of cities decreases with the increase in size in a smoothly geometric pattern.[2] Unitary states such as France, Austria, Denmark tend to follow the primate distribution. Federal states lie in the other category. Perhaps most striking in this connection in the concentration or lack of concentration of clearings or debits to bank deposits. At the end of the 1960s, Paris handled 91.3 per cent of the clearings in France, and London 87 per cent of those of the United Kingdom, as compared with Canada where Toronto had 37.3 per cent, Montreal 25.5 per cent and Vancouver 6.3 per cent. Jean Labasse who presents these figures in a book on the geography of finance notes that Japan lies between these extremes, with 51.2 per cent of clearings in Tokyo and 19.7 per cent in Osaka.[3] Handy on my shelves are no

* Published as 'Communita Europee: gerarchia o federazione', in Paolo Foresti (ed.), *Il Diagolo con gli Stati Uniti e il Malessere Europeao*, Bologna: Il Mulino, 1986, pp. 149–58.

current figures for the United States, but the historical data put out by the Federal Reserve Board show about the same pattern as for Japan, with 52 per cent of bank debits in New York and 34 per cent in 140 other centres. Clearings are a little more concentrated with New York having 61 per cent in 1929 (45 per cent in 1936 when security markets were less buoyant) compared to Chicago 8 and Boston and Philadelphia 3 per cent each (somewhat more in all cases in 1936).[4]

In preparing for this task I went through a certain amount of the literature on federalism which was particularly flourishing in the late 1960s and early 1970s as the European Economic Community emerged. A federalized state, in one definition, is one in which the several units and their respective powers are constitutionally and otherwise united under the ultimate power of a central state and government.[5] The essential is that the subordinate units retain or have reserved some irreducible powers in the same territory.[6] It is sometimes held that federalism involves checks and balances that anchor the powers of government midway between a centralized state and a series of small separate ones. Building up from anarchy to a unified state, one finds a series of possible steps: league, confederation, federation, united—as in the United Provinces, or the United States, and a union, where the degree of oneness reaches a little more emphasis. Still higher of course is the unitary state which gives no hint of the existence of constituent parts in its title.

I find no agreement on why some states are federal and some unitary. At least two theories exist. In one the question turns on size. The United States, Canada, and Australia are so large that powers have to be left to local entities. Switzerland might be thought to be an anomaly on this showing, but it can be held that the various cantons are quite distant from each other in economic and political space, set as they are in narrow valleys with difficult communication from one another, despite what a two-dimensional map shows. The other theory lays emphasis on the age of states and cities. It is hypothesized that geographical units need certain administrative services. In old states, these have already been provided with an infrastructure in place. When such states are fashioned into larger units, the central government finds many of the services required by a state already being furnished. But this theory is readily falsified by the fact that new states like Canada and Australia are federal, not unified, and a number of old states, fashioned from smaller units, are unitary. The unitary character of France and England perhaps furnishes a counterexample to the hypothesis, but the late unification of Germany and Italy certainly does.

The third theory turns on the question of the degree of leadership or dominance in the unifying process. German unification was led by Prussia under Bismarck, Italy's by Piedmont under Count Cavour. In both cases, Austria and in the German case additionally France served as an external challenge that helped produce a unit. But external challenges are thought to be helpful in the formation of federations, too.[7] The United States moved from a confederation to a federation at the end of the 18th century as the struggling country continued to feel threatened by Britain. It moved to become a union during the Civil War. Some analysts find that unitary states may expand but do not permit secession.[8] The fact that Switzerland (in the Sonderbund war of 1847) fought to prevent secession is noted, but Friederich holds that 'ability to secede may make it the distinguishing criteria (*sic*) of an international federal union'.[9] The United States typically adopts the terminology of a federation but acts much more than Canada and Australia as a unitary state. The Federal Reserve system was established on the theory of twelve separate financial districts with primarily housekeeping functions and a limited input into policy. In turn the Federal Reserve Bank of New York was subsequently replaced as the pivot of the system by the Federal Reserve Board in Washington.

What does this have to do with the European Economic Community? In my judgment a great deal. It seems to me to lead to the prediction that unless and until there is stronger leadership in the EEC, it runs a grave risk of falling apart as did a number of other post-war federations in East Africa, the West Indies, Rhodesia and Nyasaland and Malaysia.[10]

The history of the British application for membership is informative. France wanted a community of *patries*, with no derogation of sovereignty to the centre. It wanted to be the leader, but was unwilling to pay for the privilege, as Prussia had done in forming the *Zollverein* and working slowly to unification. The free-rider principle means that followers are usually unwilling to pay their proportionate share of the expense of forming a country and the leader has to take on a disproportionate share. France was unwilling to do this, and in fact wanted to receive benefits from the European Investment Bank, the European Overseas Fund (to which Germany contributed, but lacking colonies did not benefit), and in the Common Agricultural Policy. When France failed to get its way in the CAP, moreover, it threatened to break up the market by secession. The British application for membership was originally seen as a threat to French leadership, and de Gaulle said 'Non'.

As time went on, it became clear that the French bid for the leadership role was failing, and a more likely candidate for it was the Federal Republic of Germany. The Netherlands, Belgium, Luxemburg and to a lesser extent Italy were prepared to follow a leader, and turned from France to a reluctant Germany. At this stage, France welcomed the accession of Britain to dilute the opposition to the French position. The British entry, undertaken as a consequence of the breakdown of both the Commonwealth and the special relationship with the United States, was accompanied by hard bargaining, especially by the French, in which Britain acceded to the agricultural programme which was contrary to her own programme and to her interest, and to an unfavourable budget arrangement. When the Conservative government under Mrs Thatcher found that the economic benefits of expanded markets for exports and stimulating competition from imports were less than anticipated, it sought to revise CAP and the budget arrangement. Two summits at Athens and Versailles have failed to reach a compromise between Britain and all the others, with the most intransigent being France. The result is a threat to the continued survival of the Community.

One symptom of the difference between a real community and a synthetic one that is likely to break apart is furnished by the question of the *juste retour*. This principle, adopted in the Common Market under French insistence, requires that in common projects, procurement from each state much match the state's contribution to the project. To an economist, this is an horrendous principle. Efficient resource allocation demands that funds be raised in these cases on the basis of ability to pay and be spent where goods are produced most efficiently and cheaply. To buy only from those that buy from you (or contribute to the project) is called by Adam Smith 'the sneaking arts of underling tradesmen . . . A great trader purchases his goods always where they are cheapest and best, without regard to any little interest of this kind.'[11] Some years ago, Seymour E. Harris wrote a book on New England in which he complained that the Federal government spent in New England less than it collected in taxes.[12] This complaint was taken by most economists to reflect an attitude antithetical to union. In a union, taxes are levied throughout the country according to one set of principles, and monies are expended throughout on another, without regard to the balance of income raised and monies spent in any geographical unit. To be sure a certain amount of log-rolling of pork-barrel projects takes place in the Congress along regional lines, but this runs contrary to the implicit contract in the country and is thoroughly disapproved of in high-minded quarters.

It is sometimes claimed that the European Monetary System (EMS) is a great success.[13] Eight revaluations of currencies in five years suggest that the constituent members of the EMS, which does not cover Britain, have failed to reconcile their differing tastes in matters of employment, inflation, income-distribution and the like. One of the crucial features of a single state—whether federation or unitary state—is a single money and coherent macroeconomic policy throughout the affected territory to sustain the money. Changing exchange rates are the antithesis of a single money, which is defined as the only asset fixed in terms of itself. The members of the EMS may congratulate themselves for their success in quickly recognizing divergences in the values of their constituent national monies. They remain far from having sealed their union by the adoption of a single money such as the *ecu* was intended to be.

The most hopeful prospect for the emergence of the European Economic Community from its present slough of despond would be for West Germany to perceive that leadership and an hierarchical organization were missing and to move into a leadership mode. I am not a political pundit, but this outcome does not seem likely. For one thing, Germany is very shy of the *Fuhrerprinzip* these days, and for understandable reasons. It is prepared to be a good citizen and to support other positive initiatives in building Europe, but is reluctant to move into the vanguard. Secondly, some of the assertiveness of the country has been beaten out of her after ten years of war and two defeats 1914–18 and 1939–45. Like France after Waterloo, it will be some time before the country again feels ebullient. Thirdly, it has its own national agendum: reunification. To the extent that leadership in the onward march of the European community is disapproved of by the Soviet Union, reunification with East Germany and the rise of the European Community are in conflict.

In 1950 in a talk at the School for Advanced International Studies, then summering in Peterborough, New Hampshire, I predicted that the Common Market would have to move forward to political integration or it would fall apart. I thought there was no half-way house in which it could long rest. Whether that prediction has already been falsified or not, depends on one's intellectual rate of interest. In any event I am persuaded that the high-water mark of economic integration has been reached with the tide now receding. I could be, and hope I am, wrong.

NOTES

1. C.P. Kindleberger, 'The Formation of Financial Centers', *Princeton Studies in International Finance*, no. 36, 1974, reprinted in C.P. Kindleberger, *Economic Response*, Cambridge, Mass.: Harvard University Press, 1978, pp. 66–134.
2. Brian J.L. Berry, 'City-Size Distribution and Economic Development',

Economic Development and Cultural Change, vol. 9, no. 4 (July, 1961), pp. 573–88.

3. Jean Labasse, *L'espace financier: analyze géographique*, Paris: Colin, 1974, pp. 144–5.

4. *Historical Statistics of the United States, 1789–1945*, Washington, DC: Department of Commerce, 1949, p. 270; Board of Governors of the Federal Reserve System, *Banking and Monetary Statistics*, Washington, DC: 1943, pp. 238ff.

5. Frank, N. Trager, 'On Federalism', introduction to Thomas M. Franck, editor, *Why Federations Fail, An Inquiry into the Requisites for Successful Federalism*, New York: New York University Press, 1968, p. x.

6. *Ibid.*, p. xi.

7. Ivo D. Duchacek, *Comparative Federalism: The Territorial Dimension of Politics*, New York: Holt, Rinehart and Winston, 1970, p. 154.

8. Carl J. Friederich, *Trends in Federalism in Theory and Practice*, New York, Praeger, 1968, p. 85.

9. *Ibid.*

10. Thomas M. Franck (ed.), *op. cit.*, Chapters 1–4.

11. Adam Smith, *An Inquiry into the Nature and Causes of the Wealth of Nations* (1776), New York: Modern Library, 1937, p. 460.

12. Seymour E. Harris, *The Economics of New England*, Cambridge, Mass.: Harvard University Press, 1952.

13. Robert Triffin, 'The European Monetary System: Tombstone or Cornerstone?', a talk given at the Federal Reserve Bank of Boston Conference on 'The International Monetary System: Forty Years after Bretton Woods', at Bretton Woods, New Hampshire, 19 May 1984.

13 Standards as Public, Collective and Private Goods*[1]

I

Adam Smith postulated three types of public goods: safety, justice and public works which it would not pay private individuals to produce, all three summed up in the word 'magistracy', which was the necessary prerequisite for free trade (1776, pp. 653, 669, 681–2). Magistracy can be extended from this group or made to include within it such elusive 'goods' as macroeconomic stability, redistribution of national income, the monetary system, and of interest here, standards of various sorts. Standards of measurement—whether linear, weight, bulk, temperature, time or value (i.e. the unit-of-account function of money) clearly fall within Samuelson's definition of public goods in that they are available for use by all and that use by any one economic actor does not reduce the amount available to others (1954). In fact they are a strong form of public good in that they have economies of scale. The more producers and consumers use a given standard, the more each gains from use by others through gains in comparability and interchangeability.

My concern goes beyond standards of weights, measures, temperature, time and value, though they play important roles in what follows, to include standards determined by various groups—governments, trade or professional associations, and even companies—limiting the characteristics of goods or products, and to deal with the setting, diffusion, and changing of standards.

* A seminar paper given to the Institute for International Economic Studies, University of Stockholm 16 November 1982 and published in *Kyklos*, vol. 36, Fasc. 3, 1983, pp. 377–95.

II

At least two classes of standards can be distinguished: those designed to reduce transactions costs, and those in which there are physical economies external to the firm. Under transactions costs can be included not only the ease of concluding transactions because both parties to a deal mutually recognize what is being dealt in, but also the prevention of adulteration, short measure, or short weight, debasement and the like that may make a transaction unsatisfactory to one of the parties. In recent times the state has set standards of weights and measures and maintained surveillance to see that they were adhered to. In the Middle Ages, the cloth guild of Florence controlled yardsticks (Origo, 1957, p. 77). Linear measure in retail trade is today probably left to the consumer to patrol, but most cities check up on the more complex machines to weigh, say, meat, to ensure against short weight. Quality counts as well as quantity. In the Middle Ages most trade was conducted on consignment because the buyer wanted to inspect the merchandise to check for quality (de Roover, 1966, p. 143). Some goods today are incapable of being described in a standard designation because of the unevenness of nature or man-made uniqueness. On this account diamond, furs, wool, race horses, art and antiques are sold in quantity only at auctions after inspections. Where possible, however, transaction costs on commodities are reduced by standardizing quality by grades. At a primitive stage of international trade, India sold cotton in the famine created by the American Civil War full of dirt (Landes, 1958, p. 71), and Turkish wheat entering world markets for the first time in the early 1950s was said to suffer from an admixture of stones and dead mice. Standardization and grading, resulting in such short-hand descriptions as middling cotton, 1 3/8ths inch staple, No. 2 medium-grain rice, Straits quality tin, Santos No. 4 coffee, prime western slab zinc, etc. save time in description, allow for conventional discounts or premiums for divergences from the standard, and permit trading over distance without inspection. There may be provision for testing, as in taking a core sample of a loaded railway car of wheat. Where standards of quality can be established, however, trade is expedited and transaction costs reduced.

Some standards are imposed by government in the interest of the consumer, notably in the testing of drugs and inspection of meat. For the most part, however, standardization was originally undertaken by merchants. In a previous paper, I have suggested that a distinction could be made between the gains-from-trade merchant who arbitraged goods in their existing condition, buying cheap and selling dear, and the value-added merchant who was especially interested in upgrading and controlling quality (1978a, pp. 37–8). These are ideal types and in actual practice most merchants combined the two functions. Part of the value added of such a stapling centre as Amsterdam in the seventeenth and eighteenth centuries was the sorting, grading, packing and storing undertaken by the Second Hand after the First Hand of great merchants had brought the goods to the entrepot centre. Adam Smith's belief that the merchant exchanging corn from Königsberg for wine from Portugal brought both to Amsterdam because he felt uneasy separated from his capital and wanted to see it badly enough to be willing to pay the double charge of loading and unloading (1776, pp. 421–2) was based on a complete misunderstanding of this central point. The merchant had a strong interest in ensuring that the goods were sorted by grade and conformed to the qualities demanded. The 'gentlemen merchants' of Leeds paid more attention to quality of the woolens they bought than to price (Wilson, 1971, pp. 56–7). It had been especially efficient to do so two or three centuries early at a time when goods were sold at semi-annual or quarterly fairs, or shipped in an annual convoy to such as destination as Newfoundland, since goods rejected by the buyer would tie up the merchant's capital for an extended period.

The function of the merchant in commercial development in fixing and maintaining standards of quality is underlined when one contemplates the difficulties encountered in quality by Socialist countries, where producer performance and bonuses are usually related to quantities of output, which, given goods shortages, does not have to meet a rigorous quality test in the market. Competitive markets that clear allow consumers to reject altogether or to price down low-quality output, and thus provide strong incentives to merchants to enforce quality control on producers.

Governments and merchants are of course not the only instruments for standardization. When Denmark entered the international (largely British) market for butter at the end of the nineteenth century, much of its output was so-called 'peasant butter' of uneven taste and texture. Before this could be sold in quantity abroad, it had to be upgraded to the quality of 'manor butter', a process carried out, after the invention of the cream separator, through a newly-created institution, the marketing cooperative. This had the advantage of allowing production to continue on a small labour-intensive scale of the family farm, while marketing, after standardization and grading, of eggs, bacon, cheese as well as butter, was done on an efficient large scale (Faber, 1931). These standards were of course collective as contrasted with public, goods or the quasi-private goods of merchant standards. The twentieth-century equivalent of such collective goods is the control by wine-growers of the labelling of champagne and other 'appellations contrôlées' wines from particular regions. Here the standards are set by the vintners but enforced by government in an effort to protect consumers from adulteration on the one hand and to limit competition on the other.

After a certain stage of development and for certain classes of goods the efforts of merchants to standardize and grade output can become dysfunctional. It was said that the wholesale merchants dealing in cotton goods in Lancashire in the twentieth century maintained 34 grades of poplins when the ultimate user could distinguish at most three different qualities (Robson, 1957, pp. 92–5). In the British machine-tool trade, merchants have been regarded as inhibiting quality change and the development of new tools by standing between the producer and the consumer, telling the producer with an idea for a new machine 'They don't want them like that', and the customer looking for a new device 'They don't make them like that' (Beesley and Throup, 1958, pp. 380ff). Chandler (1962) notes that when the local and regional corporation in the United States grew to national size at the end of the nineteenth century, it gave up the services of independent wholesalers and jobbers and drew the marketing function back into the firm so as to maintain direct contact with customers. Without the interposition of the merchant, it was possible for producer and consumer to explore together possible improvements and their costs and benefits. This gain seems to have outweighed the diseconomies of scale in administration from combining in one company such different functions as production and marketing.

Machine tools were long an industry in transition from standardized lathes, milling machines, grinders and the like to special machines for special purposes. Between these limits a large and growing class of goods exists in which the hardware is standardized but requires instruction or software for its effective use. The claim has been made that the need for software first developed in the chemical industry at the end of the nineteenth century as instruction in the use of nitrate fertilizers was necessary to prevent the peasant-farmer from blowing himself up (Hohenberg, 1967). In today's world complex manufactured products leads naturally to the spread of the multinational corporation as products require instruction in use and repair, plus depots of spare parts, both leading to the creation in each national market of subsidiaries that evolve with some high degree of probability into local manufacture (Carlson, 1978). The standards set by makers of automobiles, electrical appliances, other durable consumer goods and industrial equipment are private goods, supported by advertizing to reinforce the claims for quality, rather than collective or public goods. The maintenance of these quality standards has perhaps little effect in economizing on transactions costs except where a customer satisfied with a given product is content to replace it with the same item from the same producer without search.

Where government lays down standards for the protection of ignorant consumers it may do so in the interest of producers, as Lindblom asserts was true both for meat inspection and for pure food and drugs, with policy formulated by business control parading as democratic reform without an important contribution from popular demand (1977, p. 191). If this be true, an ostensible public good is effectively a collective good, although the two sorts of good can be complementary. Similar examples can be found in land zoning, with perhaps different private groups having different interests in the outcome of zoning decisions, and policy leading to standards with costs and benefits that have particular distributions. Governmental standards may also turn out to be dubious public goods and at the same time collective bads, as in building codes designed to protect the public from shoddy construction, but frequently piling up requirements, such as provision for handicapped persons in areas where few if any exist, at costs which are only casually considered and prove to be exorbitant. Governmental standards of this sort for the protection of consumers or investors are difficult to bring under the rubric of 'reducing transactions costs' and perhaps deserve a separate category.

To return to standards set directly by producer or marketer, they save transactions costs in improving recognition and avoiding buyer dissatisfaction, with perhaps the disability of impeding quality changes if merchants inhibit exchange of information between producer and consumer. But standardization can reduce transaction costs in other ways, notably in standardization of working time, of statistics, and of monies. The saving in transactions costs, it may be noted, may well involve other types of costs which in particular cases exceed the transactions benefit.

Milton Friedman once applied the analogy of daylight saving time to flexible exchange rates. Instead of changing our habits when we wish to extend the hours of daylight, we change our clocks. By the same token we should change exchange rates instead of trying to change prices and wages (1953). He neglected to point out that to be efficient, daylight saving time has to be adopted for an entire zone at once, and optimally for all time zones around the world by the same amount on the same day of the year. When New York is in touch with London or San Francisco or Singapore or Bahrein, exchange rates for time zones must be fixed (Kindleberger, 1981, pp. 34–41). The point can be generalized: standardization of working time facilitates transactions by having people on the assembly line or in offices that need to interact available to work together. There is no such necessity for novelists or scholars, but for factory or office workers there is likely to be, despite the heavy costs in excess capacity in buildings and equipment, in transport congestion, and to the extent that everyone takes a holiday in the same weeks or month, in resort facilities. The Soviet Union experiment with varying the day or days of rest within the week, and currently popular proposals in the west for 'flexitime' working arrangements focus on one cost of standardized work days, weeks, months and years, but neglect the benefits. Standardized worktime in the factory makes possible the simultaneous or sequential application of labour to materials; in urban occupations where interpersonal communication at a high level is needed, as in advertizing, law, finance and administration, it makes it likely that the person needed will be found when sought at his or her desk (Vernon, 1960; Winston, 1982).

Standardization of economic information reduces transactions costs in various ways for the most part too obvious to require illustration. The European Economic Community had to establish a common tariff nomenclature before it could impose a common tariff. Comparison and aggregation of national trade data require standardization of trade statistics whether by the Hague convention of 1913, the interwar League of Nations standard, or the United Nations Standard International Trade Classification (SITC). Today the United Nations and such bodies as the International Monetary Fund, the World Bank and other specialized agencies, national governments, their ministries and statistical bureaus, private research organizations, and individual scholars like Kuznets, Leontief, Friedman and Schwartz, Maizels, Bairoch, Rostow etc. spent countless hours and sums trying to make statistical series comparable both between countries and over time. The difficulty inherent in the process is that national statistics are shaped to separate country's conditions and needs, and statistical series over time encounter changes in underlying conditions of population, technology, resources, products and tastes which require changes in their composition. The index-number problem is insoluble both in time series and in cross-sectional analysis, despite the powerful sophisticated methods which have been brought to bear on it.

Finally in this listing is the need for money as a measure and as a medium of exchange. As a unit of account, money reduces transactions costs by assisting comparisons, converting, as is well known, the $N(N-1)/2$ comparisons of a barter system to $N-1$. Hayek (1977) and Vaubel (1979) neglect the unit-of-account function of money when they recommend the innovation of private competitive monies. They believe they take care of the objection that two or more would be subject to Gresham's law by allowing the several private monies to be traded against one another at varying prices. With monies varying in price, however—within a country and even between countries—there is in my view no national (or international) money in the sense of a standard suitable for measurements. A fixed conversion coefficient between metres and yards permits measurement to take place in either. When the relationship between the yard and the metre fluctuates, however, the public good of a standard of measurement is lost.

Even the medium-of-exchange and store-of-value functions of money that Vaubel believes should be left to the private market as private goods, subject to the prescription of *caveat emptor*, pose problems in transactions costs. The state has two reasons to set a money standard. In the first place, there is strong historical evidence that not all members of society possess the capacity adequately to safeguard their own interests. This is the reason for standards of pure food and drugs, honest measure, tolerable limits of bacteria in the water at bathing beaches and public swimming pools, enforced by the state. The state, moreover, lays down and seeks to enforce strong rules against counterfeiting or debasement of money of other sorts, such as writing bad cheques. The Federal Deposit Insurance Corporation sets limits of insured deposits, originally $10,000, then $40,000 and now $100,000, because small depositors presumably lack the capacity to judge the safety of a given bank, whereas the possessor of wealth is held responsible for protecting his own money.

In addition to this function of protection, standardization of the medium of exchange saves transaction costs. It took four months to test and count the 1,200,000 escudo ransom of the sons of Francis I in 1529—40,000 escudos more being demanded because of imperfect coins (Vilar, 1976, p. 174). To economize on weighing and assaying specie in Italy in the Middle Ages, and up to the nineteenth century in the Eastern Mediterranean, banks accumulated coin in purses marked with the amounts contained, and dealt in them without recounting, with the state levying heavy penalties against any overstatement of the amount (Udovitch, 1979, p. 174; Marlowe, 1974, p. 153). 'Bank money' developed in the seventeenth century, consisting of transferable deposits of coin in the public banks of Genoa, Venice, Amsterdam, Hamburg, etc. with the bank certifying to the existence on deposit of specie of the requisite weight and fineness (Van Dillen, 1934). Bank money in Amsterdam normally traded at a premium of 3 to 5 per cent about the equivalent coin, the premium testifying to the transaction saving in testing and counting (Smith, 1776, p. 452). As unit of account, and to a great extent in the medium-of-exchange and store-of-value functions, standardization of money—a process that has been continuing in Darwinian fashion for centuries—provides a public good that reduces transactions costs.

III

Standardization can produce physical economies as well as savings in transactions, though not necessarily in total cost. In production, the saving may lie in economies of scale through repetitive production and in the reduction of down time for changing patterns and shifting materials. In use—more often perhaps of intermediate than of final goods—the benefit is in interchangeability of equipment. A classic example is the standard railway gauge of 4 feet 8 1/2 inches, believed by tradition to have originally represented the width of the hind end of a Norfolk mule used to pull coal wagons on wooden rails. In 1846 the British Parliament enacted the Gauge Act requiring all railroads to conform to the standard gauge. The Great Western Railway that operated from London to Devon and Cornwall and had started with a gauge width of five feet resisted strenuously on the ground that its wider gauge was superior to the standard adopted, producing a smoother, more stable and safer ride. As the Great Western acquired other railroads through purchase and merger it widened their gauges by 3 1/2 inches and equipped the acquired locomotives and wagons with new axles. Cargo moving on other railroads from the Midlands to the Southwest had to be transhipped at Gloucester from standard to wide-gauge wagons, and vice-versa for shipments in the other direction. After holding out for half a century, the Great Western finally yielded to the inevitable and adopted the standard gauge in the 1890s.

Railway-gauge problems have also been prominent in wars involving Russia with a wide gauge and Germany with the standard (adopted by most countries), and in the separate states of Australia. In the Russo–German case, the Germans for a time shifted one track inward on sleepers as they conquered Russian territory in World Wars I and II, and then adopted locomotive and wagon axles with an extra wheel to fit the wider size to make transfers possible without relaying track. In Australia each state kept to its own gauge until after the middle of the present century, forcing most interstate cargo to be carried by sea between settlements along the coast, and interstate shipments by rail to be reloaded from one system to the other.

Many manufacturing processes in Britain escaped standardization for lack of government efforts, those of a trade association, or the pressures of a dominant firm. It has been said that there were 200 types of axle boxes, 40 different handbrakes in railway wagons, perhaps 200 sizes and specifications for manhole covers. The Railway Clearinghouse laid down regulations for equipping privately-owned cars with automatic brakes, but most railroads built their own stock to their own standards (Parkhouse, 1951). There were 122 channel and angle sections in England, when the Germans had reduced their number to 32 (Landes, 1965, p. 495), and 'an almost unbelievable lack of standardization' on the part of British manufacturers of ploughs (Saul, 1968, p. 212). In World War I Britain was found to have 70 electricity generating companies with 50 different systems of supply, 24 voltages and 10 different frequencies (Plummer, 1937, p. 21). British automobiles adopted the precedent of trains and drove on the left of the road with the driver in the right-hand side of the front seat, whereas virtually all other countries changed over to the American standard of left-hand drive cars on the right-hand lane of dual roads.

Standardization between firms allows for greater interchangeability of equipment not only in such items as railroad locomotives and rolling stock, but also savings for the consumer if, say, the change from 78 revolutions per minute for records and record-players is made entirely to 33 r.p.m. long-playing records, instead of one company, R.C.A., adopting for a time a different standard of 45 r.p.m. French resistance to the adoption of the United States standard in colour television of a minimum number of lines per inch and attempt to spread its own finer but more complex and difficult to maintain standard evoke echoes of the holdout of the Great Western railway except that in this case it succeeded in getting its standard adopted in Europe. It is a general phenomenon that the first major firm in the field in a country has a relatively free hand in setting the standard. This may, however, prove later to be less than optimal but at such time difficult to displace.

In Britain some part of the explanation for the lack of standardization that would have constituted a collective good for an industry lay in the numbers of small companies making a virtually simultaneous start in an industry, with none sufficiently in advance to induce others to follow its lead. In addition, both railroads and cities hired own consulting engineers with pride in their professional competence who chose specifications for railway or municipal equipment as if they were architects designing unique structures, without attention to possible external economies (Saul, 1968). (The adoption of separate building codes for cities and towns in the United States has the same origin in local pride of authorship and the same result in preventing the achievement of economies of scale in many aspects of the construction industry, though there may be some basis for regional differences—south and north, wet and dry, and the like.) There were exceptions in the British case. In tramways, John Young was a dynamic municipal engineer who persuaded the entire country to follow his standard type of overhead trolley, enabling manufacturers to gain production economies of scale (McKay, 1976, pp. 181–4). By contrast standardization in Germany and France was achieved by the success of a dominant firm in each country so far in the lead that it forced the competition to follow. Charles Mertz of Northeastern England was both a consulting engineer and a supplier of electrical equipment who achieved standardization of electricity production and distribution in the area in which he operated (Saul, 1968, pp. 231ff; Byatt, 1968, p. 272). He was of course aided by starting some time after the initial introduction of electricity in the south of England, and was able to profit from the example of that region's troubles.

Where a company is far in the lead, as the American Telephone and Telegraph Company or IBM in computers, there is strong pressure on the rest of the industry to make its equipment compatible, leading to the private and collective good of standardization, although for the lead company which may be partially displaced, the standardization might be regarded as a private bad. In international trade Jacques Drèze has explained why Belgium, a small country unable by itself to get economies of scale in its market, has to concentrate on the production of standardized commodities that can be sold in world markets, for example, semi-finished iron and steel bars, rods, shapes, wire and the like, flat glass, intermediate chemical products such as soda ash and urea, electric wiring harnesses used interchangeably on many models of foreign automobiles (1960).

Standardization may also be desirable within an organization for physical reasons. Armies, navies, air forces find it desirable to focus on a few types of weapons in order to reduce numbers of spare parts to be maintained, and to simplify the training and operations of users and repairers. What is self-evident for such a large organization as an army applies as well to firms, to railroads for locomotives, bus companies, fleets of taxis or rental cars, etc. If the equipment wears out a little at a time, and technical progress or model changes continue in the industry, the company faces a difficult choice between heterogeneous equipment or lumpy capital expenditures, which choice may or may not be assisted by the possibility of selling obsolete serviceable equipment in a second-hand market.

A variety of defences of advertizing have been put forward, notably the dissemination of information, the gaining of consumer loyalty through product recognition, appealing to consumers directly over the heads of wholesalers, jobbers and retailers (Kaldor, 1951). For consumer loyalty it is important for the company to set and maintain high standards and quality control and to persuade the public that a brand name is a guarantee of quality. Brand loyalty based on such belief is an intangible asset, included on the balance sheet under good will. Sophisticated methods of testing and quality control are required along with advertising to eliminate 'lemons' (equipment that performs inadequately or requires excessive maintenance and repair), short measure, or disappointment to public expectations in other ways. Generic foodstuffs and drugs which are cheaper than branded articles encounter difficulty where a brand name is believed to be a guarantee of quality. To the extent that generic products are gaining on higher-priced branded products, it is possible that the consumer attaches an implicit guarantee of standard quality to the retail dispenser.

IV

Standards may be imposed by government, by trade or professional association, dominant firm, or in some cases be altogether missing. Where they exist with important economies in transaction costs or physical economies of scale, or don't exist but would be useful, they are difficult to change, or to adopt late in an industry's life, because of lumpiness. A substantial capital investment is likely to be required for a smaller monetary gain over time. With perfect information on costs and benefits, and well-functioning capital markets the decision as to whether or not to change standards is readily made by a single decision-maker with due attention to discounting future benefits by some appropriate rate of interest. In practice, with many firms in an industry, the difficulties are likely to be great, partly because of the free-rider problem that inhibits the production of public goods: each firm, household, individual waits to undertake to change the standard until the rest of society has conformed and the costs and benefits to the single unit are clarified. The various forms that resistance may take can be illustrated, beyond the Great Western railway and French television already cited, with reference to right- and left-hand drives for automobiles, and the metric system in France, Britain and the United States.

Trains in Britain used the left track, and those of Sweden, Switzerland and the United Kingdom (at a minimum) still do. When automobiles came along, the British clung to the left-hand side of the road, whereas the United States chose the right-hand side. (The question was undoubtedly decided state by state, but once the first few states adopted a common standard the rest followed without question. The practice of driving on one side or the other with horses and horse-drawn vehicles may have been a factor affecting the choice in Britain and the United States, but I lack information.) When the United States moved into mass production and export of automobiles, the American left-hand drive car, appropriate to a right-hand traffic pattern, came to dominate foreign countries. Pressure for standardization was significant among contiguous countries, although a few like Austria and Sweden, held out in the British pattern. For the British Isles, with no highways running directly to foreign countries—prior to completion of the Channel tunnel—it was easy to keep to an idiosyncratic standard since there was no necessity to change sides of the road in continuous travel. A certain cost was incurred in having to have special assembly lines for left-hand drive cars sold abroad, or right-hand cars purchased from abroad, and in accidents from drivers who intuitively turned the wrong way or pedestrians who looked the wrong way. The extra cost of foreign right-hand-drive cars may have been enjoyed, however, as a non-tariff-barrier.

Sweden shifted from the left to the right side of the road after a long drawn-out process of study and decision-making. Royal Commissions studied the question once in the 1930s, and again in 1946, both with negative decisions, a national referendum voted against change in the 1950s, and a positive decision was taken only at the end of the 1960s. The early commissions thought the costs—presumably the transitional heterogeneity of the carpark as well as the more serious necessity to discharge passengers of trams and buses on the street rather than on the sidewalk—outweighed the benefits of moderately cheaper cars and a common standard with neighbouring countries. Increasing internationalization of automotive purchases and sales and of automotive travel finally tipped the decision the other way. It is of some interest that the national referendum voted overwhelmingly against change.

In Austria, I believe, there was little pressure for change up to 1938 when, after *Anschluss*, Hitler ordered the change to be made overnight. Confusion was substantial, and doubtless accidents, but an absolute authority, interested in uniformity throughout the country, decreed that it be done without ado. The contrast between the close and drawn-out decision in Sweden, made without difficulty in a democratic society, and one put into effect without discussion suggests the limits of experience in changing standards.

The French change from the weights and measures of the *Ancien Régime* to a metric system, including among the measures money, reveals a process with something of both elements, along with a failure, the decimalization of time. The basis for the metric system was laid in the seventeenth century, and with the support of the French Academy of Science, put into effect by Talleyrand who got it through the Estates General of the French Revolution. The legislation was introduced in 1790; commissions were appointed for weights and measures on the one hand and time on the other. Both were adopted. Decimal time beginning with year one from 22 September 1794 and the 12 months of thirty days each: *Vendémiaire, Brumaire, Frimaire*, etc., weeks of 10 days was adopted partly to break down the Christian system of Sundays and holy days. It lasted only ten to twelve years. Decimal time with 10 hours of 100 minutes each per day survived far less—failing to survive for two years (Carrigan, 1968). Weights and measures needed a Revolution to effect a drastic change. The substitution of the decimal *franc germinal* for the *livre* (pound) *tournois*, divided into *sous* and *deniers* (nominally equivalent to shillings and pence), a quasi duo-decimal system that went back to the Romans was perhaps more readily put into effect in 1803 under Napoleon because of the collapse of the *assignats* in 1795.

Somewhat like the Gauge Act of 1846, however, it was one thing to order the standard changed and another to have the change accomplished. In his book *From Peasants into Frenchman* (1976), Eugen Weber points out that the French peasant was still using the old measures as late as 1870, when he began to be integrated into the rest of France by virtue of military service on the one hand and national norms laid down for education on the other. The process seems extended, but it is understandable to those who are aware that the change from the old to the new franc, decreed by President de Gaulle in 1958 at the ratio of 100 to 1, is still ignored by many French today. Children and tourists quickly began to calculate in new francs, the children learning in school, the tourists starting with *tabula rasa*. People who grew up under the old franc, however, mostly cling to 10,000 francs when foreigners would say 100.

A generation for the new franc, seventy years for the *franc germinal* of 1803 were slight as compared with the century and a half for the British to adopt a system of decimal money. Immediately after the Napoleonic wars there were pressures to join the French in adoption of the decimal system. A Royal Commission in the 1840s recommended early action. Indeed, the minting of the two shilling florin was undertaken in 1847 as the first step toward a decimal money—one tenth of a pound as compared with the half crown which was a binary one eighth of a pound. Throughout Europe in the middle of the nineteenth century country after country was falling in line with the decimalization of money, Belgium, Germany, Italy, Spain, Sweden, Switzerland, although the Swedish decision lagged behind others for a time because of the objections of clergymen. A new committee was appointed in Britain in the 1850s to rubber-stamp the decision to follow suit. It happened, however, to contain the opinionated monetarist, Lord Overstone, who objected to decimalization largely because it involved change. By adroit manoeuvring he blocked the decision which was not taken favourably until a century later when computerization somewhat increased the benefits of the change (O'Brien, 1971, Vol. 1, pp. 52–9; Vol. 3, appendices D and E).

Lord Overstone's stated objections to decimalization were based on technical grounds on the one hand, and on the distribution of costs and benefits on the other. Technically he made such points as that a system of 1000 mils, which would have been required because 100th of a pound (2.4 d) would have been too large for the smallest coin, was inferior to a system of 960 farthings (1/4 d), since 27 numbers can be divided into 960 without a remainder and only 15 into 1000. He also felt that it would have been necessary to change the normal system of counting since he found it awkward to quote a price of, say, 10 pennies for a dozen eggs. As to distribution of costs and benefits, he acknowledged that the change would benefit banking, insurance, and finance of all sorts for which reckoning, especially of percentages, would be eased, but felt that the change in money would be hard on the lower classes and the poor. While Overstone was generous in gifts to charity, it is not evident that he had an intimate knowledge of these groups. In general he opposed change. Final British action in 1951 was taken after Australia and New Zealand had adopted decimalization, and long after the change had been made in Canada and South Africa.

The United States is today engaged in the process of changing, especially linear and liquid measurements and temperatures from the British to the continental decimal standard, doing it with deliberate slowness and increasingly meeting resistance from politically conservative groups who oppose change, especially change that involves adopting foreign standards. To an amateur in such matters, it seems to have been psychologically wrong to proceed so slowly, posting temperatures in public places both in Fahrenheit and in Celsius, and distances and speeds both in kilometres and in miles. The process of change requires the public first to convert from the new to the old, and, when the new becomes sufficiently familiar, to stop converting and use just the new. If both measures are given simultaneously, the necessity to convert is eliminated, and the second stage of relying on the new scales to economize on conversion may not be reached. It may be in the short run, however, that the benefits of a common set of measures between the United States and the rest of the world are declining as neomercantilism spreads, and that the benefits appear to decline as the costs seem heavier.

V

Apart from international statistical standards which have to be changed anyway and where countries have a strong motive to agree, it is hard to think of international standards that did not start out as the public good of some particular country, usually one with high international standing because of its economic and/or military power. During World War II, the United States and the United Kingdom harmonized the pitch of the screw thread between them to make screws of the same size interchangeable. Since the economy of the United States was several times that of Britain, the most costly changes were made by the latter. The Justinian and Gregorian calendars in macro-temporal measurement were produced by Rome and adopted generally in Europe and throughout its colonies, though not by Russia or the Moslem world. Greenwich mean time became the world standard when Britain ruled the waves. As noted, decimalization emerged from France, the gold standard from Britain, and the dollar-exchange standard from the United States, the last with some political holdouts such as France. It is not a random result that international air traffic, where the benefits of a common standard of communication are high, communicates in English, except for the one expression for planes in distress, 'M'aidez', which is usually transliterated into 'Mayday'. Like a dominant corporation in a new industry producing steel shapes, left-hand drive automobiles, IBM 360 computers, the big countries 'ram it through'.

When countries are more evenly matched in size and importance, agreement on international standards for output, regulations, taxation etc. is likely to lag or to be weakened in compromise. The original Rome treaty envisaged not only abolition of tariffs on trade within the Community but also the harmonization of excise taxes, regulations and the like so that trucks and railroad cars carrying goods would not have to stop at the frontier. This freedom of movement for goods remains to be achieved. Local standards may be retained and new ones such as the requirement that cars in Sweden be equipped with windshield wipers for the headlights imposed as non-tariff barriers. In joint activities such as the European airbus, the equipment of NATO, the pooling of research in space and nuclear physics, the principle of allocating work to the low-cost source has been compromised in favour of the *juste retour* in which each country gets a share of output allocated to it according to its financial contribution. The possibility exists that the Common Market may end up like early British industry with only limited harmonization and interchangeability as the free rider or the holdout hoping to have its standard adopted, makes easy adoption of common standards impossible. Merchants were responsible for most standardization at the international level in earlier times, though some international standards were imposed by strong governments, and a few by the power of superior performance. In today's world in highly competitive national markets and in the international economy with no one country any longer leading or dominant, there is risk of market failure in the sense of failure to adopt widely accepted standards in new goods, to keep old standards up to date as improvements become possible, and especially to achieve the international public good of world standards.

NOTES

1. This paper brings together, extends and generalizes a number of previous observations on the subject (Kindleberger, 1964, pp. 149–52, 1978a, pp. 137, 228ff., 1978b, pp. 6–7, 1982, pp. 203–16). The analysis and illustrations accordingly are to a considerable extent repetitious.

REFERENCES

Beesley, M.E. and Troup, G.W., 'The Machine-Tool Industry', in: Duncan Burn (ed.), *The Structure of British Industry*, 2 vols., Cambridge: Cambridge University Press, vol. 1, pp. 359–92.

Byatt, I.C.R., 'Electrical Products', in, Aldcroft, D.H. (ed.), *The Development of British Industry and Foreign Competition, 1875–1914*, London: George Allen & Unwin, pp. 238–73.

Carlson, Sune, 'Company Policies for International Expansion: The Swedish Experience', in, Agmon, Tamir and Kindleberger, C.P. (eds), *Multinationals from Small Countries* Cambridge, Mass.: MIT Press, pp. 49–71.

Carrigan, Jr., R.A., 'Decimal Time', *American Scientist*, Vol. 66 (1978), no. 3, May–June, pp. 305–13.

Chandler, Alfred D. *Strategy and Structure: Chapters in the History of Industrial Enterprise*, Cambridge, Mass.: Harvard University Press, 1962.

de Roover, Raymond, *The Rise and Fall of the Medici Bank*, New York: W.W. Norton, 1966.

Drèze, Jacques, 'Quelques réflexions sereines sur l'adaptation de l'industrie belge au Marché Commun', *Comptes rendus des Travaux de la Société Royale d'Economie Politique de Belgique*, no. 275, 1960.

Faber, Harald, *Co-operation in Danish Agriculture*, 2nd ed., London: Longmans Green, 1931.

Friedman, Milton, 'The Case for Flexible Exchange Rates', in, Friedman, M.

Essays in Positive Economics, Chicago: University of Chicago Press, 1953, pp. 157–203.

Hayek, F.A., *Choice in Currency: A Way to Stop Inflation*, London: Institute of Economic Affairs, Occasional Paper no. 48, 1977.

Hohenberg, Paul M., *Chemicals in Western Europe, 1850–1914: An Economic Study of Technical Change*, Chicago: Rand McNally, 1967.

Kaldor, Nicholas, 'The Economic Aspects of Advertizing', *Review of Economic Studies*, vol. 28 (1951), pp. 1–27.

Kindleberger, C.P., *Economic Growth in France and Britain, 1851–1950*, Cambridge, Mass.: Harvard University Press, 1964.

———, *Economic Response: Comparative Studies in Trade, Finance and Growth*, Cambridge, Mass.: Harvard University Press, 1978a.

———, 'Government and International Trade', Princeton, NJ: Essays in International Finance, no. 129, 1978b.

———, *International Money*, London: George Allen & Unwin, 1981.

———, 'International Monetary Reform in the Nineteenth Century', in, Cooper, R.N. *et al. International Monetary System under Flexible Exchange Rates*, Lexington, Mass.: Ballinger, 1982.

Landes, David S., *Bankers and Pashas*, Cambridge, Mass.: Harvard University Press, 1958.

———, 'Technological Change and the Development of Western Europe, 1750–1914', in, *The Cambridge Economic History of Europe*, VI. Vol. 1, Cambridge: Cambridge University Press, 1965, pp. 274–601.

Lindblom, Charles E., *Politics and Markets: The World's Political–Economic System*, New York: Basic Books, 1977.

Marlowe, John (pseudonym), *Spoiling the Egyptians*, London: Deutsch, 1974.

McKay, John P., *Tramways and Trolleys: The Rise of Urban Mass Transport in Europe*, Princeton, NJ: Princeton University Press, 1976.

O'Brien, D.P. (ed.), *The Correspondence of Lord Overstone*, 3 vols., Cambridge: Cambridge University Press, 1971.

Origo, Iris, *The Merchant of Prato*, New York: Knopf, 1957.

Parkhouse, S.E., 'Railway Freight Rolling Stock', *Journal of the Institute of Transort*, vol. 24 (1951), pp. 211–18, 242.

Plummer, Alfred, *New British Industries in the Twentieth Century*, London: Pitman, 1937.

Robson, R., *The Cotton Industry in Britain*, London: Macmillan, 1957.

Samuelson, Paul A., 'The Pure Theory of Public Expenditure', *The Review of Economics and Statistics*, vol. 36 (1954), pp. 387–9, reproduced in *The Collected Scientific Papers of Paul A. Samuelson*, Vol. 2, Cambridge, Mass.: The MIT Press, 1966, pp. 1223–5.

Saul, S.B., 'The Engineering Industry', in, Aldcroft, D.H. (ed.), *The Development of British Industry and Foreign Competition, 1875–1914*, London: George Allen & Unwin, 1968.

Smith, Adam, *An Inquiry into the Nature and Causes of the Wealth of Nations*, 1776 (Cannan ed.), New York: Modern Library, 1937.

Udovitch, Abraham, L., 'Bankers without Banks: Commerce, Banking and Society in the Islamic World of the Middle Ages', Center for Medieval and Renaissance Studies: *The Dawn of Modern Banking*, New Haven: Yale University Press, 1979, pp. 255–74.

Van Dillen, J.G. (ed.), *History of the Principal Public Banks*, The Hague: Martinus Nijhoff, 1934.

Vaubel, Roland, 'Free Currency Competition', *Weltwirtschaftliches Archiv*, vol. 113 (1977), pp. 435–59.

Vernon, Raymond, *Metropolis, 1985*, Cambridge, Mass.: Harvard University Press, 1960.

Vilar, Pierre, *A History of Gold and Money, 1450–1920*, London: NLB, 1976 (Spanish original 1969).

Weber, Eugen, *From Peasants into Frenchmen*, Stanford: Stanford University Press, 1976.

Wilson, R.G., *Gentlemen Merchants: The Merchant Community of Leeds, 1700–1830*, Manchester: Manchester University Press, 1971.

Winston, Gordon, *The Timing of Economic Activities*, New York: Cambridge University Press, 1982.

14 Dominance and Leadership in the International Economy

EXPLOITATION, PUBLIC GOODS, AND FREE RIDES*

In 1960, before the balance-of-payments troubles of the fall of that year, I wrote an article on 'The End of the Dominant Role of the United States and the Future of World Economic Policy'. This was a response to a request from an American Commission on National Policy, if I recall its name, appointed by President Eisenhower and headed by John J. McCloy, to explore future courses of actions. (The exercise is an ancient one in American public life, undertaken by Francis A. Walker in the 1880s and by Wesley C. Mitchell for Herbert Hoover in the 1920s, as well as by Nelson Rockefeller, when he was contesting the Republican candidacy for the presidency in 1968.) My article was written hurriedly, in a couple of evenings in a hotel in Paris, and was not welcomed in the United States. It saw the light of day only in the French version (Kindleberger, 1961). It concluded, rightly I still think, that the United Stats could no longer dictate to other countries what was needed to be done in the field of economic foreign policy; it was obliged at that time to ask, not tell them. Dominance was giving way to leadership.

Dominance was a concept introduced into economic discussion, especially French economic discussion, by François Perroux, professor of economics at the *Collège de France* and director of the *Institut Scientifique d'Economie Appliquée*. One country, firm or person dominated another when the other had to take account of what the first entity did, but the first could ignore the second. It was a peculiarly French idea, with strong overtones of resentment at alleged domination by the United States in fields of foreign exchange, trade policy, multinational enterprise and the like.

---

* This chapter originally appeared in *Hommage à François Perroux* (Presses Universitaires de Grenoble, 1978), and republished, slightly revised, in *International Studies Quarterly*, vol. 25, no. 2, June 1981, pp. 242–54.

Leadership may be thought of at first blush as persuading others to follow a given course of action which might not be in the follower's short-run interest if it were truly independent. As will be suggested below, it has strong elements of both arm-twisting and bribery. Without it, however, there may be an inadequate amount of public goods produced. This last is a relatively new concept in economics of great salience for political science.

A public good is one the consumption of which by an individual, household, or firm does not reduce the amount available for other potential consumers. The classical example of the pure public good is the lighthouse. By no means are all public goods pure, and one can conjure up complex mixed cases. Radiodirectional signals for navigation require the consumer to have a radio receiver: a private good to receive a public benefit. Roads can be so congested that the last car on it converts it from a public good to a public bad. General education is a mixture of public and private good. It increases the productivity and enjoyment of the individual, his capacities for citizenship, and his responsiveness to economic stimuli from others. The theory of clubs invokes goods which are consumable without being exhausted by a collectivity, but exclude others outside the group. One could go on. For present purposes, however, it is enough to note that within a single country, many public goods are provided by the government through a budget, most private goods by the market.

In the theory of representative democracy, Downs (1957), Breton (1974), Olson (1965), Buchanan (1965) and others in economics, and Froelich *et al.* (1971) in political science suggest that public goods are underproduced relative to private goods because of the fallacy of composition, or what some call the 'free rider'. The voter will get it anyhow; why then should one work and lobby, undertaking transactions costs which are expensive, if in any event one is going to get a full share? When no one pushes to vote expenditure on a public good, it may not be produced at all. Thus, vested interests whose benefits are sufficient to warrant exertion get a disproportionate share of the public goods they are interested in. This accords with the commonplace view that governments take better care of producers than of consumers and accounts for the success of the military–industrial complex and the automobile–gasoline–highway lobby in having government spend money on public goods congruent with their interests. There need not be corruption. Choice among competing public goods is expensive, and the principle of the free ride means that those with only limited benefits from public goods do not get their full share. Public goods are underproduced. Note that this is quite different from the Galbraith view that private goods are overproduced because of the power of advertizing. It assumes that producer and consumer are both rational. Until Froelich *et al.* produced *Political Leadership and Collective Goods*, this was the position. The public good was a useful concept for research. The economic historian Jonathan Pincus (1977, 1972) applied the theory of public goods to tariff formation, proving through multiple regression that interests in the United States which were concentrated did better, that is, received higher tariffs, in the tariff of 1824, than those which were widely spread. 'A commodity is known by the senators it keeps', as the saying goes. It paid, in 1824, to be concentrated, owning a large piece of a few senators, rather than a small portion of many. And in an interesting article, Koichi Hamada (1977) calls monetary integration a public good which is underproduced because its benefits are too widely spread.

This theory of representative democracy, however, needed a place for leadership. Froelich *et al.* provided an economic theory of leadership to go with it. Leaders work for something called 'leadership surplus'. They compete with other potential leaders for ascendancy, and once in office maximize their surplus or profit by providing collective goods against taxes, donations or purchases promised in their election process. A leader's personality may play a role, as he or she derives pleasure or utility simply by being head of the administrative office. In this instance, costs to the leader of exertion are matched by rewards of a non-pecuniary nature. Froelich *et al.* allow little room in their theories for the hereditary leader, or for leadership responsibilities, unless the last can be regarded as a negative surplus which is minimized through fulfilment of explicit or implicit commitments.

Leaders of course are subject to moral decay, as Lord Acton noted in saying, 'Power corrupts, and absolute power corrupts absolutely'. Responsibility can degenerate into exploitation. Exploitation has been defined, unsatisfactorily in my judgment, as a position in which a country, firm, individual, and the like gets more income or product than the lowest possible amount it would be willing to accept in the circumstances (Penrose, 1959). This implies a close to nonsense position in which two parties to a transaction can each exploit the other when both receive a higher price than the reserve price or minimum return at which it would be willing to operate. Johan Galtung, the Norwegian sociologist, has defined exploitation as dependence,[1] which also strikes me as bizarre.

Interdependent entities—husband and wife, two countries trading with another, professor and student—are mutually exploiting each other (in a private aside, Martin Bronfenbrenner believes such mutual exploitation occurs frequently. Take a married couple: he treats her as a servant, and she treats him as a meal ticket). The essence of exploitation is that one party exerts power to produce a result more favourable to it than if that power had not been exerted. The typical illustration is a monopolist or monopsonist (monopoly buyer), which restricts his or her sales (purchases) to force buyer (seller) to pay a higher (accept a lower) price than would obtain in a perfectly competitive market in which all sellers and buyers were without power to affect the price.

When there are big rents, as economists call them, or a surplus that vastly exceeds what is necessary to get the work done, there is a strong possibility that the two sides to a transaction will each see itself as exploited when it may be only trying to provide leadership. The operation is regarded as a zero-sum game whereas most economists (and political scientists?) would regard it as a non-zero sum game from which both parties can benefit. Take the multinational corporation that discovers oil in a poor country. Is it leading or exploiting? The answers turns on the counterfactual, or what would have happened in other circumstances. And when both parties choose different counterfactuals, the room for disagreement is enormous. The corporation compares the existing situation with that before its discovery of oil, the country with circumstances in which one of its own citizens had discovered the oil and furnished the necessary technology to develop it. The company resents any and all taxes, until its counterfactual shifts to nationalization as a possibility. The country resents the company's profits. In these circumstances, extramarket power is likely to be applied by the country, whether as leadership, or exploitation of the company is difficult to determine.

Leadership can degenerate into exploitation. It can also degenerate into confusion and anomie. Pincus believes that a public goods theory of tariff-making, as exemplified in the tariff of 1824, is akin to the view of Schattschneider (1935) who wrote on the Hawley–Smoot tariff revision of 1930. That is not my interpretation. I regard Schattschneider as concluding that the Hawley–Smoot tariff was the result of Hoover's abdication of his responsibilities, of failure to lead. There were tariffs for every industry, and rates were fixed by lobbyists after they had sent the congressmen from the committee room.

For Adam Smith, within an economy public goods consisted of defence, law and order, and a minimum number of roads and bridges. To this list, John Stuart Mill added tranquility. Other economists noted that the government must provide the public goods of money, to the extent that the economy did not rest on the pure gold standard without banking (which could be said to be privately produced) and rules for the conduct of enterprise. With Keynes, the list of public goods was enlarged to include stability of national income, sought through fiscal as well as monetary policy. Today we recognize other public goods, such as control over private negative externalities, as in pollution.

The analysis of public and private goods is also applicable to the international economy. For private goods, read national benefits, and for public, cosmopolitan goods, for the maintenance of the world economy. The question is how to distinguish domination and exploitation from responsibility in the provision of cosmopolitan goods in the world economy, and whether there are not occasions when the world suffers from the underproduction of the public good of stability, not because of greedy vested interests and domination or exploitation, but because of the principle of the free rider.

This was the theme of my book on the world depression of the 1930s (Kindleberger 1973). I argued that for the world economy to be stable, it needs a stabilizer, some country that would undertake to provide a market for distress goods, a steady if not countercyclical flow of capital, and a rediscount mechanism for providing liquidity when the monetary system is frozen in panic. Today I would add that the world leadership must also manage, in some degree, the structure of foreign-exchange rates and provide a degree of coordination of domestic monetary policies.

Britain, with frequent assistance from France, furnished coherence to the world economy along these lines during the nineteenth century and through the *belle époque*. The United States did so from 1945 (or perhaps 1936) to 1968 (or 1963 or 1971). From 1919 to 1939, Britain could not, and the United States would not, act in the capacity of world leader. I find great difficulty in accepting the views of Williams, Kolko, and other revisionists who maintain that the United States sought world dominance as early as World War I, or 1898. The beginnings of world power can be seen in the spread of New York finance abroad, to be sure, but in spite of Wilson, the leading political figures such as Hughes, Lodge, Harding, Coolidge, Hoover, and the first-term Roosevelt were isolationists, ready to intrude on the world scene only briefly and wanting no part of Europe's or Asia's problems.

There is a legitimate debate, perhaps, between French and American positions, whether the United States sought domination or was only trying to provide the public good of world stability in the period after World War II. François Perroux suggested it was also exploitation. At least through the period of the Marshall Plan, the American case that its purpose was leadership, even though domination was inadvertently involved, is not *prima facie* wrong. But whatever elements of domination were intended, I believed and believe that they had run out by 1960.

Part of the world's economic problem today is that the United States has resigned (or been discharged) as leader of the world economy, and there is no candidate willing and acceptable to take its place. We have not only the end to the domination role which I detected in 1960, but also faint signs of the end of United States leadership. The leadership persists perhaps in Middle East peace-keeping. It is hard to detect in matters of trade, aid, capital movements, monetary reform, and the like.

How should one distinguish exploitation from leadership? The issue is complex, and the answer not obvious. Management of the gold-exchange standard by Britain from 1870 to 1913 and by the United States from 1945 to 1971 can be viewed as provision of either the public good of international money, or the private good for itself of seignorage, which is the profit that comes to the seigneur or sovereign power, from the issuance of money. Of course it can be both. Public goods are sometimes competitive with private goods—as when there is a choice between taxing to build a lighthouse or a public park, and not taxing—and sometimes complementary: maintenance of *Pax Britannica* or *Pax Americana* provides peace for the world as well as the status quo for the provider. Or Prussia accepting a disproportionately small share of the revenues of *Zollverein* as against the smaller states and principalities it seduces into joining.

This is a leadership trait according to Olson and Zeckhauser (1966), who observe that the leader of the alliance pays more than a pro rata share of the general benefits of the alliance because of the free rider principle. In return for its side-payment to Bavaria, Wurtenberg, Baden, and other small states, Prussia earned a leadership surplus in prestige and power from forging Imperial Germany. The difficulties of the European Economic Community may be traceable to lack of a leadership willing to bear the burdens of the group, or perhaps to the fact that the long-time leader, France, was interested in the private national goods of *gloire*, trade benefits for the *Communauté*, as well as the cosmopolitan good of the Community.

But my concern is with those instances where the abundance of free riders means that the public good is underproduced, and that there is neither domination nor self-abnegation in the interest of responsibility.

Take first the position of small countries. In international economics, we have the so-called 'small-country assumption', which means that a country cannot affect its terms of trade (the prices at which it buys its imports and sells its exports), and if capital is mobile, the outside world determines its money supply and its interest rate. Small countries have no economic power. At the same time they have no responsibility for the economic system, nor any necessity to exert leadership. They seem to pose no problems for the international economy, and in a number of instances—Sweden, Canada, New Zealand, and so on—they can usually serve as examples through generous aid, or the provision of troops to the United Nations, and the like. But it is of some interest that on two occasions—in 1931 and again in 1971—it was the small countries, more or less simultaneously and in pursuit of their private interest, that pushed Britain first, and then the United States, off the gold standard.

It may be appropriate to regard these actions as *causa proxima*, rather than *causa causans* which was one of the number of *causae remotae*. When actions of small countries are not independent but stimulated by the same forces as others, and either concerted or more usually stimulated by what the Supreme Court calls 'conscious parallel action', the small become powerful willy-nilly, for good or ill for the system.

Parenthetically, I have a strong bias against conspiracy theories of history. I do not believe in the notion that the extreme left, the extreme right, the power elite, the establishment, oil companies, professoriat, military–industrial complex, and so on, can be regarded as single decision-making units with detailed programmes for imposing their will on the unsuspecting world. We know from Speer's diaries how chaotic were the governmental processes under the Nazis. The 'true believer' finds or suspects omniscient, omnipotent, and omnipresent opposition everywhere.[2]

The problem of middle-sized countries is a delicate one, as I have indicated in a paper on France's conversions of dollars into gold in 1931 and again in 1965 (Kindleberger, 1972). Big enough to do damage to the system, but not substantial enough to stabilize it, the question is whether middle-sized countries should run a large risk of private hurt in the interest of public stability, or seek to protect themselves at the expense of the system. I have a British friend who becomes indignant when he hears the rats criticized for leaving the sinking ship. 'What,' he asks, 'do they want the rats to do? Stay on the bridge with the captain and salute?'

Countries powerful enough to take leadership responsibility may discharge it, may become corrupted into taking dominant advantage of it, may do the one and be perceived as doing the other, or may abdicate responsibility. It is also possible, as already indicated, that they will exercise leadership and do well out of it. But the system is essentially unstable, subject to entropy. Even if it is not perceived as domination, leadership is not regarded as legitimate. 'What has he done for me lately?' is the apposite tag. And the country with, let us say, rising imports as it struggles to keep markets open, an overvalued exchange rate as it accepts the devaluations of others, an undue share of the burdens of NATO or of foreign aid, begins to concern itself with the free rides of others and talk of more equitable burden-sharing.

The need for a leader to assume the burden is nowhere better illustrated than in the reparations/war-debts/commercial-debts issue of the 1920s and 1930s. Britain's readiness to cancel reparations insofar as the United States relieved it of war debts is understandable in economic terms, as its war debts receivable and share of reparations receipts would just about equal war debts payable; but it could hardly gratify the United States, which had already given up a share of reparations and would lose on balance, or France, which was to be a net recipient of reparations over war debts payable to Britain and the United States. In addition, to keep commercial debts alive when it had few involved a loss for France and a benefit for Britain and the United States.

Lend–lease or the Marshall Plan were gestures more appropriate to leading. They are difficult to sustain over long years. The leader becomes corrupt, or is perceived as such; the leader becomes tired of free rides, or believes he or she is being bankrupted by excessive burdens, or both. The economic limit to the burden a country can sustain is of course much greater than the political limit, as is evident when one contemplates that the United States used half its income for war. The statement made frequently, for example, by Senator Robert Taft, that 'my country could not afford' something—say the Marshall Plan—is to be translated into a more accurate form: 'I do not want, or I believe voters in the United States do not want, to reduce the United States' standard of living by enough to carry a particular burden.'

A system of world economy based on leadership is thus unstable over time in much the same way that a *Pax Britannica*, *Pax Americana*, balance-of-power system, or oligopoly is unstable. The threat may come from the outside in the presence of a thrusting aggressive competitor anxious for the prestige, and possibly the real income, of the dominant economy. Prussia in the second half of the nineteenth century is the prime example, but one could take England with its hatred of the Netherlands in the seventeenth century, or the France of Napoleon as examples. The leader can be overthrown by the refusal of followers to submit to what they have come to think of as exploitation.

But change can also come from within. The leader grows weary under burdens which grow as more and more free riders seek more luxurious free rides. The means of stabilizing the system are self-evident.

1. Rely on long-run self-interest of the participants along the lines of

Kant's Categorical Imperative, expecting them to renounce free riding and to act in ways that can be generalized to all participants. This is a counsel of perfection.

2. Bind the members of the international community to rules of conduct, to which they agree, and which will restrain each member from free riding, and allocate burdens equitably, as a matter of international legal commitment. Not only will countries chisel on the commitments, but they will free ride the application of sanctions, as experience under the League of Nations and the United Nations amply demonstrated.

3. Form a world government.

I choose not to discuss item 3, which sets limits to free rides within national states, on the ground that its idealistic and visionary character is self-evident. Free riding or escape from what was believed to be excessive burdens by a regional unit might have to take the form of secession, but there seems no doubt that in the present state of inadequate sense of world social and political cohesion, it would do so.

For as far ahead as today's social scientists can see, I think it is necessary to organize the international community—as related to policy and economy alike—on the basis of leadership. Entropy is inevitable. After breakdown, there follows a long, drawn-out, and dangerous process of establishing a new basis of legitimacy, under a new leader. Self-consciousness in the role does not appear to be a help, and will make many candidates, as today in the economic field (Germany, Japan and Switzerland), hesitant and shy. But leadership to provide the public good of stability, properly regarded, misunderstood as exploitation, or sniped at by free riders, seems a poor system, but like democracy, honesty, and stable marriages, is better than the available alternatives.

I should perhaps add that I have not discussed the possibilities of a compromise among these systems, where two or more countries take on the task of providing leadership together, thus adding to legitimacy, sharing the burdens, and reducing the danger that leadership is regarded cynically as a cloak for domination and exploitation. In 1931, the suggestion was widespread that France and the United States together make a big loan to Germany. The French insisted on political conditions, the United States was unwilling to throw good money after bad, although that is the crux of rediscounting in a crisis.

After World War II, Ernest Bevin suggested to William L. Clayton and Lewis W. Douglas that the 'special relationship' be reinstituted by the United States undertaking a preliminary, antecedent Marshall Plan for the United Kingdom, following which both countries would undertake the economic recovery of the continent. The idea was never seriously considered, and Britain's decision in 1962 to apply for membership in the Common Market put 'paid' to the special relationship.

For a time it looked as though the European Community itself would emerge as an economic and political entity capable of rivaling the United States for world economic leadership (outside the Socialist blocs), perhaps succeeding to first place as the United States faltered. In the event, domestic economic and political concerns in France, Britain and Italy and the *Ost-bloc* policy of Germany have turned attention from world to national and regional concerns, and there appears to be no readiness in the Community to take on wider responsibilities.

A fourth idea is for the United States, Germany, and Japan to agree to a simple set of rules in the monetary field to give coherence to their policies and world stability (McKinnon, 1974). The idea is politically unattractive since it appears as an attack on the European Community—especially against France, on the one hand, and could be regarded as a division of the world into regional blocs on the other. In addition, there is no Japanese appetite for world responsibility.

I conclude that the danger we face is not too much power in the international economy, but too little, not an excess of domination, but a superfluity of would-be free riders, unwilling to mind the store, and waiting for a storekeeper to appear. No place, to quote President Truman, for the buck to stop. I say this without implication that there is any threat to the world economic system from outside. But without a stabilizer, the system in my judgment is unstable. It is perhaps too strong to say that a world of Denmarks is as unstable as a world of Prussias, but it poses the issue.

NOTES

1. At a seminar at the Institut des Hautes Etudes Internationales, March 1971.
2. Barnet and Muller (1975) hint darkly that the energy crisis was contrived by the oil companies to raise their profits, saying, 'The extent to which the crisis was a result of conspiracy may not be known until historians are given access to the oil companies' equivalent of the Pentagon Papers.' The correct position, in my judgment, is set out in Goodsell (1974, p. 85): 'Our evidence suggests that rather than being in conspiratorial alliance with oligarchic elites the (foreign) businessmen share with them a certain number of goals and values.' Conspiracy is, of course, possible, but I believe that most times its appearance is the result of like-minded people, similarly placed, responding in the same way to the same stimulus.

REFERENCES

Barnet, R. and Muller, R. (1975) *Global Reach: The Power of the Multinational Corporation*. New York: Simon & Schuster.
Breton, A. (1974) *Economic Theory of Representative Government*. New edition. Chicago: AVC.
Buchanan, J.M. (1965) 'An Economic Theory of Clubs.' *Econometrica* 32 (February): pp. 1–14.
Downs, A. (1957) *An Economic Theory of Democracy*. New York: Harper & Row.
Froelich, N., Oppenheimer, J.A. and Young, J. (1971) *Political Leadership and Collective Goods*. Princeton, NJ: Princeton University Press.
Goodsell, C.T. (1974) *American Corporation and Peruvian Politics*. Cambridge, MA: Harvard Univ. Press.
Hamada, K. (1977) 'On the Political Economy of Monetary Integration: a Public Economics Approach', in R.Z. Aliber (ed.) *The Political Economy of Monetary Reform*. New York: Allanheld, Osman.
Kindleberger, C. (1973) *The World in Depression, 1929–1939*. Berkeley: University of California Press.
—— (1972) 'The International Monetary Politics of Near-great Power: Two French Episodes, 1926–1936 and 1960–1970.' *Economic Notes* (Monte dei Paschi di Siena) 1, 2–3: pp. 30–41.
—— (1961) 'La fin du rôle dominant des Etats-Unis et l'avenir d'une politique économique mondiale.' *Cahiers de l'Institut de Science Economique Appliqée*, Série P, 5 (May): pp. 91–105.
McKinnon, R.I. (1974) *A new Tripartite Monetary Agreement or a Limping Dollar Standard?* Essays in International Finance 106. Princeton, NJ: International Finance Section, Princeton University Press.
Olson, M., Jr. (1965) *The Logic of Collective Action: Public Goods and Theory of Groups*. Harvard Economic Studies 124. Cambridge, MA: Harvard University Press.
—— and Zeckhauser, R. (1966) 'An economic theory of alliances'. *Review of Economics and Statistics* 42 (August): pp. 266–79.
Penrose, E.T. (1959) 'Profit sharing between producing countries and oil companies in the Middle East'. *Economic Journal* 69 (June): pp. 248–52.
Pincus, J.J. (1977) *Pressure Groups and Politics in Antebellum Tariffs*. New York: Columbia University Press.
—— (1972) 'A positive theory of tariff information applied to nineteenth century United States' Ph.D. dissertation, Stanford University.
Schattschneider, E.E. (1935) *Politics, Pressures and Tariffs: A Study of Free Private Enterprise in Pressure Politics as Shown by the 1929–30 Revision of the Tariff*. New York: Prentice-Hall.

15 Economic Responsibility*

'Economic Responsibility' might be taken to be the extension of my collected essays in economic history, entitled *Economic Response*. Actually my interest is different. I propose to pursue a theme initially addressed in the Graham lecture at Princeton in 1977, and extended last year at the University of Rochester in the Gilbert lecture on 'International Public Goods without International Government'. The question I propose we think about is the extent to which under our mixed capitalist-government-intervention systems, the individual person, household, or firm is responsible for the system beyond the duty of conforming to explicit rules. Do we, that is, have an economic responsibility for the public as well as for our personal private welfare? I propose to discuss the issue first at the level of a national economy of households, firms and government, and then to apply the analysis to the world.

Let me start at the beginning with Adam Smith and his 'obvious and simple system of natural liberty'. Once this has been established, you remember

Every man, as long as he does not violate the laws of justice, is left free to pursue his own interest in his own way . . . The sovereign is completely discharged from a duty . . . of superintending the industry of private people, and of directing it towards the employments most suitable to the interests of the society. According to the system of natural liberty, the sovereign has only three duties to attend . . . first, the duty of protecting the society from the violence and invasion of other independent societies; secondly, the duty of protecting, as far as possible, every member of the society from the injustice or oppression of every other member of it, or the duty of establishing an exact administration of justice; and thirdly, the duty of erecting and maintaining certain public works and certain public institutions, which it can never be for

* The Second Fred Hirsch Memorial Lecture, Warwick University, 6 March 1980, published in an abridged form in *Lloyds Bank Review*, October 1980, pp. 1–11.

the interest of any individual, or small numbers of individuals, to erect and
maintain; because the profit could never repay the expense to any individual
or small numbers of individuals, though it may frequently do much more than
repay it to a great society.
(Book IV, Chapter IX)

Dr. Smith himself, of course, had reservations. In discussing corporations, he observed that private interests were too strong to allow the
restoration of freedom of trade in Great Britain, stating that to expect
it was as absurd as to expect an 'Oceana or Utopia should ever be
established in it' (Book IV, Chapter II). He had some harsh words
for the 'mean rapacity, the monopolizing spirit of merchants and
manufacturers, who neither are, nor ought to be the rulers of mankind';
and for the 'sneaking arts of underling tradesmen' who employ chiefly
their own customers, as opposed to 'a great trader' who purchases
goods only where they are cheapest and best. Implicit in these and
similar passages is the admission that 'natural liberty' may at least on
occasion lead the economy astray.

Over two hundred years after *The Wealth of Nations* we still cling
fairly generally to Smith's conclusions about the beneficent outcome
of the market, although the analysis has been qualified and broadened
in various ways. The theory of public goods implicit in his 'certain
public works and certain public institutions which it can never be for
the interest of any individual or small number of individuals to erect',
has been extended from magistracy or law and order, national defence,
and roads and bridges to income distribution, where the market may
yield a result unsatisfactory from the viewpoint of welfare, and to
stabilization, where the fallacy of composition, of which more presently,
means that individual households and firms, maximizing their private
interest, may harm the general good. Moreover between the private
goods of individuals and firms, and the public goods produced by the
sovereign as an act of duty, there is room for collective goods, sought
by aggregations of individuals or firms to advance the welfare of the
particular group.

Smith's insight that it would not pay individuals or small groups of
individuals to erect and maintain certain works or institutions has been
generalized into the 'free rider', who lacks adequate incentive to
contribute or work for the production of public goods. Private and
collective goods are produced because their benefits outweigh their
costs to the producers; public goods are forthcoming because the
sovereign fulfils his duty. In democracies, political scientists warn us,
they may well be underproduced because of the free rider. Public
goods are available for all to enjoy whether they bear an appropriate
share of the transactions costs necessary to their production or not.

The individual or firm maximizing its own welfare will hold back from carrying its share of the cost, unless it is forced to do so through the police powers of the state. If there are enough free riders, the bus never gets out of the garage.

Note that this theory holds that public goods are underproduced in democracy, or in monarchies where the sovereign is derelict in his duty, not for the reason Galbraith holds, that private goods are advertized and a gullible public buys too many of them. The public is rational and maximizing, rather than made up of sheeplike consumers who do not know their own interest. But the fallacy of composition brings it about that the whole may differ from the sum of its parts. Each free rider is rational and a maximizer; in the aggregate they fail to produce the public goods needed by the system.

The fallacy of composition was first borne in on me in the first edition of Samuelson's *Economics, An Introductory Analysis*, and in particular his treatment of the paradox of thrift. Thrift is good for the individual and the household—at least in a period of stable prices. But when everyone tries to save more, the economy may save less as it goes into recession and incomes fall. The problem is more general. Individuals pursuing their private and collective interests may interfere with one another. This is especially the case for collective goods, where an increase in monopoly profit reduces consumers' surplus and total consumption, and in free riding, where the individual conserving his energy for his own purposes inhibits the production of necessary public goods.

The Chicago school of sociological economics is using economic reasoning to illuminate a number of problems that were formerly dealt with by sociology or political science, for example, education, procreation, crime, voting in democracy. Rational, maximizing behaviour in this approach views, say the law in a detached fashion. One obeys the law if the mean of the probability distribution of being caught times the likely penalty of being convicted is greater than the benefit from ignoring the law. Or one departs from a short-run profitable action with untoward public consequences only if it should happen that the feedback of those consequences in the long-run is negative, and has a present discounted value, at some appropriate rate of interest, that is greater than the short-run profit that must be forgone. Government is provided by politicians who can earn higher returns in this fashion than by work in private industry, or by 'leaders' who maximize a different argument in their objective function than income or wealth, perhaps *gloire*, immortality, lust for power, and similar non-economic drives.

I find the Chicago school altogether unpersuasive. As a counterexample to the theorem that profit maximization is all, let me suggest voting. Voting has positive transactions costs: one must take time and go to the polls. Moreover, the benefit of voting for the individual is derisory. Virtually no issues of consequence are decided by one vote. Accordingly, the costs to the single person outweigh the benefits and no rational person will take the trouble to vote. It is true that many people don't vote, and some nations, such as Australia, make voting compulsory in order to overcome the free rider. At times and places, votes will be bought as part of a collective good. For the most part, however, and within limits, people vote, and do so as a duty, as part of their political responsibility. What is more, while there are venal politicians in democracy, and in monarchies as well, many persons present themselves for elective office as a chance to serve the public.

My thesis is that economic, like political responsibility, takes two forms, one passive, obeying the law and acting in ways that can be generalized, to uphold the Categorical Imperative of Immanuel Kant and defeat the fallacy of composition; and an active form of positive leadership. Both are present in varying degrees and at various times in national economies and the world economy. An adequate supply of both is necessary if the economy is going to function well.

Before I pursue the argument, I wish to place on the record an admission of a strong prejudice in favour of market solutions to the greatest feasible extent. When it is working effectively, the market is a beautiful device for the decentralization of decision-making. Moreover, the analysis that underlies the defence of the market is highly useful as a pregnant hypothesis, to use Karl Popper's expression, serving to illuminate many problems in which behaviour can be analyzed as if (*als ob*) man responded in a rational way to income-maximizing motives. The presumption in favour of freedom for markets from regulation or intervention is perhaps weak, merely that the burden rests on people who oppose it to prove that they have a superior device for allocating factors of production to activities and the resultant outputs to end uses. The arguments in favour of the market are not conclusive, but merely that experience shows that, like marriage, honesty, democracy, old age and a few other tried and true institutions, it, while far from perfect, is better than the available alternatives.

The clash between the private market and government may perhaps be illustrated by the homely illustration of litter. The conduct may be prohibited by government, but the difficulties of enforcement are such that the chances of getting caught at, say, throwing a beer can from an automobile as adolescents in my country spend much of their time doing, mean that it is more economical for youth to defenestrate the empty container than to bring it home to the trash can (English translation, dustbin). Enlightened self-interest as a solution to the problem seems excluded, since one polluter or non-polluter in a beer can world would make so little difference—have such an exiguous feedback—that abstinence for the individual beer can ejector has no payoff. The state can require retailers to demand a deposit on beer containers which will be returned to the purchaser when the container is returned. This provides an economic incentive to withhold from littering. The difficulty here is that the collective interests of container-manufacturers, bottlers, and retail establishments dominate the public interest of the conservationists who find a countryside strewn with beer cans offensive. In the world of collective goods vs. public goods with free riders, the collective goods usually win, although container deposit laws have been passed in many states. The state can spend tax money to pick up beer cans along the highways and streets, and most do, albeit infrequently. A fifth means is education and peer-group pressure to instil the view that littering the highway is irresponsible behaviour.

I have deliberately chosen an unimportant issue, although it is one on which, living as I do in the country, I feel strongly. The essential point is that while self-interest within a framework of government regulation provides a useful first approximation to a description of the economic system, and even a working hypothesis for the solution of many economic problems, more is needed, and in particular a certain amount of self-restraint in some areas, voluntary compliance when enforcement cannot take us all the way in others, and active economic responsibility on behalf of the system as well.

Let me take the more serious problem of income tax. I am no tax expert, but it is clear that income tax in the United States, to the extent that it works well, relies on voluntary compliance. The Internal Revenue Service is completely inadequate to police the millions of tax returns, even with the help of social-security numbers and computers. Enforcement through audit or prosecution takes place from time to time, but on a scale so limited that there is strong incentive, at least for certain types of income, to fail to report it on cost–benefit grounds, the benefit of the tax saving being greater than the present discounted value of the chance of being caught times the penalty. There are indications that the tax system is breaking down in the United States, with a large black market in labour and goods, not to mention a white market in barter than seems to exist outside profit-and-loss statements in which income subject to taxation can be calculated. IRS lawyers work continuously to close old loopholes, while collective interests lobby to protect the old and create new.

So widespread have these collective interests become, with deductions from taxable income for interest payments, dependents, college tuition, medical expenses, old age, blindness, pensions, charitable contributions, taxes paid to other jurisdictions, expenditure for home insulation up to a limit, etc. that Joseph Pechman of the Brookings Institution has suggested that the slate be wiped clean of existing regulations and started again, taxing all income with no deductions, and reduced rates. The chances of such reform seem limited, given the fallacy of composition and the determination with which various groups protect their particular deduction, but history has at least two examples of regulation becoming so complex that it was no longer administrable and had to be abandoned. I refer to the Navigation Acts in Britain, repealed in 1847 when it was said that only three men in the Kingdom understood them in all their complexity, and the system of *Gewerbefoederung* or promotion of industry, with overlapping patents, privileges, concessions, monopolies, restrictions, prohibitions at the same time in Baden, which was swept away and replaced by *Gewerbefreiheit* or freedom of occupation. Collapsing voluntary compliance may be heading the income tax in the United States for disaster, such has overtaken those in France, Italy, Colombia, and many other countries, because it is cumulative. When groups interact, it is a mistake for one to act in the general interest if others do not. The problem is posed by game theory, or by the prisoner's dilemma. To act in the general interest when others do not is to be played for a sucker. How much voluntary compliance or economic responsibility is needed to make the system work is a difficult empirical question the answer to which may vary from problem to problem.

The fallacy of composition plus the need for equitable and consistent application of rules pose another problem. Most rules need exceptions for the hard cases. The difficulty is that the existence of loopholes for exceptional cases sooner or later attracts the attention of the run-of-the-mill participant for whom the rules were devised, who then claims the loophole for himself on the ground of non-discrimination. Numbered anonymous Swiss bank accounts served a laudable public purpose when they were illegally maintained by German Jews, fearful of expropriation. They are a threat to society when the system expands to accommodate criminals and other tax evaders, or I should say criminals including tax evaders. A small outlet for emigration is desirable in enabling citizens of a country thoroughly out of tune with the values of the society, and possibly persecuted for their behaviour, to leave. But to generalize emigration or immigration to make it available to anyone threatens to overwhelm or even destroy a state as the creation of the Berlin Wall in 1961, and the illegal inflow of Mexicans into the United States today demonstrate. Murray Weidenbaum has written in praise of tax havens, and there may be justification for them within highly restricted limits. Generalized, however, they destroy the state, and capacity to produce public goods, and enthrone individual self-interest together with economic irresponsibility.

The fallacy of composition for collective interests can be illustrated with organized business or organized labour. The latter had its origin in defence against the former, but as so often happens in multi-person games, two antagonists ultimately team up and war against a third, the consumer.

The individual litterbug can claim to have no impact on the beauty of the landscape except as the first beer can in a location attracts others, and the single taxpayer who fails to report income in cash, hardly affects the budget balance of a given year, but large trade unions can more readily be accused of achieving private gains at the expense of the public goods of price stability and sustained employment. Virtually every labour leader would deny that any union or combination of unions has responsibility for the economy as a whole. That is the task of government, they insist, even when their power frequently prevents the government from restraining unions. Or if the rise in the price of oil means that real national income must be reduced (in the United States), each union is likely to insist, along with all other organized groups in the society, that it is justified in seeking to ensure that none of the reduction falls on its members. Indexation, maintenance of wage differentials, exceptions to wage guidelines in collective bargains are the order of the day. In progressive industries, unions ask for the whole increase in productiviity, while in lagging industries wages have to increase at the pace of the average to prevent loss of the work force. With no one willing to accept wages below the average increase in productivity, the average drifts upward. There is the view that Hans Boechler, Ludwig Rosenberg, and Otto Brenner in Germany after the war were responsible labour leaders who exercised great restraint in their wage demands in the short run to stimulate expansion, stability and greater rewards in the longer period. The alternative view, however, is that these union leaders were not so much responsible as their unions, after a decade or more of Hitler and war, were weak.

Or contemplate Sheik Yamani, the Saudi representative to the Organization of Petroleum Exporting Countries, who appears on a number of occasions in the last decade to have been trying to hold down the price of oil in the interest of world macroeconomic stability, as opposed to maximizing short-run returns. Again there is an alternative view, that reality differs from appearances, and that Yamani is a master of public relations fully committed to raising prices as fast as anyone else. It is nonetheless possible that a monopoly may set a price lower than that at which marginal cost equals marginal revenue as it worries about possible feedbacks, perhaps only that of encouragement to new entry, but conceivably that of world recession with its consequences on the long-run demand for oil.

Acting responsibly for unions or firms, however, has the disability implicit in the prisoner's dilemma. If unions hold wages, corporations may not behave in such magnanimous fashion but raise prices and profits anyhow, to make the short-run sacrifice of labour nugatory. Or as Saudi Arabia expands oil production to make up for some of the shortfall from turbulence in Iran, Kuwait among the low absorbers may cut its production further to thwart the attempt to hold down prices. Economic responsibility on the part of one actor may merely encourage greater short-run maximization in another, without achieving the public (and long-run private) purpose sought.

This is nowhere more strikingly illustrated than in the lender of last resort role that Hirsch illuminated in his striking paper on the 'Bagehot Problem' in the *Manchester School*. The issue is called 'moral risk' in the field of insurance. When an individual firm or household is fully insured, it has less incentive to be careful. Banks confident that they will be rescued if they get into trouble are less wary about staying out of it. The mean of the probability distribution of disaster may rise but the penalty arising from disaster is reduced. There are devices to correct for moral risk, deductible limits, and required self-insurance in the fields of fire and casualty. In life insurance, the policy holder presumably has a big stake in the outcome just as the pilot and crew have in the safe operation of airplanes—a fact from which I have often taken comfort. The insistence of government, central bank or an organization like the Federal Deposit Insurance Corporation in the United States that it will save only sound banks, and lend only on sound collateral is not persuasive. First, it is analytically awkward, confusing a general-equilibrium problem with a partial-equilibrium one; in a financial crisis with falling prices, soundness is a function of how fast the lender of last resort responds. The longer it waits, the further prices fall, and the less sound are banks and their collateral. Secondly, however, as the crisis deepens it is necessary to rescue the sinners with the faithful, since their fates are linked.

One answer to these game-theoretic problems is to have rules, spelled out with great clarity, as to how banks should invest their funds, and how insured policy holders should protect their property. In collective bargaining, the proposal is for a social contract under which each sector of society, and each segment of each sector, exercises great self-restraint in return for the promise of others to act similarly.

As in any cartel, the problem is in enforcement, how to prevent marginal units from chiselling or as I prefer to view it, competing. Swedish and Dutch experience with social contract goes further than that of most countries, but has been marked by wage drift, profit drift, and in the case of the Netherlands, wage explosion after an extended period of constraint. In addition there are serious problems of finding the appropriate initial conditions that represent a sort of stable equilibrium because they embody wage differentials agreeable to all. Most unions are likely to assert that once their prospective negotiations are completed with a hefty raise, providing all other collective arrangements are unchanged, and provided prices stabilize at their present level, they will be pleased to accede. But the fallacy of composition assures us that there is no time when all will agree that now is the exactly right time to enter into the social contract. Correcting lags of some wages behind others, in an attempt to get the differentials right, illustrates the problem at its clearest.

Thus far we have been discussing economic responsibility in terms of the fallacy of composition, with the implication that if a party is small and operates with no feedbacks or external effects, no fear of creating a precedent, and is unlikely to give rise to demand for equal treatment on the ground of consistency, it may be tolerable to permit free riders to exceptions to general rules on the ground that no significant consequences would follow. This may be open to criticism on the ground that it allows the ends to justify the means, and that in law and in morality, small is big because precedents are set and consistency is needed. One cannot let small unions as in municipal transit get away with standard-breaking wage increases, because if any one group gets huge rents, all will insist on having them too. But there are two aspects of the question, related to what has just been said and to each other. What if the actors are large and conspicuous?

Large is almost definitionally equal to conspicuous, but not quite. It depends on the setting. Young people will behave differently in a big city than they do in their home village, because they are anonymous in the former and known in the latter. In New York, there is likely to be no feedback from loud and raucous conduct, provided one stays clear of the police, whereas if one were to behave the same way in Belmont or Lincoln, Massachusetts, the fact would be noticed, commented on, remembered. Observation affects behaviour—the Heisenberg principle applied to social science—in other ways. Some football players do better in the game on Saturday than they do in practice during the week, unobserved. And some firms behave more circumspectly when they loom large in a small town than when they fade into the background in a metropolis, or their actions may differ as between when they are, or are not, required to disclose their operations. It was long said of one major American corporation—I think General Electric, but that may be simply bad memory—that it was unwilling to have the only major factory in a small town because that inhibited its behaviour too drastically, as the community came to depend on it unduly. General Motors' response to the brouhaha raised in the early 1950s over its profits from the ownership of Holden Proprietary, Ltd. in Australia was to buy up the remaining minority stock and convert from a public to a private company which did not have to publish accounts—until that escape was cut off by Australian legislation requiring private companies owned by foreign corporations to publish regular reports. A number of years ago observers were struck that Edward S. Mason's book *Controlling World Trade* strongly condemned international cartels, but advocated the rather mild remedy of registration and disclosure of agreements. Presumably he thought that the content of international business agreements would differ substantially depending on whether or not the world—customers, potential competitors and governments—would or would not have access to the terms.

The small and anonymous individual or corporation is permitted a much wider range of conduct within the limits of legal proprieties than the large and conspicuous one. Some years ago, in 1960 the Ford Motor Company in the United States undertook to buy the minority stock in British Ford, for an amount equal to $360 million, if my memory serves, at a time when the balance of payments of the United States was weak, but there were no restrictions of any sort on capital outflows. The notion that a capital outflow of a given amount weakens the balance of payments by the same degree is of course partial-equilibrium analysis unacceptable in a general-equilibrium world. What the net effect on the balance of payments would have been could only be traced through by ascertaining how the monies were raised in the United States and what was done with them by the minority stockholders who sold out in Britain. Nonetheless the size of the operation produced a reaction by government and public alike, implying that the Ford Motor Company, conforming fully to the law, was less than responsible.

A similar episode occurred some years later in Britain when the Shell Oil Company tried to protect its assets by transferring more than £100 million abroad at a time when it was entirely legal but somewhat discomforting to the foreign-exchange position of this country. It too suffered a certain amount of obloquy. The current illustration in my country, although this slides over the issue of the social responsibility of corporations that I have been trying to stay clear of, concerns foreign direct investment in and business dealings with the Union of South Africa, the policies of which in respect of apartheid are widely judged in my country (and by me) to be obnoxious. Small companies are hardly troubled about the issue. Large ones with subsidiaries in that country are exposed to criticism by various groups—church, political, student—some with monies to invest, and some with university endowments, even though they are operating fully within the laws and policies of the government. We seem to be approaching the time when corporations and endowment funds are called upon to have their own foreign policy, necessarily more restrictive—since it cannot violate governmental limitations—than the foreign policy of the nation.

Size and conspicuousness are two dimensions affecting economic responsibility. Age and status are others. It is useful to distinguish between old money and new money, between the Establishment and the upstarts, between—at the level of individuals—the aristocracy or gentry and the *nouveaux riches*. Age, the Establishment and *noblesse* all *obligent*, i.e., have responsibilities that extend beyond those of the average citizen or firm. In the money dimension, of course, age and *noblesse* are highly correlated, apart perhaps from Southern Europe where inpecunious aristocrats are looking for heirs or heiresses to marry. The path to the gentry lay through business or financial success. But with gentlehood or aristocratic position went obligations along with perquisites. There is a certain amount of hypocrisy about this, and it is easy to be cynical about the Christmas baskets handed out by the lady of the manor which failed to deal effectively with any real social problem. Nonetheless, it seems to me useful to observe the greater responsibility of the successful than of the unsuccessful, and of the old successes as compared with the new.

It is suggested, for example, that Saudi Arabia has a major responsibility for the operations of the world economy, in holding down oil prices, providing foreign aid to developing countries, stabilizing the world monetary system, etc. etc. Anything that Saudi Arabia can readily do in these directions is of course highly welcome, especially in the moderation of oil-price increases mentioned early, but one must note that Saudi Arabia is a new boy in the school, not an old hand, and as such has its hands full coping with a variety of problems. Its responsibilities, apart from oil prices and refraining from rocking the world monetary boat, lie largely at home and in the region. My country, the Common Market and Japan cannot escape their responsibilities for the stability of the world economy by pointing to the new and enormous wealth of Saudi Arabia. Its problems are many, and its skilled hands limited in number.

A recent book by E. Digby Balzell, *Puritan Boston and Quaker Philadelphia*, speaks to the question of responsibility in a powerful way. Puritan Boston was a homogeneous city, hierarchically organized, intolerant, but with authority. It bred and trained (at Harvard) statesmen and leaders who served the city, state and nation. It was interested in money, but also in class pride, power, accomplishment. Quaker Philadelphia on the other hand went in for tolerant irresponsibility, more interested in making a fortune, but leading private and individualist lives rather than concerned with order and authority. To the Puritan the office of the magistrate was the highest secular calling, reinforcing rather than contradicting *noblesse oblige*. The Quaker, on the other hand, saw no need for magistrates, government or war if all men followed the ideals of the Sermon on the Mount. It was a prescription for anarchy. Into that void left by the Quakers with their first loyalty to the immediate family and the community, a union of such money-making, accumulating families, came political bosses and venal politics. The Quaker tradition shared with the Puritans the passive responsibility of obeying the laws, but they withdrew from active responsibility in making and administering them.

This leads us to a form of economic sociology diametrically opposed to sociological economics. The magistracy required to make the system work comes from the value-system, not from maximizing behaviour. Passive conformity to the spirit of the rules is part of the responsibility; readiness to take a role in enforcement and in adapting the rules to new circumstances is another, and more active part of it.

How does economic responsibility come into being? In my judgment it responds more to Keynes's law that demand creates its own supply than to Say's law that supply creates its own demand. My emphasis on size, prominence, position in society, the reactions of others, etc. suggests that it is pressure that pushes government into new functions, and peer pressure that pushes non-governmental bodies into positions and attitudes of responsibility. It is of great interest to me that in the nineteenth century and prior to the foundation of the Federal Reserve Act, the leading New York money market banks behaved differently than other banks in New York such as the trust companies and savings institutions, and than out-of-town banks of all descriptions. The larger group depended on the money-market leaders to provide them with cash in crisis, and the leaders knew what they were supposed to do, and prepared to meet the responsibility.

The conclusion is more general. More basic an incentive than maximizing income and wealth is obtaining the approval of one's peers. As David Riesman has suggested, most actors in today's society are outer-directed, conforming to the standards set sociologically in productive as well as consumption behaviour, and those that are inner-directed are merely running on the outer-directions received at an earlier stage and internalized. This last thought explains the responsibility of *noblesse oblige* and the responsibility of old money, although it must be admitted that some who might have been guided by tradition turn out to be more susceptible to the blandishments of the jet set in the outer-directed mode.

There is a problem here, however. To develop economic responsibility one must choose the right peer group. There is after all honour among thieves and one sociologist of my acquaintance explains much anti-responsible behaviour in France on the basis of the 'delinquent peer groups' that grew up in that society in defence against strict parents and strict schools. People are drawn into academic life, business, the professions, government, and crime by choosing different models to ape, rather than each maximizing income and wealth—as the Chicago school would have it—in different ways. The point is neatly illustrated by the behaviour of two firms in the same industry toward high-level employees on their release from jail after serving sentences for criminal conspiracy against the anti-trust acts. Though the employees of the two firms had been convicted of conspiring together, one firm, seeking the approval of its employees for loyalty, gave their men a rousing welcome, new jobs and made them heroes. The other company, interested in being judged against a different standard, fired its group.

Economic responsibility at the national level, in this reasoning, is maximizing income and wealth within the constraints of avoiding behaviour which cannot be generalized, complying with the spirit as well as the letter of the law, watching feedbacks through the rest of society, and example-setting. Such responsibility is generated by success, but old success that has settled down and internalized class authority and pride. It is difficult to achieve in young economies, or aged ones, the former because responsible standards have not yet taken sufficient shape, the latter because there are too many groups struggling for collective goods and the fallacy of composition overwhelms them. Despite Adam Smith and the Chicago school, profit-maximizing economies having too few dedicated leaders, with insufficient individual commitment to voluntary compliance, and collective groups unprepared to restrain their demands, will not function. This seems to me the insight of Fred Hirsch in his book with John Goldthorpe on *The Political Economy of Inflation*.

I have not much space for economic responsibility on the international front, but this is hardly necessary as I have written a number of times of 'leadership' in the world economy. In its active form, responsibility is leadership. François Perroux has written of dominance in international trade and investment, referring to the United States. Political scientists refer to the leadership role as 'hegemony'. On the left wing the expression is exploitation and neo-imperialism. In my judgment, Britain in the nineteenth century and the United States from perhaps the Tripartite Stabilization Agreement in September 1936 to the two-tier system in 1968 or the Connally *shocku* of August 1971 acted responsibly. It was in their interest to do so because of feedbacks and a low rate of interest on future trouble. There is a considerable question whether both countries benefited enormously from the position or paid something of a price in losing freedom of action, higher taxes for defence, carrying the free riders who held back paying a proportionate share of the world public goods of economic stability and peace.

The elements of economic leadership at the world level have been spelled out: an open market for distress goods, and a stockpile of accessible goods that are in short supply, in crisis only, not as a regular device for stabilizing prices; a counter-cyclical or at a minimum stable flow of capital (and aid) to maintain the flow of international purchasing power to all parts of the globe; management of exchange rates and of macroeconomic policies through the gold standard operation by the Bank of England in the nineteenth century, and the dollar standard of Bretton Woods after 1947; and finally the lender of last resort function, as illuminated by Fred Hirsch in 'The Bagehot Problem', preventing deflation from spreading through the system by holding upright the critical domino—be it bank or money market at the right time. It was these requirements of responsibility that Britain could no longer discharge in the interwar period, and that the United States then hung back from that made the 1929 depression such a traumatic episode in world economic history.

I have not resolved in my own mind whether economic responsibility can be widely shared. Certainly at the moment when the United States capacity for leadership is diminishing and Germany and Japan are fully responsible in the passive sense like the Quakers, but unwilling to take a forward role, one cannot require small countries or the newly rich to undertake very much of the costs of maintaining the system. We are blessed by having few boat-rockers of the Bismarck–Hitler–Stalin–Hirohito—even de Gaulle stripe who would produce a drastic change in how the system operates. Iran, the PLO, Gaddafi, the New International Economic Order are not powerful enough to rock the system beyond the capacities of OECD countries to restore it to balance, provided that consensuses on policy rather than stalemate emerge rapidly. But such position as in the International Monetary Fund where the United States, and European Economic Community and the Commitee of Twenty-four each has a veto suggests that active economic responsibility may be a scarce good in the years ahead.

Economic responsibility goes with military strength and an undue share in the costs of peacekeeping. Free riders are perhaps more noticeable in this area than in the economy, where a number of rules in trade, capital movements, payments and the like have been evolved and accepted as legitimate. Free ridership means that disproportionate costs must be borne by responsible nations, which must on occasion take care of the international or system interest at some expense in falling short of immediate goals. This is a departure from the hard-nosed school of international relations in political science, represented especially perhaps by Hans Morgenthau and Henry Kissinger, who believe that national interest and the balance of power constitute a stable system. Leadership, moreover, has overtones of the white man's burden, father knows best, the patronizing attitude of the lady of the manor with her Christmas baskets. The requirement, moreover, is for active, and not merely passive responsibility of the German–Japanese variety. With free riders, and the virtually certain emergency of thrusting newcomers, passivity is a recipe for disarray. The danger for world stability is the weakness of the dollar, the loss of dedication of the United States to the international system's interest, and the absence of candidates to fill the resultant vacua.

I beg you to excuse me from discussing Britain's responsibility to the European Community, and the price that is being charged for it. I hope, nonetheless, that I have interested you in the concept of economic responsibility as an essential ingredient of economic life, along with income and wealth maximization, and a legal framework in which every man, firm, bureaucrat and nation can pursue his, her or its interest.

16 Government and International Trade*

INTRODUCTION

My subject derives from one of the lines of attack in Frank Graham's opposition to the offer curve of John Stuart Mill:

> In any freely organized market, for any given internationally traded commodity, demand will be partly from residents of the country of the market in question, and partly from residents of other countries . . . The price of any freely traded good is unaffected by the national origin of sellers or buyers and there is, in consequence, no occasion for grouping buyers or sellers into more or less antagonistic sectors (Graham, 1948, p. 158)

The same thought was expressed almost thirty years later by Marina Whitman, in extending an analysis of Cooper. Whitman went on, however, to qualify it profoundly:

> . . . the efficiency gains from market integration are maximized by ignoring the boundaries of the nation-state; for private transactions in goods and factors of production, the optimum size of the integrated area is the world. By implication, the economic justification for the nation-state must lie in the existence of public or collective goods—including stabilization targets, the distribution of income, and the regulatory climate—and of differences in national consumption preferences for such goods (Whitman, 1977, p. 3).

I propose to explore the theory of public goods, the role of government (or, in some formulations, the justification of the nation-state), and the durability of the nation-state in a world of mobile ideas, money, goods, and people. I shall illustrate various points with incidents from economic history, with which I have been agreeably occupying myself of late.

---

* The Frank D. Graham Memorial Lecture, given at Princeton, November 1977, and published in International Finance Section, Princeton University, *Essays in International Finance*, no. 129 (July 1978), pp. 1–19.

It is, of course, impossible in a short essay to offer a full-fledged theory of government as it relates to foreign trade. Let me start by breaking down Whitman's basket category, public or collective goods, into the three functions of government identified by Adam Smith. The duties of the sovereign, he said, are to protect the society from violence and invasion by other independent societies; to protect as far as possible every member of society from injustice and oppression by every other member of it, or to establish an exact administration of justice, and to erect and maintain those public institutions the profitabillty of which could never repay the expense to any individual or small number of individuals, such as roads, bridges, canals, and harbours (Smith, 1776, pp. 653, 669, 681–2). Free trade and limited *laissez-faire*, that is, take place within a system of 'magistracy'.

Two hundred years later, other views of government are offered by economists. One that is directly related to international trade, through the problem of economic integration among territories, is provided by Cooper (1974, p. 9), extending to four an earlier classification of the functions of government: stabilization, allocation, distribution, and regulation. In his paper before the International Economic Association meeting at Budapest in August 1974, Cooper put the case for regionalism in terms of public goods: stabilization, redistribution, and regulation. He went on to consider the optimal provision of public goods from the viewpoint of three technological factors—economies of scale, external effects and effective stabilization—and from the viewpoint of the diversity of individual preferences for collective goods. Technological factors argue for one world; diversity of preferences argues for a pluralistic world of many nations (Cooper, 1977, passim).

Somewhat antithetical to this idealistic view of government is one set out by Lindbeck (1976) in his Ely lecture entitled 'Stabilization Policy in Open Economies with Endogenous Politicians'. Slightly modifying his scheme, we can distinguish three political-behaviour functions for government: the normative, as in the writing of Tinbergen and Meade, where an idealistic and well-informed government works in the overall interest, along lines not very different from those of Cooper or even of Jeremy Bentham; the negative, as in the Chicago school, where markets are regarded as highly stable but the system is upset from time to time by destabilizing government action; and the political or popularity, as in the school of Anthony Downs, where politicians maximize their own personal welfare by selling policies for votes in a manner analogous to selling goods and services for money. Lindbeck prefers to make combinations among these. The normative and the popularity functions are additive, with varying weights. Before elections, the popularity function dominates the normative. After an election and until the next one approaches the normative gains and popularity recedes. Commenting on the Chicago view, Lindbeck (1976, p. 11) states that it is better to think of both the economic-market and the political-administrative systems as containing instabilities and imperfections that interact with one another in a complex way.

These approaches are all insightful, but I shall break down the relations of government to international trade somewhat further. I propose first to discuss magistracy, or the institutional framework within which trade is carried on; second, more tangible public and collective goods, akin to the public works of Adam Smith; third, the view of government as a tool of private interests; fourth, the non-economic purposes of government; fifth, government as an ulcer, or independent source of muddle and instability; sixth, government as the filler of vacua; and, finally, the notion that the nation-state is at bay and, if true, the possible need for international public goods that can and should be provided by the international system. In all this, I shall be dealing explicitly with international trade, although some of the separate points may be more general.

MAGISTRACY

The tendency to identify free trade with *laissez-faire* arises naturally from the origin of *laissez-faire* in the physiocratic pressure to expand exports of grain and defeat the policy of restricting exports in order to feed the national population. While *laissez-faire* may be associated with minimal government, there is no necessary connection between free trade and *laissez-faire*, as, for example, Jacob Viner and Lord Robbins well knew (see Holmes, 1976). In Britain in the 1830s and 1840s, there was a movement to freer trade culminating in the repeal of the Corn Laws, timber duties, and Navigation Acts, in the elimination of restrictions on exports of machinery and coal, and in the rationalization of other import duties. Brebner (1948) has pointed out that this movement was accompanied by increasing government intervention in many other aspects of the economy, such as the conditions of work, the length of the working day, and the employment of women and children. Free trade was possible only within a framework of law, order, and equity—magistracy, to use Adam Smith's word. The suggestion has been made that Sir Robert Peel hesitated to press forward with repeal of the Corn Laws until he had been assured that the benefits would accrue to wage earners in manufacturing rather than swell the profits of the manufacturers (Chambers, 1968, p. 71).

Law and order are complements to foreign trade. The Coase theorem claims that institutional arrangements can be disregarded in economic outcomes, with certain exceptions for transaction costs. The standard illustration of the theorem is that land will be used for sheep grazing even if cattlemen own it if sheep are more profitable than cattle. Lowry (1976, p. 9) observes, however, that this illustration assumes that the disposition of the land is settled by owner use or a market rental rather than by, say, murder. Most relevant to our concerns is the problem of piracy. Safe passage on the high seas was and is a public good, historically underproduced much of the time but part of the magistracy needed for trade. 'The suppression of piracy', states Parry (1971, p. 58) 'was in almost everyone's interest, but it was nobody's specific business.' It would be hard to find a neater statement that public goods are underproduced because there is no way to exclude the free rider. Parry was talking about the eighteenth century. In the nineteenth century, protection from Moroccan pirates was from time to time a private national good rather than an international public one: when an English cruiser refused to assist a Prussian ship captured in the Mediterranean and held for ransom, the ship asked for protection from Sweden and was refused. At the end of the 1830s, German shipping was virtually excluded from the Mediterranean for lack of naval protection (Bondi, 1958, p. 53). Earlier, in the eighteenth century, Dutch East India Company vessels were heavily built to carry cannon and cannoneers for their own protection. Once Dutch naval escorts were provided to convoy merchantmen (a quasi-collective, quasi-public good), standard lightly-built fluyt ships were constructed, reducing transport costs and fostering trade.

The complementarity between magistracy and foreign-trade theory is underlined by Samuelson's defence of the social indifference curve. The existence of the social indifference curve rests on the supposition that there is a government that treats the nation as a family, providing redistributive transfers from time to time to temper the effects of income redistributions arising from trade (Samuelson, 1956). This supposition thus underlies the use of social or community indifference curves in the construction of the offer curve so thoroughly detested by Graham, as it took the place of Meade's assumption of nations composed of individuals identical in tastes, income, and wealth, or alternatively of Scitovsky's compensation principle.

Scitovsky's compensation principle can, of course, be implemented by transfers effected by government, but the only historical attempt to apply the compensation principle of which I am aware proved a failure. In the 1830s in France, tariffs on colonial and foreign sugar induced an upsurge of domestic sugar-beet production. A government proposal motivated by the West Indian colonies called for suppressing the domestic industry and paying 40 million francs in compensation to inland refiners. It was rejected. Instead, the Chamber equalized the tax between French colonial sugar and domestic beet sugar, while protecting both of them against foreign supplies (Gouraud, 1854, pp. 342–345).

Adjustment assistance (with which the United States has been struggling since the Kennedy-round tariff legislation) is not exactly the same as compensation, though close to it in spirit. I have two historical examples of adjustment assistance from the nineteenth century. It is seldom mentioned that when the Corn Laws were repealed, a fund of £2 million was established to extend the draining techniques of high farming among the landowners in England, and another fund of £1 million was established for Ireland. In France, Louis Napoleon put 40 million francs into a loan fund for adjustment assistance to producers adversely affected by the Cobden–Chevalier treaty of 1860 (Dunham, 1930, pp. 145ff.). In the two cases, government made possible freer trade, or at least softened the rigours of transition to it.

The point is an important one. To permit the competition and free trade that Graham thought natural, some institutions may be necessary to protect a country from the most untoward effects of competition from abroad. The European Investment Fund and the European Social Fund, established under the Rome treaty of 1957 to contain 'backwash' effects, point in this direction. Myrdal (1956) has noted that free trade can lead to factor–price equalization only when countries are sufficiently similar in their factor endowments to tolerate the consequences of free trade, which may then be able to close the remaining gap. At a more fundamental level, the difference between interregional and international trade explored by Ohlin lies in the existence within a nation of a government that tempers the wind to the shorn lamb through various redistributive devices, while in international trade such mechanisms (e.g., foreign aid) are rudimentary, if they do in fact exist. It has been said that international trade is between 'us' and 'them'. If 'we' are bound together in a social compact under which we undertake to modify by budgetary (i.e., nonmarket) means the undesirable hurts arising from trade, the aggregation into offer curves of trading firms within our nation can be thought of, not as antagonistic, but in Meade–Tinbergen terms as helpful to the optimization process.

One intangible public good or institution is the state itself. In economic history, we have the device of the 'counterfactual', that is, looking for causes by trying to establish what would have happened, or what the situation would have been like, in the absence of the event or institution the effects of which are being examined. Graham objected to the nation-state because he considered its counterfactual to be worldwide *laissez-faire*. This is understandable only as an a priori view. Historically, the counterfactual to the nation over wide areas was not anarchy but scores, hundreds, perhaps thousands, of smaller political units, each interfering with trade. In 1790, what later became Germany had 1,700 tariff boundaries and 300 rulers levying tolls as they pleased (Henderson, 1959, pp. 1, 21). Prussia alone had 67 local tariffs in 1800 (Böhme, 1968, p. 9). As late as 1848, despite the clearing up of barriers—first under the Napoleonic occupation of the Rhineland, second through the Maassen tariff of 1818 in Prussia, and third by the Zollverein of 1828—there were eighteen toll houses on the Rhine, three in Holland, seven in Prussia, two each in Nassau, Hesse, and Baden, and one each in Bavaria and France (Banfield, 1848, p. 30). On the whole, mercantilism has a bad name, associated as it is with the fallacies of export surpluses and gold accumulation. The appropriate counterfactual to mercantilism, however, was not internationalism but parochialism. Mercantilism enlarged rather than shrank market space, in particular as it built the national institutions necessary for trade, especially standards and national money.

Standards are sometimes a public, sometimes a collective, good. Napoleon laid down the metric system of weights and measures. British Parliament sought unsuccessfully to decree the width of railroad track in the Standard Gauge Act of 1846, a standard adopted through most of England and on the Continent (except Russia) but not by the Great Western Railroad until almost half a century later. Standards may be set by industry as well as by government, by a cartel, a dominant firm, an organized exchange, a group of merchants. A lack of standards does not prevent trade, but it adds to costs and reduces efficiency. An effort in Britain to adopt decimalization in the middle of the nineteenth century failed to overcome national resistance, and not until the computer required decimalization did the changeover occur a century later. It took a war to achieve adoption of the common British–American standard for the pitch of the screwthread. The US government's attempt to lead the United States to the metric system in distance, weights, and temperature seem to make progress by inches or, perhaps better, centimetres. The public good of standards presents great complexity. The more widely the standard is applied, the more difficult it is to abandon for a superior one. Cost-benefit problems of deciding when to change to a superior standard or to alter a universal one are among the most difficult for democratic governments. And there are benefits in parochial diversity, as is clear when one contemplates the rivalry among musicians in the courts of eighteenth-century German principalities. But consider trade in the absence of standards: Indian exports of cotton in the cotton famine of the 1860s were full of dirt;

Turkish wheat exports in the early 1950s were said to be replete with stones and dead mice. While it is true that government is not essential for setting standards, where the collective good of standards is underproduced it may be necessary to have government undertake the task.

It is probably not necessary to defend national money as a public good, again not essential to international trade but very helpful. International money would be still better, to be sure, and not every national money is managed at all times so as to minimize problems. At the two-by-two-by-two level, international trade theory proceeds in general equilibrium without the need for money. In the real world, above the primitive levels of exchanges of gifts and silent trade, trade needs money, as the inefficiencies of clearing in the 1930s forcefully demonstrated. Moreover, the fact that national monies occasionally or more frequently depart from purchasing-power parities justifies the aggregation of demanders and supplies in a given country into a national offer curve, representing net demand or net supply.

PUBLIC WORKS

It was perhaps the fallacy of misplaced concreteness that led Adam Smith to separate out 'roads, bridges, canals and harbours' from public or collective goods such as law, order, justice, weights and measures, and stable money. For trade, there is perhaps little distinction between the London docks built at the end of the eighteenth century and the collective institution, the 'liner', that replaced the casual ship in New York in 1818. That was the date when the Black Ball Company undertook to dispatch a sailing ship to Liverpool each Saturday whether it had a full cargo or not (Albion, 1939, pp. 13, 15). Until the nineteenth century, goods shipped out of London were lightered. In 1799, the British government built the West India Dock. The other London docks were undertaken privately in exchange for the government grant of a twenty-one year monopoly on imported tobacco, rice, wine, and brandy, except from the East and West Indies (Gayer *et al.*, 1953, Vol. II, p. 421). These public and collective goods helped London and Britain to pull decisively ahead of Amsterdam, where the port was too shallow for deep-draft vessels.

The role of government in the provision of these collective or public goods differed from country to country. Adam Smith (1776, p. 115) was not entirely accurate when he stated that banking, insurance, canals, and water works might need government capital but nothing else. Actually, the capital was often furnished privately in Britain (but publicly in France), but government permission was always needed. In France, the government prepared the master plan for canals and railroads. In Britain, there were no such plans, but massive local initiative had to secure government authorization. Whatever the arrangement, public work spurred trade. The construction of canals and turnpikes in the 1750s and 1760s was critical to the surge of exports in the 1770s and especially the 1780s. The woolen manufacturers of Leeds may not have depended on the Aire and Calder Canal to take their products to Hull for export, but Wedgwood's difficulties in moving his new, hard, and therefore brittle china by pack train explained his strong leadership, along with Boulton and Watt, in promoting the Grand Trunk Canal that linked Hull, the Potteries, and Liverpool via the Trent and the Mersey.

TOOL OF THE INTERESTS

When providing institutions or tangible public works, government may not always have acted, in Meade–Tinbergen fashion, in the general interest—all-wise and all just. Public works, for example, benefited some groups and hurt others. Canals were an object of dispute, at all stages, between millers who wanted a good head of water and bargemen who found the weirs a barrier to navigation (Ashton 1959, p. 8) and between the navigational interests who wanted high water and the landed gentry who wanted their land irrigated rather than drained (Gayer *et al.*, 1953, vol. II, p. 418). The necessity for government to choose among competing interests gives rise to the Marxian view that government is principally the tool of the ruling class.

In the context of international trade, we account for this possibility in the Stolper–Samuelson theorem. That theorem explains how tariffs imposed by government benefit the scarce factor in a country, with the corollary that free trade may be imposed on a country in the interest of the abundant factor (Stolper and Samuelson, 1941). On this showing, the choice between tariffs and free trade turns on which interest group controls the sinews of government. If the abundant factor does so, it may display faith in general equilibrium and in Hume's law that imports generate exports. Or it may, as Semmel (1970) seeks to show for Britain in the first half of the nineteenth century, think in more specific terms of free-trade imperialism, adopting free trade in an effort to divert investment abroad away from competitive manufacturing and into agriculture.

The theory that the tariff may be regarded as a collective good has been shown to apply to the United States tariff of 1824. Widely diffused interests did not receive tariffs as high as those obtained by industries that were concentrated in a few states, because of the willingness of the concentrated industries to bear the transactions costs of getting the tariffs levied (Pincus, 1977). Conversely, the benefits of free trade to consumers are generally neglected because their interests are diffused; in other words, the collective good, free trade, is underproduced because no one bears the transactions costs and all are would-be free riders. Analogously, the Department of State is continuously complaining that it lacks a domestic constituency like those of the Departments of Commerce (business), Treasury (finance), and Labour among government bureaus, or like the constituencies of Congress.

The notion that vested interests favour tariffs fails to take account of a number of additional factors besides the vested interest of the abundant factor, which merges so comfortably into the general interest. Theoretical preoccupation with the two-by-two-by-two model tends to neglect traders themselves, as well as collective interests that favour free trade or low tariffs. For traders, see the free-trade policies of the Dutch, who were uninterested in exports of domestic produce or output of import-competing goods but were committed to turning over goods produced and consumed abroad. Turnover was maximized by maintaining customs duties at very low levels and imposing on labour the taxes needed to support the navy that protected trade (Wright, 1955). For collective interests that favour free trade or low tariffs, see industries that process or consume imported intermediate goods. There is no duty on newsprint in the United States: the press is too powerful. Generally, effective rates of protection are well above the nominal because the influence of consumers of raw materials is exerted to keep tariffs low on those materials compared with tariffs on finished products. The free-trade movement in France was promoted intellectually by the port of Bordeaux, Lyons, and Paris, but the action came at the peaks of the business cycle in the 1820s, 1830s, 1840s, and 1850s, when iron foundries wanted relaxation of the duty on coal.

It is occasionally suggested that the movement to freer trade comes from government, which has sharper insight into the true interest of business groups than have business groups themselves. The classic example is Finance Minister William Huskisson's reduction of the tariff on silk in the 1820s, which stimulated the boroughs of Macclesfield and Spitalfields through the competitive effect more than it hurt them through the negative protective and redistribution effects. The European Common Market has also been justified on the Schumpeterian grounds that competitive imports galvanize industry. Lhomme (1960, p. 179) explains away the Cobden–Chevalier tariff, insofar as it interferes with his thesis that bourgeois forces ran France, with the dubious proposition that Louis Napoleon knew the interests of the powerful classes better than they did themselves. A less tortured explanation is that Louis Napoleon was buying a non-economic value—British neutrality towards his anti-Austrian and pro-Italian foreign policies—in an economic coin that had little value for its own sake.

NON-ECONOMIC OBJECTIVES

Not all public and collective goods are complementary to private goods—like more, or less, foreign trade—and some may indeed be substitutes. Nationalism is one such good. In some circumstances, nationalism can be thought of as an investment good. The nationalistic euphoria of Germany in the *Gründerzeit* was a strong stimulus to economic expansion that rode through the depression of the 1870s. But Johnson (1970, p. 50) thought of Canadian nationalism and xenophobia as consumption goods. A country may choose autarchy for nationalistic reasons, including national defence or just a national mood of exaltation, of togetherness. Developing governments build pyramids, including inefficient manufacturing industry, at a net cost in national income, because such non-economic or uneconomic goods are arguments in the national objective function (Cooper and Massell, 1965).

This is nation building, not unrelated to the mercantilism discussed earlier, and each may or may not be productive. Nation building appeals far more to political scientists than it does to economists. The heroes of political science, by and large, are not the internationalists—Smith, Cobden, Chevalier, or even Marx—but the strong nationalists—Bismarck, de Gaulle, perhaps Kissinger—who tend to think of economics as uninteresting in itself but possibly useful in the conduct of foreign policy. Before 1875, Bismarck was content with low tariffs since they embarrassed Austria by preventing her from joining the Zollverein. After Austria was defeated in 1866, he finally found foreign-policy virtue in the union of iron and rye. For a time in 1878, Bismarck showed some interest in the Frenchman Molinari's suggestion that the Continent form a customs union to secure Europe's future in the face of American, British, and Russian competition (Epstein, 1967, p. 111), as the Zollverein had been used to advance Prussian political ends in 1828. In 1879, domestic politics drove the country in the opposite direction, in a manner one might predict by invoking the Stolper–Samuelson theorem. De Gaulle attributed his advocacy of the gold standard to the analysis of Jacques Rueff, who attacked the gold-exchange standard on the grounds of inflation and instability. But de Gaulle's real opposition was based on the fact that the dollar, and not the French franc, had displaced gold. The question arises particularly with respect to colonies. Were they acquired for economic ends, as Hobson, Lenin, Magdoff, and others maintain, or for *la gloire*? It is hard to make the case that any colony acquired after 1880 was economically justified, save for the Belgian Congo and the Witwatersrand of the Boer War. Elsewhere, colonies served to bolster national prestige at the general expense. Certain groups in society benefited—in Britain the upper classes, for whom the Empire constituted outdoor relief, or in France the army, the ports of Marseilles and Toulon, and the cotton interests of Rouen and Mulhouse. Typically, these were not interests that could dictate governmental decisions. The matter is better put by D'Estournelles de Constant *à propos* the French budget of 1899: 'First the joy of conquest, and then the necessity to pay' (Brunschwig, 1960, p. 144).

ULCER OR MUDDLE

Graham would have been sympathetic with the Friedman view that government may be well-meaning but is certainly incompetent. In a footnote in *The Theory of International Values*, Graham wondered how it was that the US government, created to win the rights of its people to buy and sell freely in the most advantageous markets possible, should so often deprive its citizen of those rights (Graham, 1948, p. 22n).

The Anthony Downs view of politicians as being in business for their own ends is perhaps epitomized by the deathbed remark of Louis XIV: 'Too many palaces, too many wars.' But even when government is properly motivated, *à la* Meade and Tinbergen, it may make a mess of it. The princes of Serendip, who did everything badly with fortunate results, are outnumbered by the disciples of the engineer Murphy, for whom anything that can go wrong will go wrong.

Part of the difficulty may be that government typically uses too simple a model, usually a partial-equilibrium model that assumes other things unchanged, when, in fact, an action can set in motion forces that change 'other things'. Charging reparations after wars, getting exchange rates wrong, attempting to maintain independent monetary policies in money and capital markets that are joined, imposing import-substitution policies, and propping up commodity prices are among the many examples. If one wants a lavish recent example, contemplate the attempt of the US government to improve its balance of payments by tying aid, applying the Interest Equalization Tax, and then chasing the capital flows via the Gore amendment, the Voluntary Credit Restraint Program, and the expansion of this programme, and Mandatory Restraint Program. In the end, it proved useful to sweep all the restrictions away. A similar recommendation has been made by Joseph Pechman for income tax: Start over again. ('When everybody is somebody, nobody is anybody.') Economic history affords two outstanding examples. *Gewerbefoederung*, or the promotion of industry through patents, privileges and monopolies granted to individuals under restrictions as to exporting, employment, conservation, education of workers, etc., became so complex in Baden that in the end *Gewerbefoederung* was junked in exchange for *Gewerbefreiheit*, or freedom of occupation (Fischer, 1962, p. 82). In the same fashion, the Navigation Laws in Britain, started in the seventeenth century and increasingly detailed in their application in the nineteenth became so intricate that finally, according to W.L. Harle, they were 'understood only by a few official persons and a few inquirers in political economy' (quoted by Clapham, 1910, p. 161).

GOVERNMENT ABHORRING A VACUUM

A somewhat undeveloped theory of government suggests that government may be called upon to undertake tasks that the private economy happens not to undertake spontaneously and to act, so to speak, like nature in filling the resultant vacua. Earlier I indicated that some goods, like standards, are occasionally produced collectively, sometimes by government. Gerschenkron's (1952) theory of backwardness asserts that the more backward a country as it begins economic development, the more likely it is that government (and banks) will substitute for private entrepreneurship in markets. Railroad building, education, financing of housing, and technological improvements in agriculture furnish ready examples. A more general statement can be offered as a theory of the second best: when markets don't work efficiently don't use them. In these circumstances, government is often substituted for the market.

Examples are less abundant in international than in domestic trade, and are not always successful. Markets may not work well, but—because of the muddle of government—they may work better than the substitute. In many circumstances related to particular countries and conditions, it is debatable whether markets or governments are more effective in allocating and distributing income, even when it is clear that neither perform these tasks perfectly. Bulk purchasing and international commodity agreements are among the most contentious issues in international trade. I maintain, nevertheless, that there are occasions when government intervention is required because of market failure or breakdown, if one assumes governmental ability no worse than one standard deviation below the average. Let me cite three examples, the first from trade and the others from finance.

In 1938, with much more foresight than the private market, Herbert Feis, the economic adviser to the Department of State, foresaw that the outbreak of war might disrupt the flow of commodity imports to the United States and that for purposes of national defence it would be advantageous to undertake a programme of stockpiling imported raw materials. As so often happens with government, sound advice was produced but there was no one to receive it. Eventually, however, the office of the economic adviser in the Department was assigned the task of stockpiling, and Feis, with his assistants Horace White and Leroy Stinebower, embarked on a programme of importing for government account. The market may have failed to anticipate the need for stocks of raw materials because the need was further forward than the 90 or at most 180 days in which future markets for a limited number of assets work effectively (Arrow, 1974, p. 9). Or it may have failed because national stocks, like insurance, are a collective rather than a private good, although no stockpiling companies comparable to insurance companies sprang into being to provide the service (Feis, 1947, Episode One).

Let me turn to finance. The Italian capital market is underdeveloped, and an Italian company that is solvent but facing liquidity problems is sometimes unable to borrow in the local market. One solution is to sell the company to a multinational enterprise with access to adequate liquidity abroad. But if this is possible only at a sacrifice price, it may be better to let government credit substitute for the inadequate capital market and have the firm acquired by IRI, ENI, EMI, or another of the various semi-state agencies.

Finally, in Brazil, a liquidity crisis was precipitated some years ago by an attempt to follow the advice of the International Monetary Fund. The prices of stocks of a number of Brazilian companies collapsed, and controlling interests in some of them were bought by foreigners. Present Brazilian controls on direct investment are so rigid as to inhibit trade and investment unduly, but the origin of such controls is perhaps understandable.

Government is often called on to fill the vacuum as lender of last resort, both nationally and internationally. A minority, a small minority if my estimate is right, think that there is never a need for a lender of last resort because markets always appropriately discount the information available to them in correcting today's prices for future events and that, in any financial crisis, worthy borrowers can obtain the loans they need at some interest rate. I do not propose to dwell on the subject, as I discuss it in a forthcoming publication, but I have doubts. It may nevertheless be granted that last-resort lending has costs as well as benefits. If firms, banks, and institutions know that they will be bailed out when they get into trouble, they will be tempted to take greater risks and to be less self-reliant.

The existence of a government that will take on neglected tasks may tend in many circumstances to undermine the readiness of private institutions and individuals to look after themselves. It is often first-best to improve the functioning of markets by assisting entry and exit, limiting monopoly, and providing better information. Nonetheless, there will be occasions when government is needed to repair omissions of the market. Public, collective, and private goods constitute a continuum in which the lines are drawn differently in different societies and in the same society at different times. Government should be ready to fill in, though perhaps not aggressively, when the collectivities of the economy and the private market leave important gaps.

SOVEREIGNTY AT BAY?

My taxonomic approach to government and international trade has suggested that national government sometimes produces useful public goods, sometimes makes difficulties, sometimes serves the ends of narrow groups, and sometimes is called upon to come to the rescue when markets break down. Whatever the role of national government, it exists, and its existence and that of national governmental policies undermine Graham's contention that firms within a given state should not be aggregated into a national offer curve representing net demands for some commodities and supplies of others.

In the seventeenth and eighteenth centuries, Graham's contention was more nearly right. In *The Wealth of Nations*, Adam Smith wrote:

A merchant, it has been said very properly, is not necessarily the citizen of any particular country. It is in great measure indifferent to him from what places he carries on his trade; and a very trifling disgust will make him move his capital, and together with it the industry which it supports, from one country to another (Smith, 1776, p. 395).

Violet Barbour extended the time frame:

The international capitalist from his earliest to his latest appearance has generally been, where business was concerned, a Man without a Country, and the seventeenth-century Amsterdammer though by no means a man without a city, was strikingly uninhibited by abstract considerations of patriotism or by theories of economic nationalism (Barbour, 1966, p. 130).

To bring the literature from Smith, Barbour, and Graham down to the last few years, it is necessary only to cite Cooper's Wicksell lecture, entitled 'Economic Mobility and National Economic Policy' (Cooper, 1974), or Lindbeck's little book, *The National State in an Internationalized World Economy* (Lindbeck, 1973). Analogous views can be found in current discussions of relations between multinational firms and the governments of countries in which they operate. The firms are described as cosmopolitan, transnational actors that refuse to submit to the typically second-best economic (and frequently non-economic) policies of the countries in which they are located.

It is evident that national sovereignty is increasingly undermined by the mobility of goods, capital, enterprise, and people. At the same time, international trade and some of the public goods needed to optimize it are being damaged by strong demands at the national level for collective goods: full employment, particular distributions of income, independent rates of inflation. A number of political scientists object to the growth of the optimum economic area to a world scale; they believe it undermines the nation-state and subverts its functions. Even economists tend to become nationalist in orientation as they contemplate monetary, fiscal, employment, and labour policies, and they turn to supposed panaceas such as floating exchange rates that are believed capable of providing national autonomy.

Optimization of international trade is perhaps not the *summum bonum*, but interference with the mobility of goods, capital, enterprise, and people runs grave risks of muddle. It is preferable to try to provide some of the public goods needed as complements to trade at the international level, notably international money harmonization of policies to forestall private capital movements that respond to policy differences rather than to basic scarcities, organs for responding to market breakdown, and lenders of last resort.

Political scientists properly place a high value on pluralism (see, e.g., Hoffmann, 1977) and object to such hierarchical structures as are implicit in a gold standard managed by London or a dollar standard dominated by the United States. The same pluralism, it should be noted, argues for restraint on national government when it dominates the local level. But pluralism tends to underproduce vital public goods and to overproduce a public bad, neo-nationalism. The fallacy of composition ensures that, at least in a few instances, if each locality, region, or nation takes care of itself, the wider national and international interest may suffer, and with it the interests of all lesser units.

The free rider is the bane of pluralism, just as the imperious leader—exploiting others, allegedly in its own interest—is the bane of hierarchy, or what some observers call the hegemonial system.

Lacking a world government or any reasonable prospect of one in the immediate future, the task is the delicate one of performing certain limited functions at the international level. There is insufficient space to address the nature of a new world order after the breakdown of the dollar system—if it has in fact broken down. But the elements, some of which have already been mentioned, would not depart widely from Whitman's (1977) list: stabilization, redistribution of income, and regulation of abuses.

Let me conclude by going some distance with Frank Graham on the subject of separate firms, though not so far as to deny the validity of the offer curve. I agree with the view implicit in the Graham–Smith–Barbour position that business and government should specialize and exchange, the one producing profits and the other providing the setting of magistracy—public works and regulation—in which business is free to maximize. I do not go so far, nor do I think would Graham, Smith, or Barbour, as to condone the Dutch traders and financiers who were willing to trade with and lend to the enemy when they were not busy arming privateers to prey on the shipping of their countrymen (Barbour, 1966, pp. 130–1). To be sure, I ignore some complex grey areas, such as whether business can legitimately shape the laws through lobbying or whether foreign business should obey the letter of the law when the local population does not. It makes little sense, however, to ask a firm to help achieve macroeconomic targets in national employment, to improve the balance of payments, or patriotically to carry out ill-defined national objectives not embodied in law. The breakdown of national magistracy calls for internationally agreed rules to be observed by traders and investors rather than for appeals to patriotism.

Hirschman's analysis in *Exit, Voice and Loyalty* (1970) is useful in this connection. Exit means ceasing to buy, moving away, resigning. Voice means speaking up, putting forward one's own ideas, attempting to effect change. Loyalty slows down resort to exit. In Hirschman's analysis, exit, modified more or less by loyalty, is the appropriate response to economic dissatisfaction, while voice is the appropriate response to socio-political dissatisfaction with the family, tribe, church or state.

If you believe that government is dominated by business interests, you believe that business already exercises voice. If, on the contrary, you think of government as a muddle and of business as innocently engaged in making money, to use Samuel Johnson's phrase, the appropriate response for business in unsatisfactory circumstances is exit, to take advantage of the world's increasing mobility and move on. The government has no right to demand brand loyalty if it fails to provide safety, justice, and needed public works, or if it fails to exercise restraint and moves too far in the Anthony Downs (Napoleon, Bismarck, de Gaulle) direction.

But exit should not allow trade and investment to escape altogether from their obligations to civilization. Mobility may provide an appropriate escape from danger, injustice, and insufficient public goods in a given country, but the international system must ensure macro-stability, a Meade–Tinbergen redistribution to temper the harsh edges of competition, and equitable allocation of the system's costs. There may be too much government at the national level, as Graham thought, but there may also be too little government internationally. World government is not yet, and in any case would have to be limited to a few functions. But the need to build world federal functionalism, to use Cooper's (1974) phrase, has surely arrived.

REFERENCES

Albion, Robert G., *The Rise of New York Port (1815–1860)*, New York: Scribner, 1939.

Arrow, Kenneth J., 'Limited Knowledge and Economic Analysis', *American Economic Review*, 64 (March 1974), pp. 1–10.

Ashton, T.S., *Economic Fluctuations in England, 1700–1800*, Oxford: Clarendon Press, 1959.

Banfield, Thomas C., *Industry of the Rhine*, Series II, *Manufactures*, 1848: reprinted New York: Augustus M. Kelley, 1969.

Barbour, Violet, *Capitalism in Amsterdam in the Seventeenth Century*, 1950; reprinted in paperback, Ann Arbor: University of Michigan Press, 1966.

Böhme, Helmut, *Prolegomena zu einer Sozial- und Wirtschaftgeschichte Deutschlands in 19. und 20. Jahrhundert*, Frankfurt-am-Main: Suhrkamp Verlag, 1968.

Bondi, Gerhard, *Deutschlands Aussenhandel, 1815–1870*, Berlin: Akademie-Verlag, 1958.

Brebner, J.B., '*Laissez-Faire* and State Intervention in Nineteenth Century Britain, *Journal of Economic History* 8 (1948); reprinted in E.M. Carus-Wilson (ed.), *Essays in Economic History*, Vol. 3, London: E. Arnold, 1962, pp. 252–62.

Brunschwig, Henri, *Mythes et réalités de l'impérialisme colonial français, 1871–1915*, Paris: Colin, 1960.

Chambers, J.D., *The Workshop of the World: British Economic History, 1820–1880*, 2nd ed., London: Oxford University Press, 1968.

Clapham, J.H., 'The Last Years of the Navigation Acts', *English Historical Review*, 25 (Two parts, July and October 1910), reprinted in E.M. Carus-Wilson (ed.), *Essays in Economic History*, Vol. 3, London: E. Arnold, 1968, pp. 144–78.

Cooper, C.A. and Massell, B.F., 'Towards a General Theory of Customs

228 *International Public Goods*

Union for Developing Countries', *Journal of Political Economy*, 73 (October 1965), pp. 461–76.

Cooper, Richard N., 'Economic Mobility and National Economic Policy', *Wicksell Lectures*, Stockholm: Almquist and Wicksell, 1974.

——, 'Worldwide vs Regional Integration: Is There an Optimal Size of the Integrated Area?' in Fritz Machlup (ed.), *Economic Integration: Worldwide, Regional, Sectoral*, New York: Halstead, 1977.

Dunham, Arthur L., *The Anglo-French Treaty of Commerce of 1860 and the Progress of the Industrial Revolution in France*, Ann Arbor: University of Michigan Press, 1930.

Epstein, Klaus, 'The Socio-economic History of the Second German Empire', *Review of Politics*, 29 (January 1967), pp. 100–12.

Feis, Herbert, 'Rubber before Pearl Harbor', in *Seen from E.A.: Three International Episodes*, New York: Knopf, 1947, pp. 3–90.

Fischer, Wolfram, *Der Staat und die Anfänge der Industrialisierung in Baden, 1800–1850*, Vol. 1, Berlin: Duncker und Humblot, 1962.

Gayer, Arthur D., Rostow, W.W. and Schwartz, Anna Jacobson, *The Growth and Fluctuation of the British Economy, 1790–1850: An Historical, Statistical and Theoretical Study of Britain's Economic Development*, Oxford: Clarendon, 1953, Vols. I, II.

Geschenkron, Alexander, 'Economic Backwardness in Historical Perspective', in Bert F. Hoselitz (ed.), *The Progress of Underdeveloped Areas*, Chicago, University of Chicago Press, 1952, pp. 3–29.

Gouraud, Charles, *Histoire de la politique commerciale de la France et son influence sur le progrès de la richesse publique depuis les moyen age jusqu'à nos jours*, Paris, August Durand, 1854.

Graham, Frank D., *The Theory of International Values*, Princeton, NJ: Princeton University Press, 1948.

Henderson, W.O., *The Zollverein*, 2nd ed., London: Cass, 1959.

Hirschman, Albert O., *Exit, Voice and Loyalty: Responses to Decline in Firms, Organization and States*, Cambridge, Mass: Harvard University Press, 1970.

Hoffmann, Stanley, 'The Uses of American Power', *Foreign Affairs*, 56 (October 1977), pp. 27–48.

Holmes, Colin J., '*Laissez-Faire* in Theory and Practice: Britain 1800–1875', *Journal of European Economic History*, 5 (Winter 1976), pp. 671–88.

Johnson, Harry G., 'The Efficiency and Welfare Implications of the International Corporation', in C.P. Kindleberger (ed.), *The International Corporation*, Cambridge, Mass: MIT Press, 1970.

Lhomme, Jean, *La grande bourgeoisie au pouvoir, 1830–1880*, Paris: Presses universitaires de France, 1960.

Lindbeck, Assar, *The National State in an Internationalized World Economy*, Rio de Janeiro, Conjunto Universitario Candido Mendes, 1973.

——, 'Stabilization Policy in Open Economies with Endogeneous Politicians', *American Economic Review*, 66 (May 1976), pp. 1–19.

Lowry, S. Todd, 'Bargain and Contract Theory in Law and Economics, *Journal of Economic Issues*, 10 (March 1976), pp. 1–22.

Myrdal, Gunnar, *An International Economy: Problems and Perspectives*, New York: Harper, 1956.

Parry, J.H., *Trade and Dominion: The European Overseas Empires in the Eighteenth Century*, New York: Praeger, 1971.

Pincus, Jonathan J., *Pressure Groups and Politics in Antebellum Tariffs*, New

York: Columbia University Press, 1977.

Samuelson, Paul A., 'Social Indifference Curves', *Quarterly Journal of Economics*, 70 (February 1956), pp. 89–110.

Semmel Bernard, *The Rise of Free Trade Imperialism, Classical Politial Economy, the Empire of Free Trade and Imperialism, 1750–1850*, Cambridge, England: Cambridge University Press, 1970.

Smith, Adam, *An Inquiry into the Nature and Causes of the Wealth of Nations*, 1776 (Cannan ed.), New York: Modern Library, 1937.

Stolper, Wolfgang F., and Samuelson, Paul A., 'Protection and Real Wages', *Review of Economic Studies*, 9 (November 1941), pp. 58–73.

Whitman, Marina v.N., *Sustaining the International Economic System*, Essays in International Finance No. 121, Princeton, NJ: Princeton University, International Finance Section, 1977.

Wright, H.R.C., *Free Trade and Protection in the Netherlands, 1816–30: A Study of the First Benelux*, Cambridge, England: Cambridge University Press, 1955.

Index

states' rights, 145
Stigler, G., 123
Stein, Harold, 41
Stein, Herbert, 135
Stinebower, L., 223
stock-market crash of October 19,
   1987, 3, 4, 8
Strange, S., 151
Streeten, P., 155–6
Strong, B., 26, 119
Strousberg, B.H., 114
Sukarno of Indonesia, 66
swaps, 46, 64
Sweden, shift from driving on left,
   178
Switzerland, as federation, 161–3

Tax Act of 1981, 61
   1986, 13
Temin, P., 19, 54, 69, 76–7, 80, 123
Thatcher, M., 164
Third World debt, 11, 24–5, 40, 62,
   66, 87ff, 116
Thornton, H., 26, 44, 117
Three Mile Island, 139
Tinbergen, J., 212, 215ff
Tobin, J., 10, 14
tragic choices, 126
transactions costs, savings in, 172–3
   and standards, 168
transitions as periods of danger, 119
Tripartite Monetary Agreement, 22
troop pay accounts, 41–2
Truman, H.S., 41, 194

unified states, 130
Union Générale, 119
United Kingdom, financial crisis,
   1967, 64
   1961, 64
   as a unitary state, chap. 12
United Nations Charter of Economic
   Rights and Duties, 144–5
   Conference on Trade and
   Development, 144
   Resolution on Permanent
   Sovereignty over Domestic
   Resources, 144
   Standard International Trade
   Classification (SITC), 172
United States, as aging economy,
   27, 50, 209

balance-of-payments deficit, 87
rescue loans for Britain, 1931, 26
United States National Bank of San
   Diego, 23, 84–5

van Dormel, A., 108
Vaubel, R., 69, 70, 80–1, 125, 172–3
Vernon, R., 132
Viner, J., 97

Walker, F.A., 185
Walzer, M., 125ff
Wanniski, J., 4, 21, 114
Warburg, J.P., 100
Warburg, M.M., 113
Warburg, P., 52, 113
Watson, M.W., 91n
Weber, E., 179
wedge between high- and low-grade
   bonds, 54, 79–80
Wedgwood, J., 146, 218
Weidenbaum, M., 201
Westgate California, 84
White, E., 69, 75, 81
White, H., 223
Whitman, M. v.N., 211, 226
Wicker, E., 69, 76ff
(WIDER) World Institute of
   Development Economics
   Research, 30
Wilson, W., 189
Wilcox, J.A., 70
wealth effect (of stock-market
   crash), 7, 54
William Deacons Bank, 20–1, 52, 55
Wolfe, T., 95
World Bank, 27 and see
   international institutions
World Economic Conference of
   1927, 42, 158
   of 1933, 42, 137, 150
   proposals of small countries, 150
World Health Organization (WHO),
   134
Wriston, W., 59, 116

Yamani, Sheik, 202
Young, O.R., 154
Young Plan, 11

Zeckhauser, R., 190
Zollverein, 220